MONEY, POLITICS, AND CORRUPTION IN U.S. HIGHER EDUCATION

Books by Dan E. Moldea

The Hoffa Wars:
Teamsters, Rebels, Politicians, and the Mob
1978

The Hunting of Cain:
A True Story of Money, Greed, and Fratricide
1983

Dark Victory:
Ronald Reagan, MCA, and the Mob
1986

Interference:
How Organized Crime Influences Professional Football
1989

The Killing of Robert F. Kennedy:
An Investigation of Motive, Means, and Opportunity
1995

Evidence Dismissed:
The Inside Story of the Police Investigation of O. J. Simpson
(With Tom Lange and Philip Vannatter)
1997

A Washington Tragedy:
How the Death of Vincent Foster Ignited a Political Firestorm
1998

Confessions of a Guerrilla Writer:
Adventures in the Jungles of Crime, Politics, and Journalism
2013

Hollywood Confidential:
A True Story of Wiretapping, Friendship, and Betrayal
2018

Money, Politics, and Corruption in U.S. Higher Education:
The Stories of Whistleblowers
2020

MONEY, POLITICS, AND CORRUPTION IN U.S. HIGHER EDUCATION:

The Stories of Whistleblowers

By Dan E. Moldea

Interviews with Jon Oberg, David Halperin, Rod Lipscomb, and James Keen

Introduction by Louis Clark

Second Edition

Washington, D.C.

Interior design: Elite Authors

Portions of this book have appeared on Dan Moldea's website,
www.moldea.com, where updates about this work will appear.

Library of Congress Cataloging in Publication Data
Moldea, Dan E., 1950
Money, Politics, and Corruption in U.S. Higher Education:
The Stories of Whistleblowers

1. Moldea, Dan E.——Department of Education.
2. Student-loan program.
3. For-profit colleges.
4. Government animal research and academia

ISBN-13: 978-1-7350984-1-8

Second Edition

To America's whistleblowers,
as well as to those who honor and protect them

"[T]he exercise of ethical whistle blowing requires a broader, enabling environment for it to be effective. There must be those who listen and those whose potential or realized power can utilize the information for advancing justice. Thus, as with any democratic institutions, other links are necessary to secure the objective changes beyond the mere exposure of the abuses. The courts, professional and citizen groups, the media, the Congress, and honorable segments throughout our society are part of this enabling environment. They must comprehend that the tyranny of organizations, with their excessive security against accountability, must be prevented from trammeling a fortified conscience within their midst. Organizational power must be insecure to some degree if it is to be more responsible. A greater freedom of individual conviction within the organization can provide the needed deterrent—the creative insecurity which generates a more suitable climate of responsiveness to the public interest and public rights."

Whistle Blowing:
The Report on the Conference
of Professional Responsibility (1972)

Edited by Ralph Nader,
Peter Petkas, and Kate Blackwell

CONTENTS

PART ONE: JON OBERG
The Student Loan Program and the 9.5-Percent Scheme

PART TWO: DAVID HALPERIN

For-Profit Colleges

RODNEY LIPSCOMB

ITT Tech

PART THREE: JAMES KEEN

Academic Corruption in the World of Animal Research

PART FOUR:
A DISCUSSION AMONG OBERG, HALPERIN, KEEN, CLARK, AND MOLDEA

"You guys are warriors"

CHARACTERS

Jon Oberg associates

Laura Berthiaume: Personal attorney for Jon Oberg

Louis Clark: Executive director and CEO, Government Accountability Project

Michael Dannenberg: HELP committee counsel, Senator Ted Kennedy

J. James Exon: Governor of Nebraska

Dr. John Hartung: Iowa-based friend and colleague of Jon Oberg

James Kvaal: Aide to Senator John Edwards; co-author of a major white paper with Bob Shireman

Dr. Mark Schneider: Jon Oberg's director and colleague at IES/NCER

Robert M. Shireman: President, The Institute for College Access and Success (TICAS)

Clayton Spencer: Counsel, U.S. Senate Committee on Health, Education, Labor, and Pensions, chaired by Senator Ted Kennedy

Lynette Whitfield: Neighbor of Jon Oberg in Rockville, Maryland

David Halperin associates

Paula Abernathy: Vice president, TICAS

David Boren: U.S. Senator (D-Oklahoma)

Howard Dean: Former governor of Vermont; 2004 presidential candidate

Dennis DeConcini: U.S. Senator (D-Arizona)

Gerhart Gesell: U.S. District Judge, Washington, D.C.

Rod Glaser: Former vice president, Microsoft

Adam Gonyea: Navy veteran, ITT whistleblower

Thomas Harkin: U.S. Senator (D-Iowa)

Zach Messitte: Staff member, U.S. Select Committee on Intelligence

Ralph Nader: Citizen activist

John Podesta: Co-founder and director, Center for American Progress

Jimmy Robertson: Co-counsel with Halperin; former state supreme court justice, Mississippi

Rashida Smallwood: Whistleblower, ITT Tech

Gene Sperling: Director, National Economic Council under President Obama

George Tenet: Staff director, U.S. Select Committee on Intelligence; CIA Director

Lawrence Tribe: Law professor. Harvard University

Sarah Wartell: Co-founder and director, Center for American Progress

Rod Lipscomb associate

David Scher: Attorney for Rod Lipscomb, The Employment Group

James Keen associates

Don Beerman: Director, UNL veterinary school

Louis Clark: Executive director and CEO, Government Accountability Project

Tom Devine: General counsel, Government Accountability Project; author, *The Corporate Whistleblower's Survival Guide*

David Grotelueschen: Director at GPVEC

Amanda Hitt: Attorney, Government Accountability Project

Hannah Keen: James Keen's daughter

Mohammad Koohmaraie: Former director of U.S. MARC

Will Laegreid: Keen's supervisor at the Animal Health Unit at U.S. MARC

Derek Morton: Senior auditor, Inspector General's Office, USDA

John Pollak: Former director of U.S. MARC

David Hardin: Interim director at Great Plains; director of the veterinary school at UNL

Wayne Pacelle: President and CEO, Humane Society

John Recknor: Attorney for James Keen

Gary Rupp: Former director, Great Plains

Department of Education

Jeff Andrade: Deputy Assistant Secretary, Department of Education, 2001-2003; EVP, U.S. Education Finance Group

Dr. Earl Crisp: Department of Education, Dallas Regional Office

Betsy DeVos: Secretary of Education, 2017-present

Arne Duncan: Secretary of Education, 2009-2016

Donald Feuerstein: Advisor, Guarantor and Loan Oversight Service (GLOS)

Matteo Fontana: Office of Federal Student Aid (FSA)

William Hansen: President, Education Finance Council; Deputy Secretary of Education, 2001-2003; Managing director, Chartwell Education Group; CEO, United Student Aid Funds, 2013-present

Frank Holleman: Deputy Secretary of Education under Secretary Riley

Diane Auer Jones: Assistant Secretary of Education for Postsecondary Education under Secretary Spellings and a top higher-education advisor to Betsy DeVos

Helen Lew: Auditor, Inspector General's Office, Department of Education

Fred Marinucci: Attorney, Office of the General Counsel, Department of Education

Roderick Paige: Secretary of Education, 2001-2005

Daniel Pollard: Office of Postsecondary Education, Department of Education

Richard Riley: Secretary of Education, 1993-2001

Angela Roca-Baker: Worked in the Office of Federal Student Aid (OFSA) at the Department of Education, which ran the student-loan program

Theresa S. Shaw: COO, Office of Federal Student Aid, Department of Education under Secretary Spellings

Brian Siegel: Attorney, Office of General Counsel, Department of Education

Mike Smith: Deputy Secretary of Education under Secretary Riley

Margaret Spellings: Secretary of Education, 2005-2009

Sally Stroup: Counsel, Pennsylvania Higher Education Assistance Authority (PHEAA); counsel, U.S. House Committee on Education and the Workforce, chaired by Rep. William Goodling (R-PA), 1993-2001 and Staff director, 2008-2009; Director of industry and government affairs for the Apollo Group Inc./

University of Phoenix; and Assistant Secretary for Postsecondary Education under Secretary Spellings, 2002-2006.

Dr. Grover "Russ" Whitehurst: Director, Institute of Education Sciences (IES)

Dr. Michael Wiatrowski: Director, National Center for Education Research (NCER); Oberg's supervisor

Academia

Robert B. Archibald: Professor, College of William and Mary

Christopher Avery: Professor, Harvard University

Sandy Baum: Professor, Skidmore College

Harney Perlman: Chancellor of the University of Nebraska at Lincoln

Laura W. Perna: Professor, University of Pennsylvania

Alison Van Eenennaam: Professor, University of California at Davis

Authors and Journalists

Anne Applebaum: Columnist/editor, *Washington Post*

William Bainbridge: Reporter, *Florida Times-Union*

Paul Basken: Reporter, *Chronicle of Higher Education*

Nicholas Bergin: Reporter, *Lincoln Journal Star*

Stephen Burd: Reporter, *Chronicle of Higher Education*

Michelle Celarier: Reporter, *New York Post*

Anne Marie Chaker: Reporter, *Wall Street Journal*

Patricia Cohen: Reporter, *New York Times*

Amy Connolly: Reporter, United Press International

Sam Dillon: Reporter, *New York Times*

Lee Fang: Reporter, *Republic Report*

Larry Gladieux: Co-author, *Congress and the Colleges*

John Hechinger: Reporter, *Wall Street Journal*

Stephen Martin Kohn: Author, *The Whistleblower's Handbook*

Tim Lacy: Blogger on education matters

Bethany McLean: Co-author, *The Smartest Guys in the Room*

Gretchen Morgenson: Reporter, *New York Times*

Michael Moss: Reporter, *New York Times*

Suze Orman: TV personality, best-selling author, testified with Oberg

Amit Paley: Reporter, *Washington Post*

Charles Peters: Editor, *Washington Monthly*

Christopher Quinn: Documentary filmmaker

Greg Winter: Reporter, *New York Times*

Tom Wolanin: Co-author, *Congress and the Colleges*

Non-profit and for-profit-college community

Richard Blum: Investment banker, investor in two of seven biggest for-profit colleges

Lindsey Burke: Director, Center for Education Policy, Heritage Foundation

Lanny Davis: Washington attorney

Scott Giles: Vice president, Vermont Student Assistance Corporation (VSAC)

Don Graham: Owner, *Washington Post* and Kaplan University

Janet Hansen: Vice president, The College Board

James Lintzenich: USA Funds in Indiana

Joe McCormick: CEO, Kentucky Higher Education Student Loan Corporations (KHESLC)

Steven McCullough: CEO, Iowa Student Loan Liquidity Corporation (ISLLC), a non-profit; Board member, Education Finance Council, the lobbying association

Marc Morial: President, Urban League; board member, Corinthian Colleges

Lawrence O'Toole: EVP, Sallie Mae; CEO, Nellie Mae; CEO, America's Charter School Finance Corporation; Founder and CEO, Aurora Consulting

Richard Pierce: MELMAC Education Foundation of Maine

Heather Podesta: Lobbyist for DeVry University

Robert Raben: Former U.S. assistant attorney general; lobbyist for Kaplan

Mitt Romney: Principal, Solamere Capital LLC, which invested in Full Sail University and Vatterott Colleges

Sheila Ryan-Macie: Managing director, Aurora Consulting

Kathleen Smith: Worked for Rep. John Boehner, the Education Finance Council, and was chief of staff for Postsecondary Education in the Department of Education; senior vice president at PHEAA

John Sperling: Founder, University of Phoenix

U.S. political figures

Haley Barbour: Chairman, Republican National Committee

John Boehner: U.S. Representative; Speaker of the House (R-Ohio)

George H. W. Bush: U.S. President, 1989-1993

George W. Bush: U.S. President, 2001-2009

Bill Clinton: U.S. President, 1993-2001

Hillary Clinton: U.S. Senator (D-New York)

Susan Davis: U.S. Representative (D-California)

Robert Dole: Former U.S. Senator (R-Kansas); lobbyist for Bridgeport

John Edwards: U.S. Senator (D-North Carolina)

Mike Enzi: U.S. Senator (R-Wyoming)

Dick Gephardt: Former U.S. Representative (D-Missouri); lobbyist for Corinthian Colleges

Newt Gingrich: Former U.S. Speaker of the House (R-Georgia)

Bill Goodling: U.S. Representative (R-Pennsylvania)

Al Gore: U.S. Vice President, 1993-2001

Jamie Gorelick: Former attorney, Department of Justice

Steve Gunderson: Former U.S. Representative (R-Wisconsin); CEO, Career Education Colleges and Universities

Tom Harkin: U.S. Senator (D-Iowa)

Johnny Isakson: U.S. Senator (R-Georgia)

James Jeffords: U.S. Senator (I-Vermont)

Ted Kennedy: U.S. Senator (D-Massachusetts)

John Kerry: U.S. Senator (D-Massachusetts)

Dale E. Kildee: U. S. Representative (D-Michigan)

Trent Lott: Former U.S. Senator (R-Mississippi); lobbyist for APSCU

John McCain: U.S. Senator (R-Arizona)

Howard McKeon: U.S. Representative (R-California); Chair, U.S. House Sub-committee on Higher Education and Workforce Training, which had jurisdiction over the student-loan program

George Miller: U.S. Representative (D-California)

Patty Murray: U.S. Senator (D-Washington)

Barack Obama: U.S. Senator; U.S. President, 2009-2017

Carl Perkins: U.S. Representative (D-Kentucky)

Colin Powell: Former Secretary of State; advisory board member, Leeds Equity Partners

President Ronald Reagan: U.S. President, 1981-1989

John Tower: U.S. Senator (R-Texas)

Donald Trump: U.S. President, 2017-present

Chris Van Hollen: U.S. Representative (D-Maryland)

State political figures

Andrew Cuomo: Former state attorney general (D-New York)

Tom Kean: Former governor (R-New Jersey); Coalition for Educational Success

Patrick Lynch: Former state attorney general (D-Rhode Island)

Christopher Madaio: State assistant attorney general (D-Maryland)

Stan Matzke: Former director, Administrative Services for the State of Nebraska

John McKernan: Former governor (R-Maine); CEO, Education Management Corporation

Pat Morehead: State Senator, Nebraska

Kay Orr: Governor (R-Nebraska)

Ed Rendell: Former governor (D-Pennsylvania); Coalition for Educational Success

Eric Schneiderman: Former state attorney general (D-New York)

Other whistleblowers

Kathryn Bolkavec: Bosnia human trafficking

Richard Bowen: Citibank whistleblower

Thomas Drake: National Security Agency whistleblower

Dan Graves: Whistleblower, ITT Tech

R.J. Infusino: Student, Dream Center

Sherron Watkins: Exposed corruption at Enron

Key characters in Jon Oberg's legal battles

Tracie L. Bryant: Attorney for PHEAA

John Dean: Attorney, Dean, Moskowitz, and Cipriani

Michael A. Glick: Attorney for PHEAA

Timothy Guenther: Chief Financial Officer, PHEAA

Judge Claude Hilton: Judge, U.S. District Court, Eastern District of Virginia

Andrew Mehalko: Vice president of public finance, PHEAA

Christopher Mills: Attorney for Oberg, Wiley Rein

Jeffrey Nekrasz: Office of Inspector General, Department of Education

Stephen J. Obermeier: Attorney for Oberg, Wiley Rein

Scott Oswald: Attorney for Oberg, The Employment Law Group (TELG)

Matthew T. Regan: Attorney for PHEAA

Bert Rein: Attorney for Oberg, Wiley Rein

David Scher: Attorney for Oberg, The Employment Law Group (TELG)

Howard Sorensen: Legal counsel, Inspector General's Office, U.S. Department of Education

Michael Sturm: Attorney for Oberg, Wiley Rein

Richard Willey: President, PHEAA

Jason Zuckerman: Attorney for Oberg, The Employment Law Group (TELG)

INTRODUCTION

By Louis Clark

Executive Director and CEO,
Government Accountability Project

After years of lecturing about whistleblowing on college campuses and at many other venues across the country, I have heard every conceivable question on the subject of whistleblowers. The one question that students, professors, and members of the public alike have asked more frequently than any other is: "Who are these people who blow the whistle?"

Like Dan Moldea, the author of this book, I often look to whistleblowers themselves to answer this question. On the occasions when I am fortunate to be sharing the stage with such notable whistleblowers as Dr. Daniel Ellsberg, Coleen Rowley, Thomas Drake, Sherron Watkins, Frank Serpico, Dr. Susan Wood, Dr. Mona Hanna-Attisha, and Dr. Jon Oberg, all I need do is keep quiet and let them speak. These whistleblowers enthrall, inspire, and inform the understanding of each and every audience they address.

It is fitting that Moldea has chosen to keep whistleblowers' identities at the forefront of his readers' minds in this ground-breaking new book. I have known Dan since we met more than forty years ago at the influential Institute for Policy Studies. He was already working his way toward becoming one of Washington's most courageous investigative reporters, and I had just helped found the Government Accountability Project, a whistleblower-support organization.

Now, my organization has become the most prominent whistleblower advocacy group in the world, having helped more than 8,000 whistleblowers along the way. My experience and familiarity with whistleblowers, including two whistleblowers featured in this book (Dr. Jon Oberg and Dr. Jim Keen), has illuminated the struggles and triumphs of whistleblowers and exposed the many misconceptions surrounding them. Like audience members at the lectures I have given, many people still wonder: What kind of person blows the whistle?

In his book, Moldea foregrounds the question of "Who is a whistleblower?" Moldea focuses on three whistleblowers: Dr. Jon Oberg, Rod Lipscomb, and Dr. Jim Keen, as well as attorney David Halperin, a well-known and respected advocate of whistleblowers. Moldea traces the origins of the complex scandals that these whistleblowers exposed, identifies the allies and enemies they attracted, and illuminates the retaliation they have courageously endured. From these case studies, a powerful narrative emerges: Moldea shows his readers what happens when good people decide not to remain silent when confronted with rampant corruption in higher education.

It is noteworthy that Moldea has now turned his attention to the once hallowed halls of higher education, the bureaucratic machinery of the federal government, and specialized financial entities that have profited handsomely, and sometimes corruptly, at the expense of both students and taxpayers. In an interesting twist on this theme, one of the case studies focuses on a major university, the Department of Agriculture, and the farm animals whose excruciating pain and suffering resulting from mistreatment that was inconceivable.

As Moldea describes in detail in Part I, student-loan companies have stolen up to one-billion dollars in illegal payments from federal taxpayer coffers, their crimes aided and abetted by leaders of the federal Department of Education. In Part II, Moldea exposes how under-regulated for-profit colleges soak up twenty-five percent of all federal student loans while spawning 55% of student loan defaults despite the fact that they represent a much smaller percentage of student enrollments. Since these colleges are totally dependent on these loans for profit, many have adopted rapacious practices to lure students into decades of heavy debt, leaving them near destitute with few repayment options. In Part III, Moldea concentrates on the University of Nebraska and the Department of Agriculture in their joint venture to conduct painful and wasteful experiments on cattle, hogs, and sheep and the ensuing cover-up attempt of the resulting carnage.

With each of these case studies, Moldea keeps the question of the whistleblower's identity at the forefront of the reader's mind. Moldea not only describes them in detail, he allows whistleblowers to speak for themselves, even including a casual conversation in Part IV of the book.

The courage, diligence, focus, and tenacity of the three whistleblowers that you will soon meet on these pages mirror our experiences with the thousands of whistleblowers with whom we have engaged through the years. While they represent a wide variety of backgrounds and also differ in terms of educational level, socio-economic status, and racial, ethnic, and gender identity, our clients share unique characteristics which are distinct and worthy of special mention. As you read, I hope you will agree with my observations.

Whistleblowers do not see themselves as heroes

Overwhelmingly, whistleblowers do not see themselves as heroes. In fact, they don't even perceive themselves as whistleblowers. Instead they self-identify as employees who are just trying to do their jobs to the best of their abilities. It is usually well into the struggle to expose wrongdoing or to defend themselves that they begin to accept the whistleblower label, frequently because that is how the media, fellow employees, friends, or the law itself legally defines them.

Whistleblowers usually are the hardest working employees in an office and adhere to the highest personal and professional standards.

In other words, these three truth-tellers and their compatriots everywhere are exactly the type of employees that most employers say they want to recruit.

It is because these ethical employees are committed to these higher standards that they have difficulty accepting, signing off on, or looking the other way when they observe dishonesty, malfeasance, corruption, or waste. Obviously, companies or agencies that tolerate or promote wrongdoing are likely to target those most likely to challenge the status quo.

Compared to every other whistleblower I have ever known, Jon Oberg may have suffered the least. In fact, as you will read, his punishment for committing the truth was to strip him of responsibility for the student loan program which ironically made him eligible to sue fraudsters on behalf of taxpayers and to prevail, returning tens of millions of dollars to the United States Department of the Treasury.

Whistleblowers almost always try to resolve problems internally before going public

As hardworking employees with high moral standards, whistleblowers almost always raise their concerns with their fellow employees or their immediate supervisors before going public. Before they blow the whistle more formally, they tend to first pursue the available institutional processes for identifying and reporting problems. It is only after becoming exceedingly frustrated with the failure of these channels that they consider going outside the organization. Again, the employees of conscience such as those discussed in this book each spent torturous years trying to challenge corruption by pursuing reform through internal means, before cooperating with the media as a last resort.

* *Most whistleblowers would make the same choice to raise concerns publicly again, even if they did not prevail*

In my experience it is rare to find a whistleblower who regrets having blown the whistle in a public forum, even those who lost their jobs and even their careers, as Rod Lipscomb did. They might wish they had approached their disclosures in a different manner and might even hesitate to recommend that others follow their lead, but virtually always they say they would make the same decision to speak up if they had the chance to do it over again. They recognize that there is intrinsic value in making the right, ethical choice in the workplace.

Essentially, even if their careers are left in tatters and they find themselves unemployed or eventually employed in another field, they can claim pride when they look at themselves in the mirror in the morning or receive feedback from grateful victims of fraud who benefited from the disclosures.

Doing what is right provides a sense of principled personal integrity that can surpass the material benefits of remaining silent. Those who do not stand by their principles and instead compromise their integrity exemplify the wisdom of Edmund Burke: "All that is necessary for the triumph of evil is that good men do nothing."

As you read about the trio of whistle-blowing men of courage that Moldea has presented, I believe you will agree that each one is worthy of high praise and intensive study. Also interwoven throughout this book are descriptions of those intrepid reformers whose strong support has been critical in the defense of these whistleblowers and in ensuring that their disclosures have a nationwide impact.

David Halperin is one such person—a journalist, attorney, and public policy activist rolled into one superhero. For a decade he has helped to guide a national campaign to expose corrupt practices that appear endemic to for-profit higher education.

Social policy advocates, such as Halperin, require the information and documentation that whistleblowers can provide, and whistleblowers need the reformers to have maximum impact for their disclosures; otherwise the risk and sacrifice of whistleblowing could have no impact and, thus, no reform.

The alliance between whistleblowers and public interest activists is not just important, it is pivotal to ensuring that violations of public trust and institutional integrity come to light. But it is not enough. For truth and justice to triumph, there needs to be a much broader movement and social engagement to ensure that there is significant transformation.

For example, as Moldea chronicles, federal government bureaucrats at the U.S. Department of Education have allowed highly subsidized financial institutions to victimize students and to swindle taxpayers. For-profit educational institutions have essentially manipulated economically disadvantaged students into signing up for a lifetime of indebtedness without a quality education that could provide a means to escape their economic plight.

The U.S. Department of Agriculture Office of Inspector General has essentially allowed a major university and the Department to escape responsibility for subjecting animals raised for food to inhumane, cruel, and inappropriate experiments. It is not enough to know about the corruption; rather we must act, each according to our ability and means of doing so.

In the early days of the movement in support of whistleblowers, we would often portray them as rugged individualists who alone would stand up, speak truth to power, and oftentimes prevail because truth matters. We called it "the power of one." We now know that a more accurate assessment is that whistleblowers are a catalyst that will inevitably drown in the waves that they create unless reformers, public officials, elected representatives, academics, media and concerned citizens who care about truth, integrity, democracy, and transparency join in the struggle against corrupt institutions and leaders who profit from the status quo.

PREFACE

"THE FIVE REAL AUTHORS
OF THIS BOOK"

S ince 1974, I have been an investigative journalist who has concentrated on
investigations of organized crime and political corruption. I have written
books about the rise and fall of Teamsters leader Jimmy Hoffa, a contract killing
in Ohio, the Mafia in Hollywood, the underworld's influence on professional
football, the killing of Senator Robert Kennedy, the O. J. Simpson murder case,
the suicide of Vincent Foster, and the Anthony Pellicano federal conspiracy case
in Los Angeles. I also published my memoir, detailing the stories behind all of
the investigations that resulted in my published books.

To be sure, I never expected to write a book about blatant corruption in
higher education, but I was simply blown away by the whistleblower accounts
I first learned about on the front pages of the *New York Times*.

Following up, I met Dr. Jon Oberg, featured in one such story in the *Times*,
page one and above the fold. His brilliant work fighting student-loan fraud
among lenders led to my interest in whistleblowers at for-profit colleges and,
inevitably, to investigative journalist and public-interest attorney David Halp-

erin, along with his detailed exposés of predatory schools that ruin students' lives.

Then, I saw a front-page article in the *New York Times* about the whistleblower, Dr. James Keen, a respected professor and veterinarian, who became the object of frightening retaliation at the hands of a land-grant university and a federal agency.

Meantime, I also learned about Rod Lipscomb, who, at great personal sacrifice, blew the whistle on ITT Tech, a for-profit college. He wasn't the subject of a front-page story in the *New York Times*, but he certainly deserved to be.

Also, I couldn't even consider writing about whistleblowers without asking for the participation of one of the greatest protectors of America's whistleblowers, Louis Clark, the executive director and CEO of the Government Accountability Project (GAP), who wrote the Introduction to this book. I have known, admired, and respected Louis for nearly forty years.

These whistleblowing stories, all from the world of higher education, provided the trail to this book. I never would have imagined that there was such waste, fraud, and violations of basic humanity in institutions of higher education. But there was and still is.

Notably, I have been able to interview these three whistleblowers and two of their greatest champions—the five real authors of this book—at length and to put their stories into one volume as a clarion call to all who believe that the world of higher education is exempt from bad behavior and even flat-out corruption.

—◊◊◊—

I am responsible for the contents of this book. And, as with my previous nine books, I have always worked hard to get my facts straight. However, I do make mistakes, and I am more than willing to atone for them. When informed about any problems, I will immediately list provable errors on an errata sheet on my website, _www.moldea.com_, and I promise to make any and all necessary corrections in future editions of this book as quickly as possible.

Further, I have attempted to be as scrupulous as possible to credit those reporters who broke major news stories about the events discussed in this book. Their important works are referenced either in the main text or in the footnotes.

Once again, I would like to thank the heroes of this book: Jon Oberg, David Halperin, Rod Lipscomb, and Jim Keen, as well as to Louis Clark and GAP.

Also, I must express my deep appreciation to executive director Danielle Brian, COO Keith Rutter, and senior investigator Nick Schwellenbach of the Project on Government Oversight (POGO), along with Conrad Martin, the executive director of the Fund for Constitutional Government.

In addition, I would like to thank my great friend and personal attorney, Roger C. Simmons of Frederick, Maryland, and his talented associate, Susan Eisner, along with one of my oldest and most trusted friends, George L. Farris of Akron, Ohio, who has been the Moldea-family attorney for over thirty years.

Also, I want to express appreciation to my lecture-booking agents, Jodi Solomon and Bill Fargo of Jodi Solomon Speakers in Boston. In addition, I want to extend my deepest gratitude to investigative journalist and long-time friend, Kristina Rebelo, for her outstanding editorial assistance and heartfelt encouragement, as well as to Claudia Vess for her artistic advice and Jeff Goldberg for his solid counsel.

Finally, many thanks to my good friend, Tom Von Stein, and, most of all, thank you dear Mimi.

For the first two years of publication, 2020-2021, all royalties earned by this book will be contributed to the Fund for Constitutional Government.

Dan E. Moldea
Washington, D.C.
March 10, 2020

THE STUDENT LOAN
PROGRAM AND THE
9.5-PERCENT SCHEME

CHAPTER ONE

"VINDICATED"

The remarkable headline above the fold on the front page of the *New York Times* said it all, "Whistle-Blower on Student Aid Is Vindicated."

A good and decent man had finally received well-deserved recognition for exposing blatant cases of civil fraud within the federal government, engineered by private special interests and for saving taxpayers billions of dollars. The *Times* reported in blow-by-blow detail how the whistleblower's efforts led to legislation passed by Congress to stop the fraud.

The *Times's* account, like this book, is about Big Government, Big Business, and Big Media, as well as power politics in Washington, D.C., while simultaneously detailing tribulations of whistleblowers who have demonstrated integrity and dedication for their work within and outside the federal bureaucracy. It is also a story about those they influenced and those who influenced them.

—⁓—

The United States Government gingerly embraced the concept of direct federal loans to students to finance their educations in 1958 as a response to the Soviet Union's successful launch of the Sputnik satellite. The Eisenhower

Administration and Congress put money into what were called National Defense Student Loans (NDSL), hoping to produce more college graduates who could help America compete in the space race.

The idea was simple: Federal funds were provided to colleges on a matching basis as a reservoir of student-loan capital. As graduates repaid these loans, more loans could be made with the recycled money.[1]

In 1965, Congress passed the Higher Education Act, which was signed into law on November 8. The act created a second, bank-based student-loan program, known as Guaranteed Student Loans (GSL), which would soon become much larger than NDSL. It provided for customarily ten-year terms for students to repay their loans with interest rates that were capped by law. Banks making loans were protected from default by a federal guarantee on the loans. Congress offered lenders subsidies to induce them to make student loans through special allowance payments (SAPs).

Robert Shireman, a former deputy undersecretary at the Department of Education, noted:

> When Congress started guaranteeing student loans in 1965, it was an economist's nightmare and a politician's dream come true. For Congress, placing the full faith and credit of the United States behind a bank loan appeared to have no cost at all, because the defaults and interest subsidies would occur in later years and thus would be someone else's problem. Economists cried foul, concerned that financial commitments were being made without accounting for the ultimate costs.[2]

---

1   The NDSL loans were renamed Perkins Loans, after Congressman Carl Perkins (D-Kentucky), the principal advocate of the program. Perkins was the chairman of the Committee on Education and Labor from 1967–1984. Representative Perkins was also integral in the creation of the Economic Opportunity Act of 1964 and Head Start.

2   Robert Shireman, *CSHE* (University of California, Berkeley), Research & Occasional Paper Series," 2004.

Even though the federal government guaranteed the bank-based loans in the event of student defaults, the banks still did not want their capital to be tied up in long-term, low-interest student loans. Consequently, secondary markets were soon created, modeled after those in the housing industry.

In the housing market, banks could sell their mortgage loans to secondary markets, quasi-government agencies known as Government Sponsored Enterprises (GSE). So, in 1973, using the Federal National Mortgage Association, aka Fannie Mae, founded in 1938, and the Federal Home Loan Mortgage Corporation, aka Freddie Mac, created in 1970, as models, the federal government created a national secondary market for the student-loan program, called the Student Loan Marketing Association, aka Sallie Mae, that facilitated student-loan banking.

In addition, states created their own individual secondary markets to provide more capital markets for the buying and selling of student loans. Governors were authorized by federal law to designate state agencies or create non-profit entities to administer the guarantees of the loans, funded by administrative fees.

Secondary markets raised capital on Wall Street through bond offerings in both the commercial and tax-exempt markets. Those issued by state agencies and non-profits were considered municipal bonds—for which investors did not have to pay federal taxes on the interest they earned.

By the end of the 1970s, an elaborate industry of private banks, non-profit guaranty agencies, and secondary markets had built up around the GSL program. GSL had far outgrown the federal government's other loan program, NDSL (Perkins) loans.

In 1979, in the midst of The Great Inflation, the student-loan industry complained that interest rates had skyrocketed into the double-digits while the interest on student loans had remained low. Federal special allowance subsidies cushioned lenders against high rates but created considerable inequities between those whose investments were financed in commercial markets and those financed in the tax-exempt markets.

To ease the inequity and to protect taxpayers from over-subsidizing loans, in 1980 Congress passed legislation to pay holders of loans financed with lower cost tax-exempt bonds only half the federal special allowance for commercial loans, but with a floor of 9.5 percent. Thus, if a student was paying a four-percent interest rate on a loan financed by a tax-exempt bond, the subsidy gave the loan-holder an extra 5.5 percent return (9.5% minus 4% equals 5.5%.). This was known as the "half SAP" or "9.5 floor" provision of the law. It provided a semblance of equity for student-loan financiers in the high interest rate environment of the time. Although interest rates stabilized at lower levels in the 1980s, the cost of the GSL program grew as more students came to rely on student loans. At the end of the decade, Congress began to look for a more efficient way to provide the loans rather than paying banks and other loan-holders large subsidies. This would set off a fight to the death between competing student-loan programs.

Student-loan-reform advocate Bob Shireman explained:

> In 1990, the economists' concerns were addressed. With President George H. W. Bush's signature on the Credit Reform Act, all government loan programs—whether guarantees of commercial loans, or loans made directly from a federal agency—had to account for their full long-term expenses and income. Every loan program now has an estimated "subsidy cost"—put simply, the amount of money that needs to be set aside when the loan is made in order to cover the loan's costs to the government over the life of the loan. The GAO explains that the old approach "distorted costs and did not recognize the economic reality of the transactions," while the new approach "provides transparency regarding the government's total estimated subsidy costs rather than recognizing these costs sporadically on a cash basis over several years as payments are made and receipts are collected." This more rational approach changed the nature of policy discussions on Capitol Hill. Student loans were among the first programs to be affected. . . .

Congress, prompted by a memo leaked from the Bush administration that indicated direct loans would be less costly and simpler to administer than guaranteed loans, responded by creating a pilot program of direct student loans. The next year, as newly elected President Clinton focused on erasing the budget deficit, estimates showed that the direct loan program would deliver the same loans to students at a much lower cost to taxpayers than guaranteed loans. So Clinton proposed replacing the guarantee program with the new direct approach.

In 1993, concerned about GSL program costs, Congress killed the 9.5 percent floor return to holders of the tax-exempt-financed loans as a cost-saving measure, except for those already issued. As those loans were paid off, the 9.5 floor subsidies were to disappear. There was no longer a great need, as there had been in 1980, to have different SAP rates.

To all intents and purposes, the 9.5-percent subsidy appeared to have ended, and with it an exorbitant cost for the GSL program, now renamed the Federal Family Education Loan Program (FFEL). Congress in 1993 also fully implemented the Direct Loan program (DL), which it had created as a demonstration program in 1992 at the urging of Thomas Butts of the University of Michigan, with Bush Administration concurrence, to cut costs further by circumventing banks altogether.

Shireman continued:

> When the Republicans took over Congress the next year [1994], the new leadership targeted direct lending for elimination. But they did not anticipate the enormous support that the new approach would have from colleges and universities. The reality was that many college officials couldn't stand the guaranteed loan system, because it forced financial aid administrators to deal with what the GAO labeled a "complicated, cumbersome process," disconnected from other federal aid and involving thousands of middlemen. College and university officials were cautiously optimistic

about a direct loan program that would operate in tandem with the other federal aid programs. So even with the election in 1994 of a Republican Congress that was hostile to it, the direct loan program took off with the enthusiastic participation of hundreds of colleges and universities. Instead of eliminating the new program, the Republicans demanded that the Department of Education stop encouraging or requiring colleges to switch. The new mantra was college choice: Universities would choose to participate in one program or the other. But the trick was that the banks and middlemen could use all of their money and people to coax and cajole, while the Secretary of Education had both hands tied behind his back by the Republican Congress. Not surprisingly, campus participation in the Direct Loan Program has dropped.

In 1998, the Department of Education under the Clinton Administration delivered to Congress an amendment to the Higher Education Act that would have repealed the entire 9.5 subsidy for FFEL loans previously grandfathered in the 1993 legislation. Budget analyses showed that the SAP to the industry was overly generous and would be better spent in other higher-education access programs.

The amendment was opposed by the U.S. House Committee on Education and the Workforce, which had jurisdiction over the student-loan program. Rep. Bill Goodling (R-PA), the chairman of the committee, adamantly opposed the amendment as breaking with the 1993 legislative loan grandfathering agreement.

After the inauguration of President George W. Bush in January 2001 and the terrorist attacks in New York and Washington the following September 11, the Federal Reserve lowered interest rates to virtually zero in its effort to stabilize the economy. The secondary markets in the student-loan program still holding pre-1993, grandfathered loans soon started making huge profits on their federal 9.5% floor subsidies.

Some secondary markets began funneling new loans—no longer eligible for the 9.5 percent rate—through existing pre-1993 tax-exempt bond trusts to make them appear to be loans eligible for the high subsidies. Premiums rose across the industry as secondary markets sought to acquire loans to wash them through the old trusts. Secondary market managers apparently believed that they could get away with this scheme without scrutiny.

And, surprisingly, they were right, as the government continued to pay the subsidies for several years. Several top officials of the Department of Education, who had previously worked in the student-loan industry, allowed the loan-washing scheme to help the industry compete against the upstart Direct Loan program, to appease the industry's political patrons on Capitol Hill, and to keep the revolving door spinning between Congressional staff, the student loan industry, and the Department of Education. The scheme's cost to federal taxpayers was headed into the billions of dollars.

Until one man stopped it.

CHAPTER TWO

"EVEN WALL STREET GOT INTO THE PROGRAM"

B orn on March 10, 1943, and raised on a farm near Lincoln, Nebraska, Jon Oberg, a fifth-generation Swedish-American, was the embodiment of the stereotypical citizen of the Cornhusker State: modest, down to earth, and dignified. He received his Bachelor of Arts degree in psychology from the University of Nebraska, where he also earned his master's degree in political science, specializing in public policy and public finance. Later he completed his doctorate at the Freie Universität Berlin, also in political science.

While serving as a Naval officer from 1966 to 1970, Oberg's assignments took him to Southeast Asia for two sea duty tours during the Vietnam War, and then to Germany. He received a Joint Services Commendation for "exceptionally meritorious achievement" at the Defense Communications Agency–Europe for his cost-saving work on international communication networks. After four years of active duty, Oberg spent a year as an instructor at the University of Maryland, European Division, teaching political science. After returning to Nebraska in 1971, he accepted a state government job as a budget analyst, expanding his responsibilities in 1976 to senior executive budget and management analyst, specializing in higher-education finance. In 1977, he became the director of the Nebraska State Office of Planning and Programming. The following year, he became Director of Administrative Services, the state's chief financial officer.

Meantime, to manage the GSL student-loan program as it was expanding in Nebraska in the 1970s, Nebraska Governor J. James Exon authorized the Higher Education Assistance Foundation, a Minneapolis-based regional guaranty agency, for the task. No state agency in Nebraska was willing to handle the job.

For his choice of a state secondary market, however, a Nebraska-based nonprofit was ready to accept the Governor's designation. Oberg explained: "For the Nebraska secondary market, Governor Exon chose a Nebraska applicant, the Nebraska Higher Education Loan Program (NEBHELP), a non-profit organization. I remember the occasion well, as it was on the day in 1978 that I became state Director of Administrative Services. My predecessor Stan Matzke, Governor Exon, and I were in the DAS director's office, signing papers to effect the transfer, executing bonding requirements, and discussing current issues in state fiscal administration.

"As we were finishing up, Governor Exon asked Stan Matzke if there was anything else to sign. The outgoing director said, yes, there was the matter of designating a state student-loan secondary market, which Matzke wanted to do as his last act before moving on to the private sector.[3] Governor Exon asked three questions: Does it cost Nebraska taxpayers any money? Are there any other applicants and, turning to me, did I know about this and did I have any objections?

"The answers to the first two questions were no. As to my involvement, I said I was not aware of the application, but I knew that NEBHELP was an offshoot of Union Bank, owned by the Dunlap family. I vouched for the family, as I had known Don Dunlap when he ran the Lancaster County Bank in Waverly,

---

3 Oberg and Matzke, who later became director of the Nebraska Bankers Association, remained good friends until Matzke's death in 2017.

the town where I went to high school and where he was civic and community minded. With that answer, Governor Exon signed the designation papers for the Nebraska secondary market."

In 1978, Governor Jim Exon was elected to the U.S. Senate with sixty-eight percent of the vote, succeeding Republican Carl Curtis.

Oberg continued: "Governor Exon asked me to come with him to Washington to set up his first office and to staff the Senate Budget Committee for him. I was also his chief legislative assistant and advised him on banking and finance issues as well as many other concerns. This was an area in which I had an interest, having been a member of the board of the Nebraska Mortgage Finance Fund (and schooled in bond finance by the estimable Robert Kutak, a national innovator). I stayed in Washington five years, leaving at the end of 1983."[4]

In the 1980s, because it had guaranteed too many student loans for those enrolled in for-profit schools around the country, the Higher Education Assistance Foundation (HEAF) of Minneapolis started having financial problems. That threatened its ability to serve GSL in many states, including Nebraska.

Oberg explained: "The higher loan amounts and lower job prospects for students who attended these for-profit schools led to high loan default rates. HEAF also had a competitor in Nebraska, the newly established Nebraska Student Loan Program. Knowing of HEAF's troubles, NSLP asked then-Governor Robert Kerrey to designate it as Nebraska's guaranty agency, replacing HEAF.

"By that time, I was back in Nebraska as executive of the Association of Independent Colleges, AICUN. Both HEAF and NSLP lobbied public higher education officials and me for support. I talked it over with the colleges and universities in our association. We concluded NSLP should be designated along with HEAF. I wrote a letter to Governor Kerrey accordingly.

"Personally, I found the NSLP proposal attractive. NSLP was also an offshoot of Union Bank and was affiliated with NEBHELP. It was based in Lin-

---

4   Oberg and Senator Exon remained close friends until Exon's death in 2005.

coln and promised that if it got the Nebraska guaranty agency designation, it would open NSLP offices in downtown Lincoln in the newly vacant J.C. Penny's building.

"I talked to federal officials about the designation, but they were reluctant to change any state's designation, once made. It was unprecedented, they said. But I pressed them along the lines of what our association members preferred, a dual designation. That was also unprecedented, but eventually the federal officials agreed. NSLP soon started doing guaranty agency work on a larger scale, renaming itself the National Student Loan Program."

HEAF in Minneapolis eventually folded, which cost $212 million in federal taxpayer funds to cover the liquidation costs.

The NSLP thrived.

Oberg continued: "Meanwhile, in 1986, I went to Jay Dunlap's Union Bank office in the College View section of Lincoln to discuss with him the growing problem, as I saw it, of students and colleges relying too heavily on student loans as a means of paying for college. I approached him about holding a small conference on the issue, perhaps inviting a leading economist from Washington to Nebraska to address selected college and state officials about the issue.

"We acknowledged frankly that his bank was in the student-loan business at the same time I was concerned about overreliance on loans. But he readily agreed to the idea of a small conference and offered $2,000 to help pay for it. Janet Hansen of The College Board came to Lincoln in 1987 and gave her paper, 'Student Loans: Are They Overburdening a Generation?' Newly elected Governor Kay Orr at first agreed to speak to the conference but, as the event approached, she abruptly withdrew. State Senator Pat Morehead of Beatrice graciously filled in.

"My concern about an over-reliance on student loans grew out of recognition that from the late 1970s through the next two decades, the federal government was shifting its student financial aid emphasis from grants, which do not have to be repaid, to loans which do."

—ɯ—

Oberg's motivation for arranging the conference was not so much Congress's student-loan legislation of 1965 and 1972, but, in 1978, congressional leaders had added an additional lure to students with passage of the Middle Income Student Assistance Act. MISSA expanded loans to students and families in all income categories, not just the financially needy. Paying for college became nearly synonymous with student-loan financing.

Oberg had worked in the Senate in 1980, when Congress increased subsidies for the GSL program. With all the subsidy incentives in place, the volume of GSL skyrocketed, to his growing concern.

The election of Ronald Reagan likewise had added even more impetus to the growth of student loans. Reagan's budgets slashed federal student-grant programs, ending a decade of preference for grants over loans.

Oberg continued: "Even Wall Street got into the GSL program in a major way by securitizing packages of student loans and selling them to investors, similar to mortgage-backed securities."

As to the 9.5% floor subsidies, Oberg gave his explanation: "One federal subsidy of particular note encouraged state and non-profit student loan secondary markets to issue tax-exempt bonds to provide student loan capital. In the high, double-digit interest rate environment of the early 1980s, Congress authorized payments to holders of loans financed by tax-exempt bonds a guaranteed return of 9.5%. That is, the federal government would make up the difference between what student borrowers paid in interest—set fairly low by Congress to encourage students to borrow to pay for college—and 9.5%. This became an especially attractive subsidy when interest rates in the nation's capital markets subsequently fell.

"Congress repealed the 9.5% guaranteed return prospectively in 1993, when it concluded it was no longer needed to support the program."

Oberg added more thoughts reflecting his experience with how government works: "The student loan entities formed lobbying associations to keep the subsidies flowing and, of course, to increase them. The guaranty agencies lobbied through the National Council of Higher Education Loan Programs (NCHELP). The secondary markets lobbied through the Education Finance Council (EFC). As often happens in Washington, a revolving door developed in the federal student loan program as staff of the lobbying groups, Congressional committees, and the U.S. Department of Education moved between positions as lawyers, administrators, and lobbyists. This classic 'iron triangle' became so strong that during much of the 1990s, subsidies for all the players in the federal student loan program came to dominate higher education policy discussions in Washington. Grants to students and other higher education programs became almost an afterthought in the battles over student-loan program subsidies."

Predictably, the guaranty agencies, among others, tried to grasp for more than they were entitled. Seeing the incredible flow of money, several of the non-profit operations spun portions of their tasks into for-profit entities— sharing personnel with the non-profits who then made self-serving deals with conflicted motives and intentions.

Although Congress held hearings during the 1990s and stopped the most egregious practices of the guaranty agencies, the closely related student-loan secondary markets soon began to exploit the federal program with the legal conversion of many non-profits into full for-profit businesses.

Ironically, this move was led by a senator who was a future champion of the Direct Loan program, Ted Kennedy.

CHAPTER THREE

"AN UNEASY COMPROMISE BETWEEN CONGRESS AND THE CLINTON ADMINISTRATION"

I n the late 1980s and early 1990s, Jon Oberg lived with his family in Berlin, where he completed a doctorate at the Freie Universität Berlin and taught in the graduate program for Troy State University, an American university with a contract to provide graduate level public administration programs to Defense Department personnel in Europe. Oberg's wife was a German citizen and their two children attended the public schools in Berlin in order for them to learn German and to live in another culture.

"Back in the States after four years in Berlin, I began working at the U.S. Department of Education," Oberg explained. "My position in the Office of Legislation and Congressional Affairs (OLCA) was congressional liaison for federal higher education programs, working under Dr. Thomas Wolanin, the deputy assistant secretary. I had long admired Tom Wolanin's work when he was a staff member in the House of Representatives. He authored many provisions of federal higher education legislation over the years. I also knew of his doctoral dissertation at Harvard and I particularly admired his book *Congress and the Colleges*, co-authored with Larry Gladieux. It remains the best history of the historic 1972 legislation that shaped the federal student grant and loan landscape for five ensuing decades.

"Also starting work at the Department of Education in 1994 was Donald Feuerstein, in a position as advisor to the Guarantor and Lender Oversight Service (GLOS). Don Feuerstein came from Wall Street where he had been chief legal officer at Salomon Brothers, an investment bank. He was a well-known figure on Wall Street because he had advised Salomon Brothers' top executives that their false bidding scheme on U.S. Treasury Bonds was illegal, for which the firm was eventually fined $290 million and their senior executives forced out.

"But he had not taken further steps beyond advising the executives of the illegalities, which the Securities and Exchange Commission in hindsight thought was inadequate in terms of his compliance responsibilities. Hence, the SEC subsequently came up with the "Feuerstein standard" of responsibility for legal officers at securities firms. Warren Buffet, who came in to rescue Salomon Brothers, ultimately asked Feuerstein to leave so as to wipe the slate clean of all who had touched the scandal, even the man who had identified it as illegal, which seemed to me unfair; someone should have given him a medal for doing what he could.

"The Salomon scandal became the subject of the books *Nightmare on Wall Street* by Martin Mayer, *Bonfire of the Vanities* by Tom Wolfe, and *Liar's Poker* by Michael Lewis. Feuerstein next worked at the Department of Education for a dollar a year, and was a valuable advisor on capital markets, and even brought to his work a few political connections: He had been a classmate of Senator James Jeffords at Harvard Law School.

"On our frequent visits to Capitol Hill to meet with committee staffs about higher education legislation, one question kept coming up from Clayton Spencer, counsel to the Committee on Health, Education, Labor, and Pensions, chaired by Senator Kennedy.

"She had been convinced by Nellie Mae, the Massachusetts-based New England student loan secondary market, that it should be allowed to convert from non-profit to for-profit. Conversion would entail most of Nellie Mae's existing assets being placed into a foundation for distribution to charities and educational institutions, in exchange for allowing Nellie Mae to make a profit for shareholders and executives on future federal student-loan subsidies.

"Clayton Spencer had Senator Kennedy's ear on the matter, but the conversion required federal legislation that was unlikely without a sign-off from Secretary of Education Richard Riley. Tom Wolanin was adamantly against the idea, as was Don Feuerstein. They warned Secretary Riley and Deputy Secretary Mike Smith not to get into a discussion on conversion with Senator Kennedy out of concern that such legislation would permit the very thing the Department, and many in Congress, had been trying to stop—the movement of federal taxpayer money subsidies away from their intended student beneficiaries and into the hands of corporate investors and executives.

"They believed it was very uncharacteristic of Senator Kennedy to go for such a scheme but understood that local Massachusetts pressures and the commitment of his counsel, Clayton Spencer, to the conversion idea kept it alive.

"Late one night in 1996, when Senator Kennedy was participating in a Senate-House conference committee on legislation unrelated to higher education, after the conference report had already been agreed to, someone slipped conversion language into the final version of the bill. It applied to all student-loan secondary markets, as it did not mention Nellie Mae specifically. The next morning, when he found out about it, Tom Wolanin felt double-crossed by the Machiavellian midnight move. That Clayton Spencer had not advised him of the conversion amendment was a breach of protocol. Feuerstein was likewise aghast and warned that this would lead to never-ending trouble in the student-loan world. And he was right."

Also, in 1996, during other status conversions and as part of his "reinventing government" program, Vice President Al Gore eased the way for Sallie Mae to move from a Government-Sponsored Enterprise (GSE) to a wholly private concern.

"Tom Wolanin opposed the conversion within the Administration in part on his conviction that Sallie Mae was not returning sufficient funds to the Treasury as a price of conversion," Oberg recalled. "Its assets had been acquired primarily because of the advantage it had, as a GSE, of borrowing at low interest rates through the Federal Financing Bank. He resigned over the matter; with his departure the Department of Education lost a great public servant."

Following Sallie Mae's lead, four other non-profit loan secondary markets became for-profit operations: the Student Loan Funding Corporation of Ohio, the Nebraska Higher Education Loan Program, the Student Loan Finance Corporation of South Dakota, and the Abilene Higher Education Authority of Texas.

In mid-2000, Consumers Union published a lengthy report, *Good as Gold*, challenging the actions of specific state attorneys general for their handling of an applicable charitable-trust doctrine with regard to converting the considerable assets of the non-profit secondary markets.

Consumers Union stated, in part:

> Only one of the five nonprofit secondary market lending company conversions, Nellie Mae, involved a publicly available valuation process. In the Ohio and South Dakota conversions, the Attorney General's review process was confidential and remains so today. In the Nebraska conversion, only a portion of the nonprofit was subject to a valuation. Although local and national community organizations urged the Nebraska Attorney General to commission an independent valuation, he chose not to do so.
>
> When Nellie Mae elected to convert, it commissioned its own valuation. Rather than commission an independent expert to review it, the Massachusetts Attorney General's office relied on its charitable trust division

staff to review the complicated financial documents. To our knowledge, there was no independent valuation.

Within nine months of the Nellie Mae conversion, the nation's largest for-profit secondary market company, the Student Loan Marketing Association, also known as Sallie Mae, purchased the for-profit Nellie Mae Corporation from its parent company, the Nellie Mae Foundation, for $320 million. This represented a premium of approximately $80 million above the original valuation figure that had been placed on the nonprofit at the time of the conversion. The foundation's sale of its for-profit subsidiary to Sallie Mae resulted in significantly increased assets for the new foundation. It also generated a huge windfall for the executive staff of the for-profit, individuals who had been on the payroll of the nonprofit secondary market company less than a year earlier. The windfall came about as a result of generous compensation packages, including stock options that these executives had negotiated for themselves when they became employees of the new for-profit Nellie Mae Corporation. A small handful of executives received $5.7 million in stock options upon the sale to Sallie Mae.[5]

One attractive feature for the for-profit secondary markets of the student-loan program in the 1996 legislation was their ability to maintain the existing tax-exempt bonds they had generated in their previous incarnations as non-profits.

Oberg noted: "Had the legislation seen the light of day before its passage, doubtless this provision would have been questioned. How much this was worth to the new companies was not clear at the time of their valuations. No attorney general conceived how this might be exploited in the future, let alone put a value on it. There is little evidence the companies themselves envisioned

---

5   Julie Stiles, Consumer Union, "Good as Gold: Preserving Community Resources in Nonprofit Conversions," June 2000.

how they might take advantage of being a for-profit company while retaining tax-exempt bond indentures. That would come a few years later."

Oberg recalled the pertinence of the Clinton Administration's attempt to wipe out advantages for loan holders with tax-exempt financing and his role in it: "During the 1998 re-authorization of the Higher Education Act, the Clinton Administration proposed doing away entirely with the subsidy that guaranteed a 9.5% return to holders of loans financed with tax-exempt bonds issued before 1993. The subsidy was a costly anachronism left over from an earlier era and was especially inappropriate for the new for-profit companies to be making money from old tax-exempt bonds.

"The Department of Education's bill drafters in the Office of General Counsel wrote the necessary language to amend the law and, as with all other such language for the re-authorization, and I took it physically to Capitol Hill to the respective committee offices working on the legislation. On the House side, I took the draft to Sally Stroup, a lawyer working for the Committee on Education and the Workforce, chaired by Republican Congressman Goodling of Pennsylvania. She had been hired by Mr. Goodling after having served as counsel to the Pennsylvania Higher Education Assistance Authority (PHEAA), an entity that was both a guaranty agency and a non-profit secondary market.

"She was not in her usual office for the delivery, but in Mr. Goodling's office in a different building. Customarily I explained the contents of the drafts and answered questions about the proposals, but not this time. When she understood that the Administration was recommending an end to the 9.5% guaranteed return subsidy, she stopped me from going any further with the words, 'Just forget it' and then repeated them with an exclamation mark. When I persisted, she tersely explained that Mr. Goodling would not go for it, and that I might as well take the paperwork back to the Department.

"When I returned to my office a few blocks away at the Department's headquarters on Maryland Avenue SW, Don Feuerstein was waiting in the hallway just outside my door. He was curious about the reception I received and if

I'd made any headway with the repeal of the subsidy that was costing federal taxpayers several hundred million dollars annually.

"When I told him of the frosty reaction, he asked if there was some other approach we might take to get the amendment considered. I said we'd have a better chance with the Senate, and then perhaps get the amendment in through a conference with the House. He said he hoped so, or we'd be sorry. 'How so,' I asked, 'beyond being sorry for losing an opportunity to kill off an expensive and unnecessary subsidy?' 'Just remember the moment,' Feuerstein told me, 'because the failure to repeal the subsidy will come back to haunt the Department.' He could not say exactly how he thought the subsidy might be exploited in the future, but he predicted that there was a scheme out there somewhere to take advantage of it. Knowing Don Feuerstein's background on Wall Street, I mentally tucked away the information. Five years later I would remember his warning when I was a researcher in the Institute of Education Sciences, and Sally Stroup was Assistant Secretary for Postsecondary Education in the Bush Administration, and Feuerstein had long since moved on."

Meantime, in the aftermath of the failure to pass the 1998 amendment, the rivalry among the secondary markets for student-loan business became intense, as huge sums of money became available to those who could best manipulate the system.

Oberg said: "Competition came in two forms: FFEL entities competing against each other—some now for-profit—and the FFEL program as a whole competing against the upstart Direct Loan program."

According to Oberg, the DL program "had its roots in the work of conservative economist Milton Friedman. Friedman suggested that the capital for federal student loans should come from the U.S. Treasury, and that students should pay loans back based on their subsequent incomes. The idea was not practical under federal accounting rules that, until 1990, showed outflows from the Treasury simply as expenditures even if they were loans that would be paid back in later years."

Elaborating on Bob Shireman's explanations, Oberg continued: "But under the Credit Reform Act of 1990, the federal government started accounting for loans in terms of their net present value, so that both the outflows and the future revenue returns could be considered together in any year's budget. In 1993, the Clinton Administration proposed a Direct Loan program that would take advantage of the Credit Reform Act, provide loans to students directly with Treasury capital, and cut out the private banks along with the guaranty agencies and secondary markets that went with them. There would be no matching requirements from colleges, unlike the NDSL program. Servicing of the Direct Loans would be done in the new program by private servicers that would bid for the work. The process of setting subsidies for all the loan middlemen through legislation, heavily influenced by lobbying and contributions to political campaigns, was to be phased out.

"Congress in 1993, on the recommendation of President Clinton, created a Direct Loan program and even planned for it to gradually take over all student loans, ending the FFEL program. But with a Republican sweep of the 1994 elections, a new Congress put a hold on the Direct Loan takeover. This effectively froze Direct Loans at about a quarter of student loan volume. An uneasy compromise between Congress and the Clinton Administration ensued, in which the two programs could compete against each other. Colleges were to make their own choices as to which program to use—DL or FFEL—to provide loans to their students."

To be sure, the popularity of the Direct Loan Program among most colleges and universities caused pressure to be applied to members of Congress. Without the simplicity and convenience of the DL, institutions would likely be reduced to the FFEL (old GSL) program as its only option.

However, Oberg added, "FFEL loan providers had advantages that they could exploit to keep colleges in their fold and even to persuade DL participating schools to come back to FFEL. One advantage was money, from generous legislative subsidies; another was more flexibility under the law to offer lower fees and interest rates than DL.

"The competitive struggle between the two systems is illustrated by debate in the Senate during consideration of the bill to re-authorize the Higher Education Act in 1998. Senator Tom Harkin of Iowa offered a Senate floor amendment to cut a fee that students must pay when they take out loans. This particular fee on an FFEL loan was to support funding for guaranty agencies; the same fee on a DL loan was to provide federal revenue to offset the cost of the DL program and to provide fee equivalency between the two programs, so as to make the competition between them on service, not on cost to students."

Oberg continued: "I assisted Senator Harkin, at his request, to estimate how much the fee could be cut without hurting the operations of the guaranty agencies. Of course, not all such agencies were in the same financial position, so we had to go with an estimate that would protect the large majority, but not all of them. The guaranty agency lobby, NCHELP, put up tremendous resistance at the thought of cutting any of their revenues, claiming it would be the ruination of all of them. The Harkin Amendment failed. But as soon as the ink was dry on the President's signature of the HEA re-authorization, many guaranty agencies cut their fees in an attempt to lure DL schools back into the FFEL program. It turns out that they really didn't need the revenues they had just told the Senate they couldn't do without. In fact, our estimates of their real needs were spot on.

"The defeat of the Harkin Amendment, which the Clinton Administration had supported as a way to cut the cost of student loans for all borrowers, did not go unnoticed by Secretary Riley and Frank Holleman, the new Deputy Secretary. I suggested to them that DL fees should be cut despite the defeat of the Harkin Amendment, under the statutory provision that it was the responsibility of the Secretary to administer the programs evenhandedly. If guaranty agencies were cutting fees for the FFEL program, the Secretary should cut them for the DL program, too. He did it. FFEL entities sued Secretary Riley over his action but eventually dropped the suit."

Notably, according to Oberg, "a similar scenario played out over interest rate reductions and rebates. FFEL lenders started offering .25% reductions to borrowers who agreed to use auto-debit loan repayment. DL matched it. FFEL lenders started to offer interest rate reductions, but DL came up with the equivalent by shortening loan repayment term.

"I did not always favor the Direct Loan program over the FFEL program from my position in OLCA. I was a civil servant, not a Clinton Administration appointee. When the DL program got behind in completing loan consolidations for borrowers, causing borrowers to wait weeks or months for action, I suggested that FFEL lenders be allowed to consolidate Direct Loans into FFEL consolidation loans, not just the other way around.

"The Two-Way Loan Consolidation amendment was the result. This worked to reduce the backlog and helped to save the DL program from a black eye. This was an action I came to regret, however, because not much later, a shady FFEL loan consolidation industry grew up. These loan consolidators operated out of boiler rooms, many in San Diego, making cold calls to borrowers to consolidate their Direct Loans into FFEL loans. They also used direct mail with misleading—if not fraudulent—letterheads suggesting that the communication was coming from the federal government. Taxpayers lost dearly from these schemes with the consolidation of every DL loan into a more heavily subsidized FFEL loan. I still sorely regret my role in it all.

"Who was behind this shadowy activity? Former House Republican staff with whom I had worked to pass the Two-Way Consolidation amendment, who saw a get-rich scheme and lost no time going for it.

"Even with formidable competition from the Direct Loan program, FFEL still dominated the student loan scene across the nation in the last years of the Clinton Administration and the early years of the George W. Bush Administration. The advent of the for-profit secondary markets and their moves into all kinds of new higher education-related activities were especially challenging to the smaller outfits. Sallie Mae used its national scope and economies of scale to expand its market share. It used vertical integration to profit from touching the student loan process at every step along the way. Some critics alleged that Sallie Mae got a subsidy for keeping borrowers in repayment but had a conflict of interest for getting an even larger subsidy for letting borrowers go into default and collecting on them. The value of the for-profits climbed, as investors saw the trends."

CHAPTER FOUR

"THE DISTINCTIONS BETWEEN THE NON-PROFITS AND FOR-PROFITS BECAME BLURRED"

S allie Mae purchased Nellie Mae shortly after the latter transformed into a for-profit operation. In addition, Sallie Mae also bought United Student Aid Funds, an Indianapolis-based non-profit, which spun off its assets to create the Lumina Foundation, providing grants to think tanks, as well as to educational and charitable organizations.

"Smaller non-profit secondary markets from coast to coast felt the pressure to go for-profit themselves or to fold and become part of one of the bigger companies," Oberg recounted. "Pressures on the non-profit executives created personal challenges for them. Some were genuinely committed to the charitable causes their organizations stood for. A few secondary markets established loan forgiveness programs to help their borrowers, and in so doing argued that colleges should remain in the FFEL program and do business with them on behalf of their students, rather than directing their business elsewhere. Several created wholly private student loan programs, especially to serve borrowers at more expensive colleges who ran up against federal borrowing limits in their institutional student financial aid packages."

But, according to Oberg, the distinctions between the non-profits and for-profits became blurred, saying: "The entities began to contract across the lines; a for-profit secondary market might contract with a guaranty agency in one part of the country for services and compete with its affiliates in another part. Non-profits used both the tax-exempt and taxable capital markets to raise funds for student loan purchases from private bank originators as well as for their own loan originations. For-profits still had billions of dollars in loan assets funded by tax-exempt bonds. Wall Street even began to put private student loans into securitization packages with federally guaranteed loans."

Oberg added: "One case in particular stands out to illustrate the conflicts and opportunities that faced student loan executives in this era. Lawrence O'Toole led the non-profit Nellie Mae in the 1990s and was instrumental in convincing Senator Kennedy to put through the midnight amendment in 1996 that allowed Nellie Mae to convert to for-profit. As Consumers Union has documented, that conversion benefitted many educational and charitable causes in New England. To this day, Lawrence O'Toole is honored by an annual award named after him, in the amount of $100,000, given out by the Nellie Mae Education Foundation and funded by the spin-off assets from the conversion.

"But executive pay for Lawrence O'Toole and others at Nellie Mae soared after conversion, especially after Sallie Mae bought Nellie Mae less than a year later. Lawrence O'Toole received a multi-million-dollar compensation package from Sallie Mae, and then quit Sallie Mae to form his own consulting firm, Aurora Consulting, after only one year at Sallie Mae. This was not an anomaly. Other former non-profit executives struck deals with for-profits that made them very wealthy: Richard Pierce at MELMAC in Maine and James Lintzenich at USA Funds in Indiana are among the examples.

"Through Aurora Consulting, Lawrence O'Toole used his commanding knowledge of the ins and outs of the student loan industry to approach another converted entity, the Student Loan Finance Corporation in South Dakota, to demonstrate his entrepreneurship in increasing SLFC's federal subsidies. For a cut of the added take, he would show them how it could be done. He secured a seat on the SLFC board and soon became CEO.

"It was during this flurry of for-profit activity that President George W. Bush's Administration came into power, which would soon place its own stamp on student loans."

With the inauguration of President George W. Bush in January 2001, Roderick Paige, a former school superintendent in Houston, Texas, became the new Secretary of Education, replacing Richard Riley, the former governor of South Carolina.[6]

For the position of Deputy Secretary of Education, President Bush nominated William Hansen, the former top lobbyist for the Education Finance Council, the trade association for the student-loan secondary markets.[7] Hansen had earlier worked in the President George H. W. Bush administration.

As Assistant Secretary for the Office of Postsecondary Education, the younger Bush nominated attorney Sally Stroup, the previous legal counsel for

---

6 Paige had made his reputation with reforms he had engineered in the Houston school system. However, after being Secretary of Education for four years, he resigned in the midst of an investigation of a scandal revolving around alleged manipulations and fabrications of student test scores in Houston.

7 William Hansen was the son of George Hansen, a seven-time-elected Republican congressman from Idaho, who was convicted and imprisoned in two separate cases for violations of the Ethics in Government Act and for his illegal role in a $30-million investment scheme. He was also convicted for failing to disclose campaign contributions, but he paid the fine and was not sent to prison in that case. The elder Hansen died in 2014. William Hansen, conversely, was given a distinguished alumni award from Idaho State University in 2003, but he later became embroiled in controversy as a director of the University of Phoenix and as a board member of the Student Loan Finance Corporation (SFLC), the loan collection company Performant Financial, Career Education Corporation, and Argosy University, which recently closed leaving thousands of students in the lurch.

the Pennsylvania agency, another powerful secondary market for student loans. Earlier, she had worked on the congressional staff for House Republicans.[8]

Oberg painfully remembered: "I was not to work with these individuals at the Department. On June 6, 2000, my wife was killed in an automobile accident in Rockville, Maryland, while taking our daughter to a class outing of the German School of Washington where she was a junior in high school. Our son at the time was in his freshman year at the Homewood campus of Johns Hopkins University in nearby Baltimore. It was a devastating blow to our family. Our daughter wanted to return to Berlin, where we had previously lived, and she did so to finish high school. Our son, after assisting in many of the arrangements for his mother's memorial service, continued on as a sophomore at Johns Hopkins.

"Trying to handle the demanding congressional liaison position at OLCA was not the most pressing priority for me at that time, so I asked for a transfer to an independent arm of the Department, the Office of Educational Research and Improvement (OERI), later renamed the Institute of Education Sciences (IES). I was transferred over at the same GS-15 civil service level I had held at OLCA and soon began work in postsecondary education research. This was a good fit for me, as I had been a researcher at times in my career. I had a doctorate in *Politikwissenschaft* from the Freie Universität Berlin; I had taught research methods in adjunct positions at two other universities. I was published in the peer-reviewed literature and from time to time worked at home on various research projects and papers.

---

8   According to Stroup's official profile at the Department of Education: " Before joining the Department, Stroup served as the director of industry and government affairs for the Apollo Group Inc./University of Phoenix. From 1993 to 2001, she was a professional staff member for the U.S. House of Representatives Committee on Education and the Workforce. As a committee staff member, she played a key legislative role in the reauthorization of the Higher Education Act Amendments of 1998. From 1981 to 1993, Stroup was with the Pennsylvania Higher Education Assistance Agency, one of the largest, full-service financial aid organizations in the nation. First serving as a staff attorney, Stroup rose to senior staff attorney and then to senior vice president of legal services and chief counsel." A native of Pennsylvania, Stroup received her law degree from the University of Loyola in New Orleans.

"By coincidence, I left my office in the Department's headquarters building on Maryland Avenue SW, the same day Secretary Paige arrived to move into his office. He and William Hansen toured the top floor of the building together, to see who might be at work. I was one of the few around, as most of the offices on that floor were for political appointees, all of whom had left with the change in administration. I shook hands with Secretary Paige and we soon found that we had former U.S. Navy service in common. He said he had been a corpsman in the Navy in the 1950s and had served, among other places, in the Western Pacific and in the South China Sea. Likewise, I served in ships in those waters and ports in the 1960s. It was a thoroughly pleasant discussion with not one word about student loans. I moved out that day and never met with him again.

"Possibly I could have worked in OLCA under the new Administration, as I was not a partisan person and I might have given some of the people the benefit of the doubt to see how things went. Perhaps I could even have influenced their thinking on some matters. I knew Sally Stroup well from our many meetings on Capitol Hill over the years. She had sent me a sympathy card on the occasion of my wife's death.

"I had worked with many Republican staffers over the years and knew their thinking. In fact, in the Clinton Administration, I was often invited over to OMB and the White House executive office buildings to explain Republicans' thinking and various other kinds of devil's advocate views in higher education.

"My reputation was as a loyalist to the taxpayers, students, and families that our higher education programs were supposed to be serving, not to parties, people, or institutions. That included the Department of Education itself, my employer. More than once I had gone to Capitol Hill to say the Department was dead wrong on a matter and that it had to clean up its act. I often said this internally as well, when the occasion called for it; Secretary Riley had appreciated it.

"On the occasion of my wife's death, he called my home and left a long, heartfelt message on my answering machine. I have since lost it, to my great regret."

Oberg continued "But I knew an iron triangle when I saw one and was content to work on research at IES, in a building on F Street over by Union Station, not far from the Senate, rather than to buck the incoming setup. I created my own research agenda, hoping to write two papers, the first of which would deal with rising tuition and whether federal grant and loan programs contributed to it. The second would deal with the opaque world of student financial aid packaging, a process conducted behind closed doors at colleges. I suspected that the goals of federal programs to help the lower income pay for college were being undermined by the colleges themselves in this closely held process.

"I finished the papers just as Dr. Grover Whitehurst took charge of IES. He showed no interest in them. He came directly from the State University of New York at Stony Brook, where he was a psychology professor with a consuming interest in early childhood education, especially reading. He seemed determined to drive the final nail in the coffin of Rudolph Steiner, the German educator who founded Waldorf Schools and their teaching methods. This was misguided, I thought, as Waldorf School methods were hardly a threat to the nation and there were more important issues to turn to, such as whether the billions of dollars taxpayers were spending on federal programs were actually doing the job they were supposed to do. When my colleague and office director Dr. Sandra Garcia inquired of Grover Whitehurst what he thought of my papers, he replied in an email to her that he did not understand why anyone would be interested in such topics and he discouraged anyone in IES from doing any research on their own.

"Nevertheless, I respected Grover Whitehurst's skills in research methods. I met with him twice to offer my assistance with his agenda to improve the quality of research done under the auspices of IES. I also brought to his attention my background in legislation and offered to assist with the drafting of an IES legislative authorization. He never took me up on either offer. In fact, his version of an IES legislative authorization omitted all references to postsecondary education. I still had contacts nearby in the Senate, who reached out to me directly to ask what was going on and why there were no provisions to include the huge topic of postsecondary education in the IES authorizing law. I said I was no longer in the legislation business and declined to offer any assistance. That was not the end of it, however; research colleagues of mine asked for my help so I wrote amendments for them, which found their way to Congress some other way because the language I wrote wound up in the law.

"It was at this point in the Spring of 2003 that I found myself thrown back into the issues surrounding federal student loan programs."

Despite the creation of the FFEL iron triangle, the Bush Administration did not make immediate changes to the policies of the Clinton Administration. According to Oberg, many in the greater higher education community were pleased with the status quo. "Colleges liked being courted by competing loan programs, which sometimes came up with programs beneficial to their borrowers, especially loan forgiveness programs. Several FFEL lenders offered loan forgiveness to those borrowers who would work as teachers, nurses, and others in public service."

Oberg continued on a darker note: "Many student financial aid officials at colleges also liked the perks being offered in the heightened competitive environment, from office supplies (with advertising logos on them, of course) to trips to student loan conventions with lavish parties. Some college financial-aid officers even accepted stock in for-profit student loan companies in exchange for listing the company as a 'preferred lender.' This went on for years until Stephen Burd at the New America Foundation revealed that student financial-aid officials at the University of Texas, the University of Southern California, Johns Hopkins University, and Columbia University had been on the take in exchange for personal favors.

"Another reason the Bush Administration was cautious about pursuing an overtly pro-FFEL policy when it first came into office was that any abrupt changes would surely upset Senator Kennedy, a Direct Loan supporter with whom the Bush Administration was trying to work on a elementary-secondary education agenda, known as No Child Left Behind. Kennedy was content with the policy of loan program competition, as he thought eventually the Direct Loan program would prevail because of its comparative simplicity and lower cost to taxpayers."

In 2002, the education department eased federal regulations with regard to recruiting practices at for-profit colleges and universities. This also affected student loans.

According to Oberg: "In response to many abuses, federal regulations had been put into effect to prohibit these schools from paying admissions recruiters based on the number of bodies they were able to enroll. The temptation was too great to enroll virtually anyone, just to get the federal grant money associated with the enrollment if the enrollees were financially needy, as they almost always were, and to make the enrollees borrowers in the federal student loan programs. This was also favored by many FFEL lenders, who saw new market opportunities. Some student loan companies even began selling 'lead generation' services to schools, to identify potential enrollees and borrowers."

Oberg explained the background: "The proprietary schools had been complaining loudly to the Bush Administration that federal regulations on paying admissions recruiters were onerous. The schools made large political contributions to senators and members of Congress, so the Department of Education also heard from Congress to ease up. In response, the Department of Education, led by William Hansen's efforts, established so-called safe harbors so that the schools could pay their recruiters in part on their recruiting performance, as long as other factors were also included in setting their pay. The Department also made clear that the punishment for violations would only be fines, not expulsions from federal program eligibility. The safe-harbor regulations were put into place by Assistant Secretary Sally Stroup, who had recently worked in the proprietary school sector for the Apollo Group, which owned the University of Phoenix.

"Despite an attempt at the Department of Education to downplay the changes as a type of regulatory reform, proprietary schools soon became the darlings of Wall Street. The Bush Administration essentially opened the floodgates of the federal Treasury to these institutions. They and their stockholders would pocket the new federal largess, even as tuition at these schools went up to take even greater advantage of the relaxed federal standards. Loan defaults of the students would become liabilities for taxpayers, not the schools. The hapless enrollees, who defaulted on their loans in increasing numbers because of the often-shoddy education the schools provided, would have their lives ruined forever by loan collectors. Who cared? Virtually no one, for years. The few in Congress who cared complained that the proprietary sector used federal money to buy up all the lobbyists in town, including several former Clinton Administration officials who could not resist the big money."

Oberg now began to tell the tale of his involvement with the 9.5 scheme: "Another change was truly more subtle if no less far-reaching. No policy change was ever announced. Many in the Department were oblivious to it. Attempts to track it down within the Department remain clouded in mystery even to this day. Someone in the Department apparently gave certain secondary student loan markets the green light to move loans financed by later bond issues into pre-1993, but still existing tax-exempt estates, in order to claim the remarkable 9.5% guaranteed return federal subsidy. The loans could even be moved in and moved back immediately, just to claim that they were loans that Congress had grandfathered back in 1993.

"Or, conversely, no one gave anyone the green light, but certain secondary markets started doing it anyway, convinced that no one in the Department would be the wiser, or if so, would dare to say anything about it. Later, I once asked a colleague why no one in the know ever said or did anything about it.

"'We assumed that was the way Bill Hansen wanted it,' he replied, even though Hansen had recused himself from such decisions because of his previous position as the secondary markets' lobbyist, and Hansen himself left the Department (for a seat on the board of a private secondary market and a position with an education services business) before the 9.5% guaranteed subsidy became grossly abused."

U.S. News and World Report simultaneously published a story about how Bush Administration officials worked to tilt federal money in any way they could toward the bank based FFEL program, citing Stroup and Hansen:

> From the beginning, the direct-loan program has been unpopular among Republican conservatives, who argue that private industry should handle the job. Soon after taking office in January 2001, the Bush team began to undermine direct loans. First, officials stopped marketing the program and competing for new schools. Then, last year, the Bush administration proposed selling the government's direct-loan portfolio to a private company. Critics called this a veiled effort to kill the program. Education Department officials deny this. "This is money we could have invested back in the student loan program," explains Sally Stroup, a senior department official. For now, the idea has been shelved.

> Bush insiders also challenged a central pillar of the direct-loan program: the notion that it saves taxpayers money. In early 2002, [William] Hansen argued inside the Education Department that when administrative expenses were included, the cost of direct loans was much higher than official figures indicated. As a matter of fact, he said, taxpayers saved no money. However, government figures don't support his claims. They show that the FFEL plan costs the treasury far more than direct loans, even after deducting administrative costs. In an interview, Hansen denies attempting to kill direct loans and says he was only trying to strengthen the overall loan program.[9]

---

9   Megan Barnett, Julian E. Barnes and Danielle Knight, *U.S. News &World Report*, "Big Money on Campus," October 19, 2003.

CHAPTER FIVE

"THIS LOOKS TO BE ILLEGAL"

During the spring of 2003, Jon Oberg of the ED's Institute for Education Sciences (IES) was curious about the fate of the overall 9.5-percent subsidy granted to the secondary markets for the federal student-loan program—five years after he had delivered to Congress legislation for its repeal. The U.S. House had rejected the proposal in 1998, allowing the subsidy to continue under the 1993 statutory phase-out.

Specifically, Oberg, still remembering the 1998 episode, wanted to make sure that those for-profit and non-profit concerns that had been beneficiaries of the pre-1993 grandfathered 9.5 benefit were now mostly paid off in full. After all, it had been ten years since the passage of the legislation cutting off the subsidy, the term of most student loans.

After a cursory review of department records, Oberg was surprised to see that the subsidy was not only on-going but was expanding. With his antennae up, he decided to search further, trying to find an explanation for what was happening and suspecting that it was possibly illegal.

Oberg pulled the financial records of two of the secondary markets: PHEAA and NMEAF, both of which were still receiving the 9.5 subsidies.[10] Oberg speculated that these two concerns in Pennsylvania and New Mexico had simply purchased other loans still grandfathered under the 1993 legislation which would show up as decreases elsewhere. However, when he did further research of the department's internal records, he discovered that the sum of the subsidies was, indeed, increasing substantially.

PHEAA, Oberg quickly calculated, could be making millions of dollars, or even tens of millions of dollars, from growing its base of 9.5 loans.

"Also," Oberg explained, "the language of the PHEAA and NMEAF financial reports was cryptic, as if it were all innocuous. The language was much too cryptic for me. It was as if the language had been worked over very carefully to give the impression that an explanation was being provided about the new-found sources of these revenues, when, in fact, the purpose of the language was to hide what was going on."

Oberg then emailed three people for their thoughts on his discovery: Brian Siegel of ED's Office of General Counsel (OGC), which performed the legal work for the program; Daniel Pollard, who worked under Sally Stroup at Office of Postsecondary Education, the office responsible for policy formulation and regulations; and Angela Roca-Baker in the Office of Federal Student Aid (OFSA), which ran the student-loan program operationally. Oberg knew and trusted both Siegel and Pollard. He did not know Roca-Baker.

In their responses, none of them could explain the scenarios and corresponding numbers that Oberg had uncovered about the 9.5 beneficiaries.

Even though he could not believe that the secondary markets would have the audacity to attempt blatant violations of law, Oberg became convinced that his new evidence showed the manipulation of bond and loan markets serving the student-loan program, for the purpose of defrauding the federal government.

---

10   PHEAA is the Pennsylvania Higher Education Assistance Agency. NMEAF is the New Mexico Educational Assistance Foundation.

"I was not about to accuse anyone in the Department of fraud," Oberg explained, "but it struck me as convenient that huge amounts of federal money were being shoveled quietly into the FFEL [Federal Family Education Loan] program, money that could be used strategically to drive the DL [Direct Loan] program out of business, as well as to help certain favored FFEL entities compete against others. PHEAA was soon to be in a battle to fight off a hostile attempt from Sallie Mae to take it over."

The Bush Administration, which had friends and allies in the student-loan industry, appeared to be turning its back on the issue of excessive 9.5 subsidies. In fact, it seemed to be knowingly allowing it to happen.

Further, supporters of the secondary markets in Congress, wittingly or not, had permitted the subsidy to continue, which resulted in an increase in campaign contributions flowing to congressional and senatorial candidates from the secondary markets, surpassing those of even the big oil and pharmaceutical companies.

Among the biggest beneficiaries were the PACs that supported Representative John Boehner (R-Ohio), who had replaced William Goodling as the chair of the Committee on Education and Workforce in 2001, and Representative Howard P. "Buck" McKeon (R-California), who chaired the Subcommittee on Higher Education and Workforce Training, which had jurisdiction over the student-loan program.

Sally Stroup had earlier worked for McKeon on the committee's staff.

With no one moving to look into the expanding subsidies, Oberg had a decision to make and then many questions to answer.

He explained, "While I was making inquiries in 2003 and had a good sense of what was going on, many secondary markets themselves were struggling with both practical and moral decisions. Where were some of their competitors getting this newfound money and should they, too, try to get in on it? Exactly how were their competitors moving loans around among bond issues to make such large claims on the federal treasury? Should they ask the Department of Education about the process and how to participate? Or was it all undercover and only for insiders? What if it was, as many suspected, illegal?

"If others were doing it, did their own secondary market have a responsibility to colleges and borrowers to do it, too, to spread the largess? If they were for-profit companies, did they have an obligation to their stockholders to get in on the game? Should they ask for private legal opinions to give them protection against knowingly committing fraud, should the scheme go awry? If so, where could they get such legal opinions, from the lawyers in Washington who were their lobbyists? Would that not be a conflict of interest? It was all a quandary."

Oberg discovered that the secondary markets differed in how they approached the hugely tempting subsidies. And he listed and explained some of them, saying:

> * Lawrence O'Toole, working through Aurora Consulting at SLFC of South Dakota, did not need schooling on the mechanics of how to move money around to make much greater claims. As to the legality of the matter, his assistant at Aurora Consulting, Sheila Ryan (she of the "steel-trap" mind, it was said)[11], had once been on a Department of Education rule-making panel in the 1990s to write regulations for the 1993 legislation that had phased out the 9.5% guarantee. During a break, she said, she told two Department employees that certain loan and bond maneuvers could potentially exploit an unintended loophole that the Department had not closed. Flimsy as that might sound, it was enough for O'Toole to propose that if he shared his manipulation methods with SLFC, he personally

---

11   Sheila Ryan-Macie was the Vice President for Government Relations and Strategy for Nellie Mae, 1987-2001; Vice President of Programs and Administration for America's Charter School Finance Corporation, 2001-2006; Managing director, Aurora Consulting, 2001-2009. She became the Senior vice president for Operations Administration for Sallie Mae in 2011 and is now the senior vice president and chief of staff for the Navient Corporation, which became the second entity in the aftermath of the 2014 split of Sallie Mae, which continued to services private student loans while Navient would service federal student loans for the government.

should receive 1% of the additional take, and Aurora Consulting should get 2%. In polite language, one might call this a finder's fee rather than a kickback. (I later calculated the amount of the extra take for SLFC at $15.4 million between 2003 and 2006.) Lawrence O'Toole impressed the SLFC board with his scheme and became its CEO.

* The non-profit Vermont Student Assistance Corporation (VSAC), early on, took the opposite approach. Its government relations vice president, Scott Giles, had worked in both the House and Senate and knew the history of the federal subsidies. His most recent employment had been on the staff of Senator James Jeffords of Vermont, a longtime member of the Senate committee with student loan jurisdiction. Scott Giles thought any claims based on moving loans back into pre-1993 bond estates was illegal and ridiculous. However, competitive pressure was building on VSAC from outside of New England. It became a question of how long VSAC could hold out.

* In Kentucky, at the non-profit Kentucky Higher Education Student Loan Corporations (KHESLC), CEO Joe McCormick decided just to follow the crowd, using one large for-profit student loan company as a bellwether. If they jumped in, so would he. He had at one time headed the Direct Loan program at the Department of Education and knew what was at stake. He was of the opinion that all the middlemen in the FFEL program were unnecessary and that the two programs should combine in some way so as to streamline operations. That was a more important agenda to him than gimmicks to game federal subsidies.

* In Iowa, at the Iowa Student Loan Liquidity Corporation (ISLLC), a non-profit, Steven McCullough was closely tied to PHEAA, which provided software known as COMPASS to help with filing federal subsidy claims. So as PHEAA went, so did ISLLC, although in considerably

smaller amounts. Steven McCullough was also the chair of the Education Finance Council, the lobbying association, and had a responsibility to all the non-profit secondary market members. This would cause him to keep close track of the way political winds might be blowing with regard to the legality of claiming the higher subsidies.

At the time, Oberg had only eighteen months before retirement, but he suspected that nothing would change unless he did something.

Feeling somewhat isolated during the summer of 2003, Oberg, with some frustration, called a department hotline, operated by the ED's Office of Inspector General, which solicited information about waste, fraud, and abuse. Those calling in expected to remain anonymous.

After receiving no meaningful response from OIG by November 2003, Oberg sent an email to his boss, Grover J. "Russ" Whitehurst, the Director of the Institute of Education Series (IES), who had been appointed by President George W. Bush and confirmed by the U.S. Senate. Oberg explained in his message how the secondary markets were creating the illusion that, through careful manipulation, bonds and loans could appear to be legally qualified for the 9.5 subsidy under the 1993 legislation. In addition, Oberg proposed a solution to the problem: "The Secretary could issue a Dear Partner/Colleague letter that would . . . disallow future increases in the amounts of 9.5% floor loans outstanding. This would be consistent with the 1993 law (OBRA 1993) that repealed the authority for new issues."

Whitehurst replied that he would forward the memo to the appropriate people, but he admonished Oberg, saying, "It's not your job to look into it," a response that Oberg took as a not-so-subtle threat.

Specifically, Whitehurst wrote to Oberg in an email, that the Department of Education ''does not have an intramural program of research on postsecondary education finance. In the 18 months you have remaining, I will expect your time and talents to be directed primarily to our business of conceptualizing, competing and monitoring research grants."

In the midst of all this, Russ Whitehurst selected Michael Wiatrowski as the new director of the National Center for Education Research (NCER). Wiatrowski also became Oberg's new politically appointed supervisor. Among the first tasks Whitehurst assigned to Wiatrowski was to change Oberg's job description, in order to prohibit him from further investigation of the 9.5 matter as part of his official position at the department.

Later, in a notable statement of partial contrition, Whitehurst would tell a reporter for the *New York Times*: "I didn't understand the issues. . . . In retrospect, it looks like he [Oberg] identified an important issue and came up with a reasonable solution. But it was Greek to me at the time—preferential interest rates on bonds? I didn't know what he was doing, except that he wasn't supposed to be doing it."[12]

Doubting Whitehurst's understanding of what was at stake, Oberg went to the Office of Ethics in the ED's general counsel's office. He requested a ruling on two matters: 1) As a federal employee, could he do further investigation into the suspected abuses of the 9.5-percent subsidy on his own time? And 2), could he contact outside agencies, such as the GAO and even Congress, to discuss the problem?

The OGC permitted both of Oberg's requests—with the proviso that he made it clear the he was not speaking on behalf of the Department of Education. The authority for this clearance, according to the OGC, was the Lloyd-La Follette Act of 1912, which protected the right of government workers to contact and furnish information to members of Congress without the permission of their supervisors. According to the Act, "the right of employees . . . to furnish information to either House of Congress, or to a committee or Member thereof, may not be interfered with or denied."

---

12   Sam Dillon, *New York Times*, "Whistle-Blower on Student Aid is Vindicated," May 7, 2007. In that story, Dillon added: "Mr. Whitehurst, in an interview, suggested that Mr. Oberg was viewed by some senior officials as an annoyance. 'I was told he was like a dog on a bone, agitating on this issue,' Mr. Whitehurst said."

Reflecting on this, Oberg said: "This to me was all routine, in the normal give and take of working in the federal government. I had not spent much office time on the 9.5 matter anyway, and I looked forward to adding it to my own personal research agenda at home, where I often worked on issues of public administration. My job description was something which I paid little attention to, and I thought revising it would be another of the dreary exercises that wastes federal employee time. I even found considerable humor in it, the idea that, somehow, I would be scared off the subject by the threat of a change in job description. My estimation of Grover Whitehurst was, of course, lowered considerably after this dust-up, even from the point to which it had already sunk after he had tried to eliminate postsecondary education research from IES's legislatively authorized mission. But holding other people's missteps against them was to me another waste of time when there were more important things to do."

Speaking of his relationship with Wiatrowski, his new supervisor, about changing his job description, Oberg added: "I worked with [Wiatrowski] on it lightheartedly, assuring him that I was amenable to virtually any language as long as there was some mention of postsecondary research, which was my field, why taxpayers were paying me, and to which the IES statute referred.

Wiatrowski apparently did not realize that postsecondary research was a sore point with Whitehurst, and the job description issue lingered for weeks."[13]

In February 2004—on his own and not government time while executing a "leave slip" to confirm this—Oberg, with permission from the department's general counsel's office, contacted an investigator at the GAO, Jeff Appel, whom Oberg knew through previous work. Appel brought three people to the meeting with Oberg, who proceeded to explain his evidence and suspicions.

Meantime, the crew from the hotline at the department's inspector general's office finally got around to looking into Oberg's allegations. He received an email and a call from Robert Rudolph, an IG investigator out of St. Paul, Minnesota.

"What's a secondary market?" Rudolph asked Oberg during their first conversation.

Oberg recalled, "I began to work with the IG's office to explain the FFEL student loan system and how loans and bonds could be manipulated to increase

---

13 With regard to Wiatrowski's fate at the Department of Education, Oberg explained: "Wiatrowski as director soon gave high personnel ratings to all five or so people in the NCER office—another time-wasting exercise—which Whitehurst would not accept and would not sign. He said surely someone among the five should be marked down.

"This troubled Wiatrowski greatly, and he brought the problem to the attention of all of us under his jurisdiction. I quickly volunteered to take lower marks to solve the problem and said it would be a badge of honor and I would hang it on my office wall. Wiatrowski saw this as a solution and acted accordingly.

"This did not satisfy Whitehurst and he essentially fired Wiatrowski, sending him to an empty desk in another building. Wiatrowski sued, which of course resulted in another wrangle with no end.

"The whole episode ruined Wiatrowski's career and drained his resources. Whitehurst went on to work at the Brookings Institution, where he himself eventually got into trouble and with poetic justice was sent to what passes there for an empty desk, or at least diminished responsibilities."

subsidies. I suggested the IG look at NMEAF in New Mexico as a starter audit to see what was actually going on within the secondary markets."

CHAPTER SIX

"GUESS WHO JUST CAME IN
TO LOBBY US?"

A gain, on his own time and on his home computer, Jon Oberg focused on specific secondary-market operations, "based on their moving loans around among bonds," Oberg said.

"The Department of Education would not provide me with any information on claims, even though such information should be public, so I had to approach Congress to get the information.

"Helping me in the Senate was Michael Dannenberg, counsel to Senator Kennedy's committee of jurisdiction over student loans, and James Kvaal, at the time on the staff of Senator John Edwards. They would demand the information from the Department of Education and then send it to me on my home computer for analysis. From this information, I could see which secondary markets were doing what, and when.

"From the changes in claims, I could back into estimates of how much pre-1993 tax-exempt bond authority they still retained and how many loans they were running in and out to wash them with the higher 9.5 subsidy."

Even though Dannenberg and Kvaal were extremely careful not to call or email Oberg at his office at the department, something happened that was so exciting to Kvaal that he had to speak with Oberg immediately—and called him at his office. When Oberg answered his phone, Kvaal exclaimed, "Guess who just came in to lobby us?"

The lobbyist was Scott Giles, vice president for government relations of the Vermont Student Assistance Corporation (VSAC). Giles told Kvaal that everything happening in the 9.5 scheme was illegal, and that VSAC, a non-profit, was getting badly hurt by secondary markets that had gone for-profit. In short, Giles asked Kvaal to help him get Congress to end all of the illegal operations.

Oberg had earlier dealt with Giles, who had previously worked for Senator Jim Jeffords (I-Vermont). Oberg liked and respected him as "a straight shooter."

Oberg replied to Kvaal, "Great! This should lead to a crackdown."

To Oberg, Giles' introduction into the 9.5-subsidy drama was the first major breakthrough, a seminal moment.

A second major breakthrough soon followed. While in the midst of exploring bond reports which had been researched and analyzed by Fitch Ratings—one of the three biggest credit-rating concerns, along with Moody's and Standard and Poor's—Oberg discovered references to the 9.5-percent subsidy.

Again, on his own time, Oberg called Fitch in New York and spoke with a company financial analyst.

Describing the conversation, Oberg said: "I explained that I was a potential investor in the company (for whom the reports are intended), but that I was also an employee of the Department of Education with some historical knowledge of the 9.5 subsidy.

"The analyst who answered the call said it was funny I was raising the question, because she had just gotten off the phone with Fitch's legal department, which expressed concerns about the 9.5 revenues claimed by the company in issuing new bonds.

"'They told me they don't think it's legal,' she said.

"That was all I needed to confirm that I was on the right track. But I persisted and asked why Fitch didn't come out and tell the public its conclusions about the illegality of the claims. In a scene that foreshadowed a similar highlight of the book and movie, *The Big Short*, the analyst explained that's not what rating agencies do."[14]

Also, in the spring of 2004, Oberg saw Dr. John Hartung of Iowa, a trusted friend and colleague who presided over an association of his state's independent colleges. Oberg had held a similar position in Nebraska during the 1980s.

In addition, Hartung was a board member of ISLLC, among other student-loan organizations.

Oberg remembered: "I told him to beware of joining the crowd and claiming excess 9.5 subsidies, because they were illegal and could get ISLLC in trouble. Little did I know at the time that ISLLC was already making the claims, based on its relationship with PHEAA, although not in sufficient amounts that they had attracted my attention."

Oberg was also unaware that two years earlier, ISLLC had been one of the targets of an OSFA financial review headed by Dr. Earl Crisp of the Department of Education's regional office in Dallas. Crisp's team found $58 million for which the ISLLC could not account. They wrote a report, noting illegal claims by the Iowa non-profit, and forwarded it to Washington.

However, in an abrupt reversal of the findings, the Department of Education—under Secretary Rod Paige—eliminated all references to the problem with the $58 million of new 9.5 subsidies.

Essentially, the report had been sanitized.

Specifically, the deleted language in Dr. Crisp's report had stated:

---

14 Explaining his analogy, Oberg said, "In [the book by author Michael Lewis,] *The Big Short*, an analyst at a major ratings firm says she cannot tell the truth about the impending crash of the subprime mortgage market, which almost brings down the world economy in 2008, because the client would then take its business to Moody's."

The regulations do not permit unlimited growth of tax-exempt funds by transferring loans from one bond issue to another. Growth from tax-exempt bonds should only occur from interest earnings, special allowance earnings, and investment earnings that are reinvested back into the bond issue. If a lender moves a loan as a qualifying tax-exempt bond to a non-qualifying bond, it may continue to bill the loan as a qualifying tax-exempt issue. However, this diminishes the available qualifying funds in the original bond subject to the minimum special allowance rate. Lenders must be able to provide documentation to support tax-exempt billing to the Department, particularly when quarterly billing on ED . . . exceeds the aggregate amounts supported by tax-exempt bonds issued prior to October 1, 1993.

The lender did not accurately categorize loans eligible for the minimum tax-exempt special allowance rate for loans made or purchased with tax-exempt funds after October 1, 1993. Therefore, average daily balances and ending balances . . . appear to be overstated for loans in the tax-exempt reporting category.[15]

Even though the department's general counsel's office believed that the scheme—which abused and exploited the 9.5 subsidy—was illegal, the Dallas investigators had no choice but to drop the case after being instructed to do so by a top department official, who told them, "Just let it go."

In a story that appeared in the *Chronicle of Higher Education*, reporter Stephen Burd wrote:

---

15   Letter from Earl W. Crisp, D.P.A., Guarantor and Lender Review Specialist, to Mr. Steve McCullough, President, Iowa Student Loan Liquidity Corporation. Dr. Crisp's original report was dated October 30, 2002. The sanitized report was dated December 9, 2003.

That report . . . stated that Education Department regulations "do not permit unlimited growth of tax-exempt funds by transferring loans from one bond issue to another."

But the department overruled those draft findings. And the leader of the team that conducted the review recently told a critic of the student-loan industry that his team had been told by Education Department leaders that the issue was "too hard" and that the auditors should just "let it go" and "close the review."

The team leader . . . was Earl W. Crisp, who specializes in monitoring lenders and guarantee agencies. Mr. Crisp made his comments to Robert M. Shireman, a senior education-policy adviser in the Clinton administration who now heads the Institute of College Access and Success, a watchdog group that focuses on the student-loan industry.

"Department officials went out of their way to overturn the findings of the investigator who found these payments to be illegal," said Mr. Shireman on Monday. Mr. Crisp 'saw this scam for what it was, and he intended to stop it,' Mr. Shireman said. Instead, he was ordered to let it go.'"[16]

Oberg could not be faulted for missing the sanitized report, as it had been done quietly. He was not in any chain of command that would have reviewed it.

Oberg now estimated from his own calculations that the illegal 9.5-subsidy scheme could be costing the federal government billions of dollars.

"When I learned of the Dallas team's program review in the summer of 2004," Oberg continued, "I wrote a note to Michael Dannenberg, James Kvaal, and Robert Shireman, a former Senate and OMB employee and old friend, that I had found the 'Rosetta Stone' of the whole 9.5 mystery. The Department had

---

16   Stephen Burd, *Chronicle of Higher Education*, "Critics Fault Bush Administration for Failing to Close a Loophole Worth Billions to Lenders," September 21, 2004. Burd repeated Dr. Crisp's allegations in a second article that appeared in the *Chronicle* on October 1, 2004.

known all along what was going on—or at least someone in OFSA had—but it had all been covered up.

"It was Bob Shireman who called Earl Crisp in Dallas and got the story on how he had been told to drop it.

"What was really going on at ISLLC? I suspect that when ISLLC told the Dallas program reviewers it needed time to check with PHEAA, it was not because they did not know but because they needed time to get to someone in the Department to kill the Dallas team's conclusions.

"Indeed, according to a confidential memo he shared with the ISLLC board, Steven McCullough of ISLLC met with Sally Stroup in her office to discuss the legality of the 9.5 scheme and the chances someone might raise trouble about it. Sally Stroup, however, assured him that he should not worry. The memo came to light later, through a reporter who investigated ISLLC and discussed her findings with me, knowing of my own interest in ISLLC claims."

In August 2004, after reviewing the claims of several of the secondary markets, the GAO gave Congress its report about the 9.5-subsity scam, which laid out its conclusion under a sensational title: "Federal Family Education Loan Program: Statutory and Regulatory Changes Could Avert Billions in Unnecessary Federal Subsidy Payments."

That was *billions* of dollars, just as Oberg had suspected.

One objection to the report came from Sally Stroup, the assistant secretary in the department. GAO included Stroup's letter at the end of its report as the official response of the department.

According to Oberg: "She said there was nothing the Department could currently do about the claims, short of starting a long process that might take many months or even years to cut off the 9.5 subsidy with new regulations, which would have to be negotiated with the very secondary markets that were making the claims. She said if Congress wanted to act, that would be faster. Clearly she was in no hurry."

The GAO report's author, Cornelia Ashby, on advice of GAO counsel, disagreed with Stroup, insisting—just as Oberg had in 2003—that the Secretary of Education could simply and unilaterally end the 9.5 subsidy without Congress or anyone else doing anything.

Oberg declared: "There was really no legal basis for the claims other than a remarkably convoluted rationale based on a sub-regulatory letter issued by the Department in 1996. The letter—actually an addendum to the letter—explained that loans transferred from one estate to another would retain the underlying SAP. It did not in any way suggest that the proceeds of such a transfer could be used to purchase new loans to put in the old estate and qualify them for the 9.5 subsidy as well. In fact, that violated an existing Department regulation, plain as day. The bizarre rationale also failed because it took the view that an attempt to answer a different question in an informal communication could totally overrule and render meaningless the 1993 act of Congress. All it would take for the Department to clarify any doubts about the meaning of a sub-regulatory letter would be another such letter, and it would all be over. But the Secretary would not act, backing up Sally Stroup's contention that the Department could do nothing, even if GAO said it could under other provisions that gave the Secretary to act in the public interest. Sally Stroup said public interest must be read as "public safety," and the 9.5 scheme did not endanger public safety.

"This became the line from the White House as well, at least for the time being. Sally Stroup even advised the White House that it was the Clinton Administration that had approved the 9.5 scheme, and she was the one now trying to undo it.

"This was a fabrication, because she knew full well that the Clinton Administration wanted to repeal the whole 9.5 subsidy so as not to allow its misuse.

"I read her letter to GAO with incredulity, because I remembered how she had personally rebuffed me when I gave her the Clinton Administration's 9.5 repeal language in 1998."

After the release of the GAO report, Kvaal contacted Bob Shireman. Like Oberg, Shireman, a warrior in the midst of an army of nine-to-five bureaucrats, felt that something had to be done.

The 9.5-subsidy story was ripe for media exposure, but Oberg was hesitant, believing that it was not his role to speak with the press. Bob Shireman wasn't so reluctant, and he brought Greg Winter of the *New York Times* into the fray, suggesting to Oberg that he speak with him.

Oberg agreed to speak with Winter—but only on background. He refused to go on the record. In the past—when dealing with financial matters—Oberg advised reporters who called him to go through the ED's Public Affairs Office.[17]

Oberg, whom Shireman lauded to Winter, said: "Bob Shireman told the *New York Times* that I was behind the discovery of the 9.5 claims, the first source to report it to Congress and the GAO, and that I would talk substance for clarification of how the scheme worked but that I would not agree to the mention of my name or my role in any story. Greg Winter of the *Times* agreed.

"I was careful not to return his calls on Department time. He gave me a special number and I called him from Union Station on my lunch breaks."

Though it did not appear on the front-page in the *New York Times*, Winter's story received a huge reaction, especially on Capitol Hill—because it appeared in the influential *New York Times*.

Winter, who based his fascinating story on the spectacular GAO report and its internal spreadsheets, wrote:

> Today, lenders are collecting a record amount of the old subsidies Congress thought it had retired, government data show, and they are busily stepping up the pace. Taking advantage of a loophole in the law, student loan companies have been billing the federal government at the rate of nearly $1 billion a year, at least four times the amount just three years ago—all for a subsidy that was supposed to have largely faded away. . . .

---

17 During the fall of 2003, Oberg spoke to a reporter for *U.S. News & World Report* for a story he was preparing, "Big Money on Campus." According to a later deposition, he spoke on background only to answer a factual question and referred other questions to the Office of Public Affairs, as was his practice.

[S]ome student loan companies say that the large subsidies they are receiving from the government, guaranteeing them 9.5 percent interest rates at a time when students pay much less than that, are hardly the best way of expanding access to college. But until either Congress or the administration closes the loophole promising them higher profits than the market offers on its own, there is little reason for them to stop using it.[18]

In the aftermath of the firestorm created by Winter's story, many congressmen and senators supported ending the 9.5 subsidies. However, they shied away from going past that, because of the campaign contributions they continued to receive from the alleged 9.5 abusers.

Oberg reflected: "Clearly this was posturing on the part of many who had been only too eager to accept campaign contributions from 9.5 sources, but that was before anyone knew where the money was coming from. Now, the rush was on to kill the scheme, although it soon became clear that to many, appearances were more important than substance. Congressmen John Boehner and Howard McKeon were among the first to insist on cutting it off only prospectively, trying to make sure no one had to pay anything back. As others found out how the scheme worked, they were interested in cutting off only part of it, so that once all the attention passed, they could get back to business as usual, albeit at reduced amounts."

In a follow-up story on September 22, 2004, Winter received additional quotes from key policy makers who supported the GAO report, including Rep. Chris Van Hollen (D-Maryland) and Rep. Dale E. Kildee (D-Michigan). And he also noted the rebuttal from the ED's Sally Stroup, who insisted that it would take years to plug the loopholes—without actually naming her.

That same month, August 2004, James Kvaal and Bob Shireman co-authored a white paper, *Money for Nothing: Skyrocketing Waste of Tax Dollars on Student Loan*

---

18   The expression "loophole in the law" did not come from Oberg, who always described the claims simply as illegal. His views were later confirmed by the Department's Inspector General and General Counsel. There was no legal loophole.

Companies' Scheme, published by The Institute for College Access and Success (TICAS), for which Shireman was the director. The co-authors recommended in their executive summary:

> **The Secretary of Education should take immediate action to halt and reverse the explosive growth in 9.5 percent loans.** His first step should be to publish a clarification—tomorrow—that prohibits the serial refinancing of loans, and limits the volume of 9.5 percent loans to the size of the original tax exempt bond.

> **The Secretary of Education should prepare to convert any remaining 9.5 loans to regular loans.** This may require requesting new, emergency authority from Congress before the end of this legislative session.

> **Congress and the Administration should restructure the student loan program** so that it takes advantage of market forces in the determination of government subsidies for intermediaries.

Just weeks before the reelection of President Bush, Congress acted to put the reins on the 9.5 subsidy legislatively, attempting to end the scam which had existed for so long. . . . Or so they thought.

Knowing that he was responsible for exposing the scandal, Jon Oberg felt relieved. With his retirement from the department looming, he believed, "My work here is done."

Or so he thought.

CHAPTER SEVEN

"THE IG ISSUED A DEVASTATING REPORT ON 'FINANCIAL PARTNERS'"

The following month, President Bush was reelected, defeating Senator John Kerry (D-Massachusetts). Although the 9.5 subsidy was not an issue during the campaign, Education Secretary Rod Paige was embarrassed by a situation earlier in his career, even though he was never charged with any wrongdoing.

Years earlier, while Houston's superintendent of schools, Paige had gained widespread acclaim as the architect behind the "Texas Miracle," the remarkable story about the city's students' rising test scores and unprecedented number of high-school graduations which had led to what appeared to be well-deserved merit pay for principals and teachers.

However, in 2003—after Paige left Houston and became education secretary—investigators discovered a massive cheating scandal had been behind the breathtaking success rate.

Among other deceptions, dropout rates were falsified.

Even though he was part of the team that created the "No Child Left Behind" program—which was modeled after his "success story" in Houston—Paige left the Department of Education as Bush began his second term.

He was replaced by Margaret Spellings, a domestic-policy advisor to the president. While Spellings was still getting settled, the department's inspector general's office ordered an audit of the New Mexico Education Assistance Foundation in May 2005. Determining that Congress's 1993 ban on the 9.5 subsidy going forward had been effectively ignored, the IG probe revealed that NMEAF had illegally grabbed $18.4 million of 9.5-percent-subsidy money and recommended that Secretary Spellings move in and recover that money.

As the IG could only make recommendations, the final decision fell on Secretary Spellings, who promptly rejected the IG's findings during a press conference she held with Rep. John Boehner in Boehner's congressional office. Also, in attendance was Kathleen Smith, who, like Sally Stroup, had worked for both Boehner and PHEAA. PHEAA was slated as another target of the IG—which provoked PHEAA and other potential targets to launch a full-scale lobbying campaign against the IG's 9.5 subsidy audits.

While present at the Spellings news conference, Smith was working for EFC, the secondary market's top lobbying operation.

Spellings tasked Matteo Fontana of the ED's Office of Student Financial Aid to notify NMEAF of her decision favorable to them. Notably, Fontana, while working for the department, held stock in a student-loan concern and was later convicted for accepting more than $100,000 worth of stock and not properly reporting it.

This experience became a cautionary tale for the IG's office, which selected a for-profit lender, not the well-connected PHEAA, as the target for its next audit. In addition to making a better description of the illegalities involved, the IG again made a case for the wrongfully obtained 9.5 money to be returned to the federal government.

The IG's excellent work—its second bite of the apple—earned the office the Alexander Hamilton award in 2006 from the Executive Council on Integrity and Efficiency, an organization of inspectors generals who serve throughout the federal bureaucracy.

Jon Oberg recalled: "On the same day, the IG also issued a devastating report on the Office of Federal Student Aid's 'Financial Partners' operation. It was written by Helen Lew, a no-nonsense auditor with whom I had been in contact about the 9.5 scheme. Lew was highly critical that the office's approach that emphasized partnership over compliance with the law.

"One such example was the leaking of pre-decisional materials to secondary markets so that they could push back before final decisions were made. This had happened in the case of the NMEAF audit. NMEAF used inside information to make the charge within its lobbying and political circles that a Democratic congressman was behind the NMEAF audit. The charge was not true, as I had been the one to recommend NMEAF for audit, solely on information contained in their financial reports."

Oberg continued: "When the second 9.5 audit hit Secretary Spelling's desk, Sally Stroup was gone. No reason was given for her early 2006 departure as the federal government's top higher education official. She went back to work as a committee staffer for Republicans in the House. Doubtless contributing to her departure were OMB officials who knew the stories she spun were not accurate. It being an election year, political people in the White House were also wary of the 9.5 scandal being used against Republicans.

"The man who personally made the Hamilton award to the IG honorees for their 9.5 audit of 2006 was none other than President Bush's close friend and political advisor, Clay Johnson. Music for the event was provided by the President's Own United States Marine Band. Talk about symbolism. This sent a message that the 9.5 scheme was not a creature of the White House."

Meantime, Bob Shireman of TICAS published another briefing paper in which he challenged procedures for converting secondary markets to for-profit businesses: "Who Benefits from Inside Deals when Non-Profits Convert?"[19] In an accompanying sidebar, Shireman wrote:

> Here are two simplified scenarios of conversions of a hypothetical non-profit entity with a market value of $100 million.
>
> **INSIDE DEAL:**
>
> * Corporate buyer pays $60 million for public assets worth $100 million
>
> --Buyer pays the facilitator of the deal (e.g. an official at the non-profit) $10 million (not disclosed as part of the deal).
>
> * $50 million (the publicly declared purchase price) is dedicated to charity (typically by endowing a new foundation).
>
> **COMPETITIVE BETTING:**
>
> * Buyer pays $100 million for public assets worth $100 million.
>
> * $100 million is dedicated to charity.

—м—

In 2006, Michael Dannenberg left Senator Kennedy's office and went to work for the New America Foundation, a Washington think tank where he ran its education programs. In the fall of that year, Dannenberg invited Oberg,

---

19   The Institute for College Access and Success, Inc. (TICAS) Briefing Paper: "How Non-Profit Student Loan Officials Get Rich: Will Californians get shorted on an inside deal?" May 26, 2005.

now retired, to participate in front of a standing-room-only crowd for a panel discussion at the foundation where Oberg was introduced as the whistleblower who blew open the 9.5 subsidy scandal.

The reaction to Oberg's presentation was remarkable. Former colleagues at the Department of Education showed up, as did Charlie Peters, the legendary editor of the *Washington Monthly* who had retired in 2001 but still wrote a column, "Tilting at Windmills," an apt description for Oberg's crusade.

"An attorney in the department's general counsel's office came up to me and declared, 'I can't get over how you did this.' That was an embarrassing moment for me, because actually I was only doing my job," Oberg said. He did not want the attention.

But even after his retirement, Oberg was pulled back into the fray.

In an unexpected turnabout in January 2007, Secretary Spellings suddenly embraced the findings of the newly released IG audit. She went so far as to declare—at long last—that the 9.5 scam had indeed been illegal from the outset. So much for Sally Stroup's bizarre defenses of her former industry colleagues. Moreover, the Earl Crisp review that called the whole scheme illegal as early as 2002, then was quietly reversed by parties unknown, was once again standing tall.

Oberg continued: "But Secretary Spellings did not act to recover any of the money. Rather, she struck a deal with the secondary markets. They could even make new 9.5 claims if they would undergo independent audits, using the IG's award-winning audit as a guide. If not, they could keep their ill-gotten gains but forever into the future they would be barred from making any additional 9.5 claims."

Oberg explained that, as far as he was concerned, this would not be the end of the issue of the illegal giveaways: "In February of 2007, just days after Secretary Spellings declared that the 9.5 scheme was illegal (and always had been), but chose to let those who had made false claims keep hundreds of millions of taxpayers' money, I was invited to testify before the Senate's HELP Committee, still chaired by Senator Kennedy."

In considering changes to the Higher Education Act, the theme of the hearing—which was conducted by chairman Kennedy and ranking member Senator Mike Enzi, among others—was the matter of paying for college.

Along with Oberg, who was expected by the chairman to explain the minutia of the federal bureaucracy in order to keep the discussion on track, others who testified on the panel were Sandy Baum, a professor of economics at Skidmore College who specialized on issues facing higher education; author Tamara Draut, who wrote about the debt burdens of average Americans; and best-selling author and television personality, Suze Orman. C-SPAN broadcast the hearing live.

During his summary of prepared testimony, Oberg stated:

> [W]when I was invited to testify, I asked your staff if I was expected to testify on the 9.5 guaranteed loan scandal. I was told that that was not the reason I was here particularly, because I had been the legislative liaison from the Department of Education for the reauthorization of the Higher Education Act in 1998 and I might have views on some of the legislation that came out of that, . . . but let me say a couple of quick words about the 9.5 problems.

> As one of my attachments to my written testimony, I suggested back in 2003, that one solution to this would be simply for the Secretary to call the loans. I still think that is a good recommendation. That was put in as a bill last year by Senator Murray and Senator Kennedy and I commend that to you again....

> There is also . . . the recovery of the forgiveness of these illegal payments that has been done in the past month. I see two House Republicans have already introduced or have a circulating letter asking the Secretary of Education to recall these funds. . . . My recommendation to the com-

mittee would be... that the Congress have an opportunity to exercise oversight on it.

Oberg recalled that the hearing quickly moved away from recovering illegally claimed funds: "Suze Orman wasted no time finding a reason to tout her latest book about financial literacy. Republican Senator Johnny Isakson broke in with a request for her book, and would she also please autograph it for his granddaughter? I threw cold water on the idea that students and families these days could learn how to pay for college just by improving their financial literacy. I described the complicated process built up around the federal grant and loan programs and gave as an illustration an actual conversation I had once had with a CPA who could not figure out how it all worked. If a CPA could not understand all the forms required for federal grants and loans, how could the average family?"

Oberg remembered: "It was at this hearing that I made the suggestion for Congress simply to do away with the FFEL [Federal Family Education Loan] program and put the resulting savings into student grants. It was just too costly, complicated, and scandal-ridden to continue, I testified."

It would take three more years of audits and exposés, but Congress finally, as Oberg recommended, shut it down, saving billions of taxpayer dollars in the process.

CHAPTER EIGHT

"A REVOLVING DOOR BETWEEN THE DEPARTMENT AND INDUSTRY"

The illegal giveaways by the Department of Education did not escape the notice of the news media.

CNN Money published a story about apparent conflicts of interest:

> [T]here's the movement of political appointees among the DOE, lobbying firms, and corporations. An incomplete list includes Sally Stroup, who was the chief lobbyist for Apollo Group, which owns the for-profit University of Phoenix, before she was appointed by President Bush to oversee post-secondary education at the DOE. In the spring of 2006, she left to become the deputy staff director at the House Education Committee. Two other former top DOE officials, William Hansen and Jeff Andrade, have ties to FFELP lenders. . . .[20]

---

20 Working for Hansen, Andrade was the Deputy Assistant Secretary for the Postsecondary Education from 2001 to 2003. Previously, he had served as a senior staffer on the House Education and Workforce Committee.

With his appearance at the Senate hearings, Oberg became a go-to person for the press on issues of higher-education finance. Anne Applebaum of the *Washington Post* invited him twice to her editorial office, and he accepted both times.

Oberg recalled: "I enjoyed her personal tour of the newsroom where Bob Woodward and Carl Bernstein broke the Watergate story, and I liked her editorials on the 9.5 scandal. But I did not consent to what the *Post* wanted—my cooperation in a story profiling me and how I had to work at home over the objection of Department of Education officials to get to the bottom of who was raiding the U.S. Treasury and how they were doing it.

"The *Wall Street Journal* and the *New York Times* called frequently to get my take on stories they were doing. Bethany McLean (*The Smartest Guys in the Room: The Amazing Rise and Scandalous Fall of Enron*) and I exchanged emails on student loans. John Hechinger and Anne Marie Chaker at the *WSJ* did an article that pointed out numerous conflicts of interest. I cooperated on the story as a 'former federal official who had long since retired.'"

Specifically, the *Wall Street Journal* was critical of Sally Stroup, saying:

> Four years ago, Sally Stroup, then an assistant secretary at the U.S. Education Department, got a memo from the agency's inspector general urging her to curb any "illegal inducements" lenders might be using to win college loan business.

> Ms. Stroup, who had previously worked for a Pennsylvania loan company and a for-profit education concern dependent on student loans, didn't take the memo's advice.

> At least eight top officials in the Education Department during the Bush administration either came from student-loan or related organizations or have taken lucrative jobs in that arena since leaving the agency. Former Ed-

ucation Department staffers say a revolving door between the department and industry has led to lax oversight of federal financial aid. Members of Congress -- including the Democrats who head committees overseeing education, Sen. Edward Kennedy of Massachusetts and Rep. George Miller of California -- say they are concerned about the industry ties. Mr. Miller plans to hold a hearing on student loan abuses this month. . . .

"I saw too much in the department that indicated that many of the people were too close to the lending industry and were making decisions that weren't in the public interest," says Jon Oberg, a former Education Department researcher.

Ms. Stroup says that until now, no one knew the extent of student loan abuses, and she says she took action when allegations could be proved. "We always wanted to run the agency right for students, families and schools," says Ms. Stroup, now a senior Republican aide on Capitol Hill.[21]

Oberg continued: "The *New York Times*, like the *Washington Post*, wanted to do a personality profile of me, whom they wanted to call a whistleblower. I was uneasy with the loaded term and declined. Instead, I suggested, why not do a story that got into the substance of the 9.5 scandal, so the public would know how taxpayer money was wasted. A good article might even serve as a warning to others who might try to defraud the government, as well as a lesson to federal officials who found it easier to look the other way when confronted with fraud.

"They agreed and dispatched reporter Sam Dillon to my home in Rockville, Maryland. For four hours, we went over the facts. After Dillon drafted his story, he telephoned me with the message that his editors liked it and it might even wind up on page one. There was one problem: they could not find any

---

21   John Hechinger and Anne Marie Chaker, *Wall Street Journal*, "Did Revolving Door Lead to Student Loan Mess?" April 13, 2007.

experts in student loan finance who could independently confirm how the 9.5 scandal worked. I suggested someone on the Inspector General's staff who had won the big award for the excellence and clarity of their 9.5 audit. Instead, Dillon suggested that I review the draft myself. He said this was unconventional, but I was the person who had brought it to the IG's attention in the first place.

"So late one evening at home, I received the draft from Dillon. He had done a remarkable job, except for one error of fact and one of opinion. He said I was a political employee of the Clinton Administration when I served in the Office of Legislation and Congressional Affairs in the 1990s. I said no, totally wrong; I was a civil servant who was employed because I knew the federal programs and, in that position, I had to have credibility with both Democrats and Republicans. He took it back to his editor, who said I was surely mistaken because jobs in such offices were given to political appointees. He knew, he said, because he had worked in Washington. Well, I told Dillon, I certainly knew my own status and if the error went to print, I would point it out publicly. His editor backed off somewhat, with language that suggested some in the Bush Administration *thought* I was a political employee during the Clinton years.

"The other error in the draft to which I took exception was the casual observation that I came to be "obsessed" with the scandal. I laughed. Anyone who knows me, I said, would know that was not true. I pointed out to Dillon that in my Senate testimony earlier that year, I had even put the 9.5 scandal into context, saying that other issues were at least a hundred times more important. His editor suggested "pre-occupied" rather than "obsessed." I said sure, I wouldn't obsess about it.

"There was one part of the story that I would have changed, but I never saw it until it went to print. In the page one headline, the story referred to me as a whistleblower. It was not the first time, as the New America Foundation had called me that the previous year, but the *New York Times* was a quantum leap beyond that, and I reluctantly accommodated myself to the term."

In his remarkable story on May 7, 2007—above the fold on the front page of the *New York Times*—Dillon wrote:

> When Jon Oberg . . . warned in 2003 that student lending companies were improperly collecting hundreds of millions in federal subsidies and suggested how to correct the problem, his supervisor told him to work on something else. . . .

> For three more years, the vast overpayments continued. Education Secretary Rod Paige and his successor, Margaret Spellings, argued repeatedly that under existing law they were powerless to stop the payments and that it was Congress that needed to act. Then this past January, the department largely shut off the subsidies by sending a simple letter to lenders -- the very measure Mr. Oberg had urged in 2003.

> The story of Mr. Oberg's effort to stop this hemorrhage of taxpayers' money opens a window, lawmakers say, onto how the Bush administration repeatedly resisted calls to improve oversight of the $85 billion student loan industry. The department failed to halt the payments to lenders who had exploited loopholes to inflate their eligibility for subsidies on the student loans they issued.[22]

That same day, Tim Lacy, a blogger on education issues, trumpeted the *Times's* story, headlined: "Modern-Day Hero: Jon Oberg, Former G-Man in the U.S. Dept. of Education."[23]

On May 8, the *Times* followed up with a devastating editorial about the 9.5 scandal, condemning the government for the colossal waste:

---

22   Sam Dillon, *New York Times*, "Whistle-Blower on Student Aid is Vindicated," May 7, 2007.

23   Tim Lacy, History and Education: Past and Present (Blog), "Modern-Day Hero: Jon Oberg, Former G-Man in the U.S. Dept. of Education," May 7, 2007.

Republicans in Congress have generally defended corporate welfare for companies involved in the student loan business: lenders that collect billions of dollars in federal subsidies in return for issuing government-backed loans that represent no real risk to the companies themselves. But support for these wasteful subsidies is waning in both parties, thanks to recent revelations showing just how corrupt and costly the program has become. . . .

The giveaway at the Education Department is closely related to the payoffs and kickbacks that lenders have recently been found to be paying to colleges that steer borrowers their way. These schemes are driven by excess money that would substantially dry up if Congress cut the subsidy rate. Beyond that, however, Congress needs to get out of the business of artificially setting the subsidy rate, as it does now.[24]

The following day, the *New York Times* reported that Theresa S. Shaw, the chief operating officer of the Office of Federal Student Aid (OFSA) for the Department of Education, was resigning—just before Education Secretary Margaret Spellings was slated to testify before Congress about several matters, including Oberg's revelations. The *Times* stated:

Ms. Shaw was appointed in 2002 by Education Secretary Rod Paige after 22 years in industry, mostly at Sallie Mae, the largest student lender.

Ms. Spellings called Ms. Shaw "a tireless advocate for students and families," saying that the aid program "now delivers more aid to more students at a lower operating cost with greater accuracy than at any point in its history."

---

24 Editorial, *New York Times*, "Congress and the Student Loan Scam," May 8, 2007.

[New York State Attorney General Andrew] Cuomo, by contrast, recently told the House education committee that the Education Department had been "asleep at the switch" in regulating the practices of lenders. . . .

Critics have warned that the department has been too cozy with lenders, choosing not to provide guidelines on permissible inducements to university officials.

The department is also being scrutinized by Congress for its failure to crack down on hundreds of millions in dollars in questionable subsidies that loan companies have collected.[25]

Secretary Spellings appeared before the U.S. House Committee on Education and Labor and was sharply questioned, particularly by Rep. George Miller (D-California), the committee's chairman. He criticized her for the predatory and unethical practices that had been tolerated by the Department of Education.

It had to be one of the worst days ever for Margaret Spellings. A clever politician, she quickly changed the subject to a new commission she appointed to look at the future of U.S. higher education.

It worked. . . . The media's attention was soon diverted.

---

25   Jonathan D. Glater, *New York Times*, "Federal Student Loan Official Is Resigning," May 9, 2007.

CHAPTER NINE

"THE OVERPAYMENTS MAY HAVE TOTALED HUNDREDS OF MILLIONS OF DOLLARS"

I n a profile that followed the earlier chronicling of Jon Oberg's work in the *New York Times*, columnist William Bainbridge wrote in the *Florida Times-Union*:

> Now retired, Oberg told me in a telephone conversation from his Rockville, Md., home: "I hope that all of this leads to reforms in student loan oversight. It was good to hear Secretary Margaret Spellings admit the system is broken and needs reform." . . .
>
> Oberg came to public attention in an effort to do the right thing for taxpayers against formidable powers, including those who spend many hours in the Oval Office.[26]

---

26   William Bainbridge, *Florida Times-Union*, "Thumbs Up for Whistle-Blower; Thumbs Down for Spellings," May 17, 2007.

The accolades aside, Oberg still viewed himself as nothing more than a federal employee who had simply done his job. He tried to divert attention away from himself.

"Yes, I had gone to considerable lengths to end the false claims on the Treasury," he said, "but I was also a political scientist with a professional career and an academic research agenda, so it was not uncommon for me to work at home on projects involving federal funds and federal programs. There was no great heroism on my part inasmuch as nothing was really at stake in my career in becoming a so-called whistleblower. I was about to retire anyway; my résumé and reputation were already in place for better or for worse. In retirement, I wanted to clean my garage."

Still, there was a public demand for the inside story of his role in the 9.5-subsidy drama.

Oberg explained: "NBC Nightly News wanted me on-camera to discuss the 9.5 scandal. This would be my third encounter with them. An earlier one was my disgust over a misguided 'Fleecing of America' segment. Earlier still was the time NBC News found me in Berlin, about 1990, to try to confirm an allegation made by Senator John Tower of Texas, who had been nominated by President George H.W. Bush to be Secretary of Defense. Tower was under pressure to withdraw his name because of certain untoward behavior episodes and started lashing out at those he thought were his detractors, to try to implicate them in their own scandals. I had been knowledgeable about one such affair, involving a Savings and Loan, when I worked in the Senate in the early 1980s. I told NBC News there was nothing to it, that it was obviously a desperate attempt to save Tower's appointment.[27]

"I went to the NBC News studios on Nebraska Avenue in northwest Washington one afternoon at NBC's invitation to talk on camera about the 9.5 scandal. They made the obligatory footage of my walking along a street and then interviewed me in a studio. The piece was ready to lead off the *Nightly*

---

27   Charles M. Pallesen Jr. and Samuel Van Pelt, *Big Jim Exon: A Political Biography* (Atlanta, Georgia: Infusion Media, 2012).

News with Brian Williams when it was pulled for an even better student loan story, with much better visuals. College student financial aid officers were meeting at a convention in New York City, and NBC News had footage of them enjoying themselves on a cruise around Manhattan. This was at the same time New York Attorney General Andrew Cuomo was launching an investigation into the relationship between such officials and the student loan industry.

"I was relieved that I did not have to appear in living rooms across the country as a whistleblower. The C-SPAN re-runs of the Senate hearings were already causing more than enough talk about me in Nebraska, my home state. When I went to see an elderly relative, Lester Spader, in York, Nebraska, he greeted me from his assisted living unit to say how excited he was to see me on television so often.

"*The Chronicle of Higher Education* wanted my estimates of how much the 9.5 scandal had cost taxpayers before it was shut down. Paul Basken wrote an article citing my estimates of perhaps as much as one billion dollars. I told him I was still at work refining them, and, so far, they were in the area of $800 million. I did not tell him that I was preparing the estimates for a potential lawsuit to recover the money."

—◊◊—

It took some time, but the *Washington Post* published its own front-page story about Oberg's extraordinary work on October 20, 2007—five months after the *New York Times*.

Post reporter Amit Paley, who quoted Oberg but did not write a profile of him, at Oberg's request, stated:

> In July, the department responded to a *Post* request for data on the 9.5 percent loan subsidies. The *Post* analyzed payments from 2001 to 2006 to lenders from across the country. . . .

Department officials contend that only comprehensive audits can determine the amount overpaid to lenders. Diane Auer Jones, assistant secretary for postsecondary education, called The *Post's* analysis flawed. "We don't believe meaningful inferences can be made" from the data the department provided, Jones said in a statement. But four experts in higher education finance who reviewed the analysis at The *Post's* request -- Christopher Avery, a Harvard University professor; Laura W. Perna, a University of Pennsylvania professor; Robert B. Archibald, a College of William & Mary professor; and Robert Shireman, president of the Institute for College Access and Success -- said it would provide a rough estimate of the potential cost to taxpayers.

Speaking of the *Post* article and praising the reporter who wrote it, Oberg said: "Amit Paley did a superb job, even putting together a panel of student loan experts from the University of Maryland, Harvard, William and Mary, and an independent think-tank to make estimates of the 9.5 scandal losses. They came up with estimates close to my own.

"When the story appeared on page one, Amit Paley called me to ask what I thought of it. He had put a tremendous amount of work into it, and I found no errors, so I complimented it. Actually, I thought it was curious that the story started out giving Secretary Spellings another opportunity to justify her forgiving so much taxpayer money to organizations that had committed fraud, while burying at the end of the story the new, empirical research that validated the extent of it. Amit Paley said the same thing, that he was shocked at how editors had changed his story. He was in Iraq, however, now covering the war and not able to do anything about it. A great reporter, a member of the extended Paley family that included media notables, he eventually left journalism."

Meantime, Congress—or at least six Democrats—moved for action, asking the Bush Administration for a detailed accounting of the overpayments resulting from the 9.5-percent subsidy.

According to a Reuters story on November 1, 2007:

> The overpayments may have totaled hundreds of millions of dollars from 2003 to 2006 and taxpayers have a right to know the actual amount, the senators said in an October 31 letter sent to the department's inspector general.
>
> "Taxpayers also deserve information on which lenders were involved, what methods they used to claim these subsidies unfairly, and why the department allowed the inappropriate subsidies to be paid," the senators in a statement. . . .
>
> The request adds to numerous inquiries into student loans and the Education Department. Not only the 9.5 percent loan program, but student loan marketing practices have been under scrutiny for months since a scandal over kickbacks and conflicts of interest embarrassed the $85 billion industry.[28]

On November 20, the *New York Times* continued its reporting, writing in its lede:

> The student loan corporation in Pennsylvania improperly exploited a subsidy program to collect $34 million from the government, said a report released yesterday by the inspector general of the federal Education Department.

---

28   Kevin Drawbaugh, *Reuters*, "US Democrats seek probe of 9.5-pct student loans," November 1, 2007.

The audit called on the department to recover the payments to the corporation, the Pennsylvania Higher Education Assistance Agency, a state-
owned company that makes and guarantees student loans.[29]

The chief executive of PHEAA denied that his agency had ever done anything improper.

Oberg continued: "Secretary Spellings again changed the subject away from
student loans to her appointment of a commission to study higher education
and to give her a report. She selected luminaries of various stripes to look at
questions of teaching and learning and everything else under the sun. It was
an immediate hit and became known as The Spellings Commission. Margaret
Spellings had been around politics a long time and knew that when all else
fails, appoint a commission."

To Oberg, a different strategy was required, and he had the standing to
deliver it.

"When I was originally researching how secondary markets were moving
loans around among bond indentures to claim higher subsidies," Oberg said,
"I merely wanted the Department of Education to put a stop to it. Hence, I
had gone to the IG, then to the Department, then to the GAO, all the while
thinking that if people only understood what was going on, the scheme would
come to an end. I was greatly satisfied when Congress finally acted in 2004
to start to kill it and thought my role in it was over.

"But then I remembered how Secretary Spellings had overruled the IG's
audit of NMEAF, and how I had written her a letter upon my retirement in
2005 as to how tawdry this was and how she could still end it all with a simple "Dear Colleague" letter and a requirement that all money falsely claimed
must come back to the federal treasury. I had shown the letter to my director
and colleague at IES/NCER, Dr. Mark Schneider, a fellow political scientist.
He was as appalled as I was about the whole situation. He made some good

---

29   Jonathan D. Glater, *New York Times*, "Audit Finds Misuse of $34 Million Student Loan
Subsidy," November 20, 2007.

recommendations for changes and I sent the letter off, never to receive a reply. He had asked me to stay on and to not retire, inasmuch as the small office had no other person who knew anything about postsecondary education finance. I said he should hire someone; I was not the only person who knew the field. For sure, I was not sticking around. In my final paperwork leaving the federal government, I candidly expressed my concern that in good conscience, I could not continue to work for an organization such as the Department of Education, as I doubted the integrity of its leadership.

"When I left the Department, I had asked for disks containing my research records and email correspondence. My colleague, Dr. Cliff Adelman, had just changed offices (he could not get along with Grover Whitehurst, whom he called "Joe Stalin"), and the Department had prepared such disks for him, so I asked for a similar download of my history from the Department's computers, too. Among the records I wanted to retain were the research papers I had written on the influence of federal student aid on the price of tuition and on student-aid packaging, papers that Grover Whitehurst thought would be of no interest to anyone. They were still my intellectual property and I thought I might seek to publish them in an academic journal.

"These disks were of great help in 2007 when I started to think seriously about a lawsuit, because of the way Margaret Spellings rewarded secondary markets for their illegal behavior. I had been vaguely aware that individuals could file suit on behalf of the United States in so-called *qui tam* actions under the False Claims Act. To qualify as the "relator" under the law, the person bringing suit had to be the original source of the information that led to uncovering the false claims. The records of my emails were perfect to document that I was the original source. I had shared my thinking process and suspicions with numerous people along the way, including the Department's program administrators, policy setters, and lawyers.

"The first lawyers I approached about such a suit, supposed experts in the False Claims Act, told me I could not qualify as a relator because I was a federal employee in the Department that administered the program. I explained that I worked in a completely different and independent branch of the Department. Especially helpful, I thought, would be the rebuff I got from Grover Whitehurst saying it was not my job to ask any questions about the student loan programs. When I showed them the email records I had, they thought long and hard about it, but in the end said it was too unusual for a federal employee to file a *qui tam* suit and wished me luck elsewhere.

"This happened three times or more and I was about to give up when I told my Rockville neighbor, Lynette Whitfield, about my frustration. A lawyer doing mostly pro-bono work (or "low-bono" work, as she called it), she said I should talk to Jason Zuckerman of The Employment Law Group (TELG) to see if they would take my case. Jason, she said, was a good man and just might think the case was winnable.

"She was right. Jason Zuckerman was a great find. He and his colleagues David Scher and Scott Oswald took me on as a TELG client and helped me greatly in preparing the lawsuit.

"For the lawsuit, I prepared spreadsheets on ten secondary markets that I was convinced had violated the law. I was careful in making my estimates, giving many secondary markets the benefit of the doubt as to how the loans that they claimed eligible for the 9.5% guaranteed subsidy had acquired their qualifying characteristics.

"Although Congress cut off the subsidy prospectively in 1993, many old grandfathered loans were still in repayment because they had been in deferment or forbearance or had their terms extended for other reasons. Also, pre-1993 bond indentures could have been re-funded at some point and the re-fundings might be considered the same as the original bonds in certain cases.

"Then there was recycling: for example, early pay-offs by borrowers might be recycled back into the bond trust from which they were originally financed. There was also the possibility of legitimate transfers of loans among bond trusts that might conceivably retain the subsidy eligibility.

"I looked back at the history of the amounts of pre-1993 bond estates and how they had fluctuated in size in the 1990s, before the illegal gaming began. I came up with conservative formulas that I applied to many secondary markets to see if there was any reasonable explanation for the growth in the subsidy claims. Even if a secondary market had deliberately gamed the system and made false claims, if the amounts were such that they could have come up with the same numbers by legal re-funding, re-cycling, and transferring, I took them off the hook.

"Jason Zuckerman, after helping me with the legal language necessary for the lawsuit, went on to work for the federal Office of Special Counsel, an agency set up to help federal employees who were in conflict with their agencies. OSC, before his arrival, had been among the worst federal agencies imaginable: long waiting lists and often nothing to show for the trouble even when it got to clients. (I knew of its reputation firsthand, as I had asked for OSC assistance in late 2003, after Grover Whitehurst told me it was not my job to report problems in student loans. I got a letter back from OSC advising me to take up my issue inside the Department of Education. Good grief, what did they think I was doing?) By the time Jason Zuckerman left OSC to start his own practice, the agency was getting top marks."

CHAPTER TEN

"THIS COULD HAVE BEEN A CASE-KILLER FOR ME"

Jon Oberg filed suit in the Eastern Division of the U.S. District Court of Virginia, aka "The Rocket Docket," on August 21, 2007. As soon as the case was docketed, the U.S. Department of Justice asked that it be placed under seal while it considered a possible intervention, a common practice in controversial litigations involving the federal government. Notably, because of the seal, the defendants received no official notification that they had been sued.

Oberg explained: "The law gave DOJ a couple of months to make a decision. DOJ instead took two years. During that time, we had many meetings between my lawyers, DOJ, IG, and other parties. The defendants were not aware of the suit during this time, to my knowledge. I had been under instructions not to say anything about the existence of the case to anyone, and not to remove any evidence from my home computer, should it eventually become subject to discovery.

"We hoped DOJ would intervene and take over the case, but in the end, it did not. They said privately that the suit had merit and they did not dispute any of my numbers, but from that point on, we were on our own.

"TELG was sorely disappointed. In most such cases, if DOJ does not intervene, the case is over.

"Non-intervention is often wrongly viewed by the public as a judgment that DOJ does not think a case has merit. In reality, other factors may be at work. In our case, it would have been awkward for DOJ to investigate ED, a sister federal agency, as to who might have given secondary markets the green light to game the system, if that in fact that had occurred. Could it even have been some of the Department's lawyers sitting around the table in the two years DOJ considered intervening? I suspected some of them for knowing more than they told DOJ. I am quite certain ED lawyers leaned hard on DOJ lawyers not to intervene. For one thing, it would have been embarrassing for them to have to admit they were aware of shenanigans going on in the Department while they closed their eyes to it. More than one ED employee told me between 2003 and 2005 that what I was doing was right, but he or she could be of no help. 'Gotta put food on the table, y' know.'

"TELG had an obligation to me, its client, to continue the case if I wanted to pursue it, but it was a small office and they did not have the ability to muster the resources required to take on secondary markets with billions of dollars in assets while DOJ did nothing. TELG needed a bigger law firm to join in or take over. It found one in Wiley Rein, a formidable K Street firm with nearly three hundred lawyers.

"Dave Scher told Wiley Rein about the case and arranged for me to give a presentation so they could get a sense of who I was and whether they might take me on as a client. Bert Rein was intrigued by the 9.5 scheme and how it worked. He quickly understood what it was about, how I had all of the emails that documented I was the original source uncovering it and committed the firm to the suit.

"It helped that the case involved hundreds of millions of dollars in false claims and that if we won, there would be a good return for Wiley Rein. In the end, however, I believe I was able to get good representation because law firms such as TELG and Wiley Rein are serious about fulfilling their responsibilities to would-be clients under our system of law. This would become even more apparent over the coming years.

"I am also deeply indebted to my personal attorney, Laura Berthiaume, for her continued oversight of my legal agreements with the firms that handled my litigation under the False Claims Act.

"Wiley Rein and TELG went to work immediately to try to take depositions and to demand discovery of documents from secondary markets, ED personnel, lawyers, lobbying associations, and other relevant parties. Four of the defendants argued they were arms of their respective states and under the doctrine of sovereign immunity, they could not be sued. The six other defendants tried to get rid of the suit on other grounds before they were required to give depositions and allow discovery.

"In the late fall of 2009, Judge Claude Hilton of the federal district court in Alexandria ruled against us on the four entities that were so-called arms of states but allowed us to go ahead with the remaining six.

"We felt that we had not had our day in court on the four that claimed sovereign immunity. Michael Sturm of Wiley Rein, in oral argument, had been cut off from discussing the matter by Judge Hilton, who said he had heard enough before Michael Sturm was even able to get out one sentence. We would temporarily set these four cases aside, vowing to come back to them at some point when the other cases were disposed of."

Describing his litigation, Oberg said: "The give and take of depositions and discovery proceeded quickly. My lawyers visited secondary markets scattered across the country to take depositions under oath. We demanded relevant documents in discovery and soon accumulated hundreds of thousands of pages, to be pored over by many Wiley Rein lawyers. Likewise, the defendants demanded all my computer records and took many hours of deposition from me, under oath.

"I attended most of the depositions that we took in Washington, DC. It was gratifying for me to hear from secondary market CFOs, to see their numbers and processes conform to my predictions. As to what legal authority they were using to make their claims, it was amusing to see them squirm, as they had trouble putting forward an explanation with a straight face, but sad to realize that these were federal taxpayer dollars that were at stake. This was what white-collar fraud looked like, personified.

"Lawyers who had tried to give the process outside legal cover were pathetic. John Dean of the Dean, Moskowitz, and Cipriani law firm, which also did lobbying work for the secondary markets, knew he would be in for a hard time and said early in his deposition that he was beset with a serious illness, was under the influence of prescription drugs and would not be able to speak clearly, or always understand what was going on in his deposition. Perhaps this was brilliant on his part, but I thought the very idea that the secondary markets would hire a Washington lobbyist to give them legal opinions—he did them for both nonprofits like Kentucky's as well as for-profits—was absurd.

"Sally Stroup testified to being unsure of how the 9.5 scheme worked but said she thought it was legal. That was her personal opinion, she said, not the policy position of the Department of Education. She didn't remember much about how it actually worked.

"After a morning of questioning by the defendants' lawyers, who desperately wanted her to exonerate them but failed in that quest, Bert Rein took over the questioning in the afternoon for our side. Walking her through the 9.5 scheme while periodically wiping off his glasses with his necktie, Bert Rein concluded her deposition only when she conceded she had no more answers by putting her head in her arms on the table in front of her and signaled that she had had enough.

"All of this was witnessed by representatives from the Justice Department and the Department of Education, and recorded by video cameras in preparation for a jury trial, where all of those giving depositions could be put on the stand to see if they could do better before a jury.

"Most of the other Department of Education personnel who gave depositions exhibited an ineptitude hard to fathom. These are the people handling billions of taxpayer dollars.

"When my turn came for deposition, I knew I would be in for an arduous grilling from defendants' K-Street and Wall Street lawyers. I had already been required to give up all of my home computer records. I did not know what was in them that opposition lawyers might give me trouble about. I was not confident that the downloads of computer records were complete and accurate. The individual who came to my house to take computer discovery was inexperienced and not sure what it was all about. He seemed to think I was a defendant who had committed a crime, instead of a plaintiff who was discovering fraud elsewhere.

"His first reaction to seeing my computer was surprise that I had a Mac: 'Oh, you have a Mac, I've never done a Mac before. I don't know anything about them.' Some months later it became clear that he did not know what he was doing. He had missed some emails that were helpful to us and I had to bring my computer to Wiley Rein offices to provide them.

"I approached my deposition trying to be well prepared but simultaneously viewing myself as an academic observer curious about the whole process. What other political scientists had been behind closed doors to witness K Street battle K Street, in the presence of the Justice Department, with the video cameras rolling?

"A defendant's lawyer who traveled to Washington from Texas began my interrogation. I was instructed by my lawyers to tell the truth, as I was under oath, and that they would interrupt if the questioning got out of bounds. I was told to be concise, just to answer the questions posed and not to go down any rabbit holes or get engaged in any long discussions.

"After many hours, the first session of my deposition was over. The highlight of it for me was when the Texas lawyer tried to ask me a key, 'gotcha' question, but stumbled over it himself, as it was a complicated mix involving issues of law and finance, expressed in convoluted grammar. He had tried to ask it without referring to his notes.

"I smiled and asked if he wanted to try that question again, nodding to the notes in front of him. He started to read it, but midway through gave up and moved on to the next question. At the end of the session, I shook hands with him and expressed concern about the condition of his eyes. He had a partial patch over one and I asked what had happened, as if we were old friends who had not been engaged in a game of wits the whole day. My lawyers were satisfied with how the day went. I had survived hours of deposition without ruining the case.

"My real attention during the first day of deposition had not been on my case at all. I don't know if it showed—I didn't say anything to anyone—that I was thinking mostly of my mother, who was in her last days in Nebraska. My brother and I had been trading off, living at her home in Lincoln for two weeks at a time, while she was under hospice care for an inoperable lung condition. She was ninety-four.

"She died on the morning of my first deposition. My brother left a telephone message for me to call him. I got it only when I arrived home. He had known I was in the middle of a deposition that day and did not want to disrupt me. That is the way my mother would have wanted it. She did not know the details of my case, but she would have been upset had my brother called to interrupt.

"Two weeks later, I was back giving the second of three days of depositions. My lawyers were particularly concerned about questioning that might come from WilmerHale, the law firm that represented SLFC of South Dakota. They had suspected sophisticated questions of law and finance, perhaps some that might have gone after my spreadsheet analyses to show that the construction of my formulas had too many assumptions to be valid. I was ready to defend them.

"Instead, their lawyers went after my inclusion of SLFC in the case. They said that I was not the original source of the discovery of what SLFC was doing. Using the email records from my computer, they said it was Paul Basken of the *Chronicle of Higher Education* who had uncovered the 9.5 scheme at SLFC. Indeed, my email records looked as if that were true.

"Basken had done an article that attempted to estimate the amounts involved in the scheme at all the participating secondary markets. He had contacted me to review his methodology. Some of our communication was by email, some by phone. In one email, I wrote that I had overlooked SLFC. It certainly looked as if SLFC had grounds to get out of the case.

"But I pieced together what had actually happened, and why I had written what I did in the email. Prior to that email, Paul Basken and I had talked on the phone and I had read off my list of secondary market suspects. For the conversation from my kitchen counter, I had grabbed only the top sheet of my list. SLFC was on the second sheet. In that sense, I had overlooked SLFC. My lawyers were relieved at the explanation, but how could I prove it? Well, my notes proved that there was a second sheet with SFLC on the list, and my computer records backed up the fact that SLFC was in the analysis before the phone conversation with Paul Basken.

"This line of questioning opened up other attacks on me. What was I doing talking to the press anyway, and had I talked to the press while the case was under seal? And what other records were out there that the opposition lawyers had not seen?

"No, I had not talked to the press about my case either before I filed it or when it was under seal. Yes, I had taken calls from the press about the 9.5 scheme itself, because I was known as the expert on the matter, and I was happy to fact-check prospective stories about it. Never did I divulge that I was going to court myself.

"In my depositions, I stressed that my lawyers had told me not to talk to anyone about the case, not the subject. My association with the issue was known to all. It had appeared in the *New York Times* on page one, after all.

"In late 2008, while the case was under seal, I was asked by Stephen Burd of the New America Foundation to review the draft of a blog he was writing on the 9.5 scandal. I sent him back my thoughts.

"After this exchange became known through discovery, all defendants wanted to claim this was spoliation of the case and to do more searches of

my computer for other such communications. New America, at first, re-
sisted giving up anything from their end, on First Amendment grounds. I
was troubled that others were now being brought into my case, but I had no
problem with New America releasing any communications they had had with
me. I had always lived by the local wisdom not to write any emails you are
not prepared or proud to see the next day in the *Washington Post*. Steve Coll,
the president and CEO of New America, eventually relented and provided the
communications at issue.

"During discovery, the sources of the numbers I used to make my case
specific with regard to each of the ten defendants came under question from
opposition attorneys. They knew how I had received numbers from Senate
sources in 2003 and 2004, but my analyses showed secondary market claims
through 2006. Had I not used public information from the Department of
Education for the later numbers, which would disqualify me from being the
original source of the false claims complaint? Relators, under the law, cannot
turn others' work into their own and then claim they are the original source.

"Indeed, I had used 2006 numbers from the Department of Education in
my analyses, but they were hardly public. I had been invited in the spring of
2007 by staff of the Senate Permanent Subcommittee on Investigations to
give them a bipartisan briefing on the 9.5 scandal. I told them in response to
their questions that I needed new information from the Department in order
to estimate what was at stake in Secretary Spellings' decision not to collect
back the illegal claims.

"Under the signature of Senators Carper and Coburn, who headed the
subcommittee, the Department received a demand for new numbers. When
the subcommittee staff received them, they sent them to my home computer,
and I gave them my analysis.

"Unfortunately, this correspondence did not show up on my computer records. I did not know that, so when I sent the helpful correspondence to my
lawyers, I thought they already had records of it from the original computer
dump. Not so.

"This raised a new issue: opposition counsel did not in fact have all my computer records. I was not really surprised, as I had not had much confidence in the man who first took my files, his never having experience with a Mac. This prompted opposition lawyers to hire computer specialists to go over my computer records keystroke by keystroke, to reconstruct messages they had never seen, which might be relevant.

"They suspected not the ineptitude of the man who had originally downloaded my files, but that I had deliberately, in violation of my own lawyers' instructions, deleted files. Sure enough, the keystroke analysis turned up relevant messages that I had deleted.

"This looked like it might be a break for the defendants, but there was a reason the records looked the way they did. On my computer, when I opened a message, there was a software malfunction that did not allow me to close the window. The 'close' window was obscured. The only way I could get the message off my screen was to delete it.

"I knew, of course, that I was not to delete any records from my computer, so I was always careful to make sure another copy of the message existed on my computer. I even took a screen shot of the missing 'close' window should this ever become a problem. My lawyers were relieved to learn the explanation and to see that I had made a record of the screen.

"But one deleted message that was not helpful turned up in the keystroke reconstruction. In a 2004 note to Michael Dannenberg and James Kvaal, I mentioned my discovery of what I called the 'Rosetta Stone' that explained how the Dallas team of program reviewers had discovered the 9.5 scheme as early as 2002 in Iowa. I said in the email that the evidence had apparently been floating around in the Department for months on one of its computer systems. I had found it by accident.

"This could have been a case-killer for me. Opposition lawyers were eager to make the argument that I was not the original source after all, that I had found the Dallas program review in the Department and then made up a story that I discovered the scheme on my own, all along having in mind a false claims suit that would make me wealthy.

"The problem with this scenario, however, was that it was nonsense and there was no evidence for it. The first I ever mentioned the program review in any record was more than a year after I had made my own discoveries, and if I were really poaching off the work of others, why would I mention the program review to anyone?

"This was a far-fetched scenario, and it was just a coincidence that a message I had deleted to get it off my screen had been one that was potentially unfavorable to me. What I needed to demonstrate that I had no ill intentions when I deleted the message, was a second copy of the message that was still in my files. I easily found one. Problem solved, but the whole computer downloading misadventure seemed for a moment to cast a cloud over our case.

"I was a credible original source on my own and didn't need to crib anyone's work. Yet one keystroke could have brought the whole case crashing down. Fortunately, because I was careful with my files, it didn't.

"Opposition lawyers seemed to give me deference on account of my background. Behind the scenes, they were scratching their heads about the arcane details of this case. One told me quietly that he wished he were on the other side, with me instead of against me. Of course, that could only have been a tactic to put me off guard.

"But as my depositions wore on, hour after hour, we almost reached a basic level of rapport. Once, after a lunch break, I was sitting in my seat and invited the still-assembling group to get to work. I was having fun, I said, 'let's get on with it.'

"One of the opposition lawyers laughed. He said that was a first. He had never seen a witness say he was having fun. He got some nasty glances from others who were company lawyers for the defendants, not the K Street lawyers brought in to help. Did he not realize that I was not only the opponent in this case, I had testified in hearings that the whole FFEL program should be done away with, and that earlier that same year, Congress had actually killed their program? No more laughing.

"I was confident I could answer even the most loaded of their questions on substance, but, nevertheless, I was relieved when their tactics seemed to play more to the video cameras than to tripping me up on the intricacies of bond finance.

"When I gave a deposition at the law offices of WilmerHale, I was strategically placed in a chair with no legroom under it and a huge glare shining off the World Bank building across a plaza.

"This seemed to me deliberate so that when opposition lawyers shoved documents in front of me and demanded that I explain them, I would appear to squint and squirm in front of the cameras. It was easy to foresee a future jury trial at which the videotape would play, and opposition lawyers would ask the jury to judge my physical reaction to being presented evidence against my case. 'See how uncomfortable the relator is to evidence that destroys his case? Just look how he squints and squirms.'

"I said immediately that I could not respond to anything with all the glare in my eyes. My lawyers asked that the drapes be lowered. A WilmerHale lawyer went to the electronic controls, pushed a couple of buttons and said sorry, they seem to be malfunctioning. Whereupon one of my lawyers went to the controls and lowered the blinds.

"Who says depositions can't be fun?

"After depositions, with no real breakthroughs to derail my case, the defendants acquiesced to settlement discussions. These would be to me more threatening than funny."

CHAPTER ELEVEN

"I WANTED THE PUBLIC TO SEE HOW THE 9.5 SCHEME WORKED"

Moving in with his story, Oberg said: "While motions were flying back and forth on the case in preparation for trial, serious settlement talks got underway. We met once at the offices of the Mayer Brown firm at 1999 K Street, once in Wiley Rein's big conference room at 1776 K, and also at other locations. Joining were lawyers from the civil division of the Justice Department and lawyers from the Office of General Counsel at the Education Department.

"At Mayer Brown, a lawyer from Wall Street came down to impress us that the defendants were preparing for trial and that no holds would be barred, so we should quickly take whatever settlement we could get. They were prepared to offer a few million and have it over with. This was a meeting that included principals, and I was present.

"The Wall Street lawyer looked at me down a long, polished table and threatened, 'We're going to make it very difficult for you at trial, Mr. Oberg.' I said nothing. Bert Rein suggested they put their offer on the table. That was too simple, so the man from Wall Street made his threat again, as if that were a line he had been flown in to recite and he wanted to make sure the defendants got their money's worth for his nine-hundred-dollars-plus hourly fee.

"Fred Marinucci from ED's OGC was present, as he always was at such meetings. This raised my eyebrows. He had been a departmental colleague of mine and we worked for many years together on various issues. We sometimes even traveled together on the Metro to and from work.

"On one such trip in 2003, I mentioned the 9.5 scheme. He expressed incredulity. He later told me at the Department, after another meeting on an unrelated topic, that although payments to secondary markets were under his jurisdiction, he and his staff had been taken off the matter. All decisions on 9.5 payments, he told me, were being made behind closed doors, by only two people: Sally Stroup and a lawyer sent over to OGC from the White House, Jonathan Vogel.

"Had Fred Marinucci told DOJ about this? Did he know about the Dallas team's program review of ISLLC? Their draft, after all, had been reviewed and perhaps even written by OGC.

"Why had Fred Marinucci not objected to being sidelined when it was apparently his judgment that the 9.5 scheme was illegal? Why had he not gone over heads to say this was all phony? Then, of course, to whom would he have objected, William Hansen, the Deputy Secretary, or Eugene Hickok, his replacement deputy who was eventually removed from the government for holding stocks in student-loan lenders?

"Perhaps he did object, to no avail. Fred Marinucci likely did what he could in a difficult situation; discovery evidence years later suggests he was giving the defendants fits as best he could.

"There was a lighthearted moment for me at the talks at Mayer Brown. Charles Rose, ED's general counsel, was present as we broke up for a quick lunch. Mayer Brown had set up some stale sandwiches and store-bought mini bags of potato chips for us in a small room with no windows. The government's attorneys, including Charles Rose, indicated that the ethics rules of the federal government precluded them from partaking, even if it was only to be a short break to keep things moving. So, four government lawyers left the building to seek out a food truck for lunch.

"They took their time. An hour later, they came back. Nice, I thought, how the government's lawyers get all-concerned with ethics over a bag of potato chips, while equivocating on a case where hundreds of millions of dollars have been fraudulently shoveled out the back door of the U.S. Treasury.

"These talks broke down. I was not the type of person to succumb to threats. The talks at Wiley Rein came closer. The defendants added a few million to the offer. Still, I said no. I felt they were still nowhere near what they would or should pay.

"I wanted a trial. I wanted the public to see how the 9.5 scheme worked and who perpetrated it, win or lose for me. The public should know how its government worked. Taxpayers should know how their dollars were being spent. Students and families should know what was being done in their name.

"Roll the dice, I said, it didn't really matter to me one way or the other. The settlement money wasn't the issue. I already had my federal retirement and social security checks and my career was coming to an end. Moreover, I was especially against participating in an exercise where big companies threw money at lawsuits to make them go away.

"As we got close to trial, my lawyers, with the assistance of a private company that helps with trial prep, set up a mock jury and held a practice trial, all videotaped so as to be able to critique their performances as well as my own. Wiley Rein lawyers also played the parts of the defendants, vigorously resisting our allegations. I gave a rendition of my legal complaint on videotape for the mock jury.

"In this trial, we did not do as well as we might have. The 'jurors' were upset with officials at the Department of Education as much as with the secondary markets and wanted to know why they weren't on trial. My lawyers thought I should allow more emotion in my presentation, rather than sounding too academic.

"As the August 2010 date of an actual trial approached, Judge John Anderson set aside two weeks of courtroom time in the Alexandria federal courthouse and started sending out jury selection notices and subpoenas. [30] He ruled on various relator and defendant motions but held some back, keeping both parties guessing as to how he would shape the issues at trial.

"A few days before the trial, as even more motions were put before him by both sides on matters such as who could or could not be expert witnesses and what information could or could not be presented, Judge Anderson called us, along with all six defendants and representatives of the Justice Department and the Education Department, to his courtroom to provide one last attempt at settlement.

"He was assisted in this attempt by Judge T. Rawles Jones, his magistrate judge-colleague at the Albert V. Bryan U.S. Courthouse.

"This was not my first session in Judge Anderson's courtroom. Once before he had tried unsuccessfully to move the settlement along. That day lived in my memory for the comedic moments leading up to the session.

"I had inadvertently brought along a cell phone, which would not be allowed in the courthouse, so I looked for a place to keep it outside where I could retrieve it later. I looked around benches and bushes outside the courthouse, where I actually saw cell phones stashed by people in the same predicament. But I had time to find a safer place, so I went across Courthouse Square to the Westin Hotel and asked the clerk at the newsstand to put my phone under his counter and I would retrieve it in a few hours. He consented.

"As I was walking out of the lobby, I saw a large group of familiar-looking people gawking at me with incredulity. There stood all the defendants and their lawyers. They had booked meeting rooms at the Westin for a strategy session before going into Judge Anderson's courtroom. In fact, they had booked all

---

30   Although Judge Claude Hilton was originally assigned the case, the defendants had approached the plaintiff about jointly seeking a replacement because the defendants did not have confidence in his abilities. The plaintiff acquiesced and the court assigned magistrate Judge John Anderson as his replacement.

the meeting rooms in the hotel so as to keep my lawyers and me from holding our own strategy session there.

I didn't know that at the time, so I merely smiled at them as I walked alone through the lobby and said, 'Good morning everyone. See you all in a few minutes.'

"After passing through courthouse security, I took an elevator up to the courtroom, alone. On stepping out, three lawyers from DOJ and ED saw me. One of them expressed surprise and needled me: 'You came alone? We thought you'd be in an entourage protecting you.'

"I said no, any entourages you saw must be lawyers. I told them I always traveled alone, coming over from Maryland on the subway, walking a few blocks from the King Street station to the courthouse. I knew they had come over in government cars in an entourage themselves.

"There was no humor at the final attempt of Judge Anderson and Judge Jones to get to settlement and avoid a trial. A trial would be expensive for the federal government in time and money. Judge Anderson had never conducted such a big trial. He and Judge Jones, it was clear, were going to be all business and do their utmost to have the parties reach settlement.

"After an opening plenary session, Judge Anderson met separately with the defendants in his chambers. Judge Jones met in other chambers with me and my lawyers Bert Rein, Michael Sturm, and David Scher, along with lawyers from DOJ and ED.

"Judge Jones began by telling us that he had familiarized himself with the case and was appalled at the behavior of the defendants and the whole 9.5 scheme. So far, so good, we thought. But then he said that Judge Anderson, the presiding judge who would conduct the trial, was nevertheless going to rule against us on one key motion and that we would therefore probably lose at trial.

"My lawyers and I were crestfallen as we took in the news. David Scher and I suddenly and simultaneously had the same question for Judge Jones: Was

Judge Anderson also giving the same information to the defendants? No, Judge Jones said, the defendants were not being told about this prospective ruling.

"It quickly dawned on us that Judge Anderson might be telling the defendants that he was going to rule against them on another key motion, and that *they* would, therefore, likely lose at trial. That was perhaps why Judge Anderson had not yet ruled on all the motions, so he could essentially force settlement by putting both sides into 'settle or lose' positions.

"From that moment on, it became a matter of settlement terms. Our group met next with Judge Anderson, who gave us his report that the defendants were ready to settle if we were. They were ready to pay substantially more than they had ever previously put on the settlement table. This would be one of the larger settlements in the history of the False Claims Act. Bert Rein handled the negotiations over the amounts through Judge Anderson.

"As the long day wound to a close, we all met again in a plenary session. Judges Anderson and Jones went over the settlement terms. Everyone agreed to the amounts. Almost as an afterthought, one of the defendants' lawyers asked if there would also be the 'standard' and 'usual' agreements between the relator and the defendants, dealing with who can say what about each other and affirming there would be no admission of wrongdoing on the part of the defendants. I knew this was particularly important for SLFC, because WilmerHale was defending the interests of two prominent people in the student loan industry, whose reputations would be diminished by public knowledge of the SLFC arrangements with Aurora Consulting.

"My counsel agreed, as everyone got up to go home. The defendants' lawyers promised to provide my counsel with agreements in draft the next day.

"In the days that followed, I started to receive on my home computer the settlement documents to sign. I had no problem with the primary, or 'merits' settlement that would be signed by all parties, including DOJ. But I objected to going beyond that.

"When I read supplemental settlements between only myself as the relator and the defendants, I immediately called counsel at Wiley Rein and told them there was no way I would ever sign them. I would not be a party to any un-balanced settlement that would limit my ability to speak out on public policy, even if this were standard practice in the financial world. I wanted to be able to address public policy on student loan finance generally. I would only agree not to single out any defendant for criticism.

"Actually, some of the defendants may have been duped into participating by *government* ineptitude or corruption, and I absolutely wanted the public to know about the way in which government processes were manipulated for private benefit from the standpoint of public policy. The student loan industry itself was not my target, because many in the industry had acted properly and not tried to take advantage of taxpayers through the 9.5 scheme. I had already made my points about the industry in Senate testimony in 2007 and Congress had killed the FFEL program earlier in 2010.

"A day later, I received new drafts of the agreements. In them, I had the freedom to speak out insofar as public policy was concerned, so long as I did not reveal what I knew about individual defendants.

"Additionally, according to existing court orders, information that had been put under seal by the defendants, including that of SLFC, were soon to be made public anyway. Of particular importance to me was Judge Ander-son's order of June 11, 2010, that unsealed all of the exhibits as of August 20th, including "confidential" and "highly confidential" information, unless the defendants made motions on particular exhibits to seal them permanently. The defendants made no such motions. That meant that if anyone wanted to see un-redacted exhibits, the court could release them. Henceforth, I could answer all questions about discovered information by saying the entire record was available through the court to anyone who wanted to see it. The revised settlement agreements did not make me the gatekeeper, a role I did not want.

"That made all the difference, so I signed the amended agreements. I would not have to be a party to any cover-up.

"The defendants were given a couple of months to pay and to come back before Judge Anderson to make the deals final. Five of the six defendants did, and it was all over for them.

"Judge Anderson was happy with the result. He complimented the lawyers on both sides for the quality of their legal work. He said he had never been involved in a case where the work had been better. He said the settlement was a victory for judicial efficiency.

"The lawyers, if not the defendants and the relator, were pleased at the outcome as well. One of them suggested loudly that Judge Anderson must also be grateful to Judge Jones and had rewarded him with a bottle of scotch. Judge Anderson grinned, then laughed that, actually, it had been a whole case.

"One defendant, SLFC, did not pay up. It claimed it could not come up with the $3 million it had agreed to pay. Collection was turned over to DOJ."

In the aftermath of the settlement, the Department of Justice issued a press release, which stated:

Four student aid lenders have paid the United States a total of $57.75 million to resolve allegations that they improperly inflated their entitlement to certain interest rate subsidies from the U.S. Department of Education in violation of the False Claims Act, the Justice Department announced today.

The settlements resolve allegations brought in a whistleblower action filed in the Eastern District of Virginia under the False Claims Act, which permits private citizens to bring lawsuits alleging violations of the Act on behalf of the United States and to share in any recovery. The whistleblower suit was filed by Dr. Jon Oberg, a former employee of the Department of Education, who alleged that several lenders participating in the federal student financial aid programs created billing systems that allowed them to receive improperly inflated interest rate subsidies from the Department of Education. The United States did not intervene in this action, which was litigated by the whistleblower, but it provided assistance at many stages of the case, including during the settlement process. . . .

"Collaboration between the federal government and citizens with knowledge of fraud is important to the successful enforcement of the False Claims Act," said Tony West, Assistant Attorney General for the Civil Division of the Department of Justice. "Whistleblowers like Dr. Oberg are critical to our efforts to recover taxpayer money lost to waste, fraud, and abuse."

"The U.S. Attorney's Office remains committed to assisting ordinary citizens who blow the whistle on wrongdoing by companies that take taxpayer dollars," said Neil MacBride, U.S. Attorney for the Eastern District of Virginia. "Through the efforts of one citizen and the government, these lenders will be paying millions back to the government."[31]

---

31   Press release, Department of Justice Office of Public Affairs, "Four Student Aid Lenders Settle False Claims Act Suit for Total of $57.75 Million," November 17, 2010. (This case was handled on behalf of the United States by the Civil Division of the Department of Justice and the U.S. Attorney's Office for the Eastern District of Virginia, with the assistance of the Department of Education Office of General Counsel.)

CHAPTER TWELVE

"AUDIENCES WERE INTERESTED IN THE RETALIATION WHISTLEBLOWERS FACED"

"Immediately after these six defendants had been disposed of," Oberg recalled, "my counsel appealed the decision by Judge Claude Hilton to exclude the four other original defendants, Arkansas Student Loan Authority (ASLA), Kentucky Higher Education Student Loan Authority (KHELSC), Vermont Student Assistance Corporation (VSAC), and Pennsylvania Higher Education Assistance Authority (PHEAA).

"These defendants had argued before Judge Hilton that they were arms of their respective states and hence protected under the Eleventh Amendment to the U.S. Constitution from suits under the False Claims Act. This appeal process, through the Fourth Circuit Court of Appeals in Richmond, Virginia, would take more years of litigation until it was straightened out.

"In November of 2012, SLFC decided to pay up. It was, to me, curious timing that SLFC had delayed paying until after Mitt Romney was defeated in the presidential election contest. Lawrence O'Toole at SLFC may have been hoping that his friend and longtime FFEL colleague, William Hansen, the Romney campaign's higher education advisor, would be coming back into power and would instruct DOJ to cease collection efforts."

—⟶⟵—

In the midst of all of this, Oberg decided to make two decisions to enhance causes associated with his whistleblowing. The first was to create a charity with the funds he received from the 2010 settlements. A second decision was to become associated with the Government Accountability Project (GAP), a non-profit organization created to support whistleblowers.

"For the charity, I affiliated with a donor-advised organization, already established as a 501(c)3 entity," Oberg said. "I selected a name to signify that the sow's ears of a federal program gone wrong could be turned into silk-purse distributions to do public good. Under this arrangement, I could personally remain anonymous. I had never undertaken anything for the attention it would bring, and I was not about to start through charity.

Oberg has since made many dozens of contributions, ranging from a few thousand dollars to hundreds of thousands of dollars. They have gone to a variety of charitable organizations from coast to coast, from Boston and Washington to San Francisco and many places in-between. Many have wound up in his home state of Nebraska and in his hometown of Lincoln. They have supported the destitute, the environment, educational institutions, and several consumer protection organizations.

"As to my association with GAP, I owe this to my first lawyer on the 9.5 scandal, Jason Zuckerman. GAP does great work for whistleblowers, he told me, and could use my assistance as a whistleblower in many of their projects. He introduced me to Louis Clark, GAP president, and I started immediately to join in GAP planning."

GAP conceived of a national 'Whistleblower Tour,' promoting the contributions of whistleblowers, as well as the need for whistleblower protection. GAP took the show on the road to colleges and universities, providing panels of whistleblowers to appear before classes in law, accounting, and journalism, to include larger events for the public as well. These events provided students and faculty with the opportunities to interact with famous whistleblowers, such as Daniel Ellsberg of the Pentagon Papers case and Frank Serpico, who had exposed police corruption in New York City decades before. And there were also more recent whistleblowers, like Sherron Watkins, who had rocked the accounting and finance world with her revelations about Enron.

"I was invited to appear at the first such Whistleblower Tour event, to be held at the University of Nebraska–Lincoln," Oberg said. "Thomas Drake would be on the panel. His name was in the headlines as he had just settled his case against the National Security Agency (NSA). I declined to appear because one of the six defendants with which I had settled was headquartered in Lincoln, and I did not want to create conflict."

Oberg was glad to appear on GAP panels at the Florida International University in Miami, at Auburn University in Alabama, at Syracuse University in New York, at CUNY's Baruch College in Manhattan, and at Saint Joseph's University in Philadelphia.

At FIU and Auburn, he was paired up with Frank Casey, who along with Harry Markopolos, had blown the whistle on Bernie Madoff to the SEC. At Syracuse, it was a big panel with Thomas Drake (NSA), Jesselyn Radack (DOJ), Susan Wood (FDA), and Michael Winston (Countrywide Mortgage).

At Baruch, he teamed with Sherron Watkins of Enron and at Saint Joseph's, with a whistleblower from the State of Indiana. On these panels were often either Louis Clark or Dana Gold of GAP, who would discuss issues of ethics involved in whistleblowing.

"I was never paired with a whistleblower from my own home state of Nebraska, Kathryn Bolkavec, but eventually Louis Clark of GAP got us together. She was the author of the book *The Whistleblower* and the movie of the same name about human trafficking in Bosnia. She had been fired as a law enforcement officer for trying to stop the abuse of Eastern European women who had essentially been kidnapped and sent to Bosnia by traffickers as prostitutes.

She filed suit in the United Kingdom and was vindicated for her actions, for which she also received a monetary settlement. It was only large enough to pay her counsel, however, and like many former whistleblowers, prospective employers did not exactly rush to her with job offers.

Oberg went on to develop numerous good relationships with other whistleblowers and was honored to keep in touch.

"When in Houston once, I had coffee with Sherron Watkins, who was trying to live a normal life after being named as one of Time Magazine's "Persons of the Year." Like other whistleblowers, she was not welcomed back into her professional community despite being a CPA who had worked at a high-level executive while at Enron. Richard Bowen, who blew the whistle at Citibank on mortgage fraud, faced the same problem. Despite great service to their professions, after becoming whistleblowers, these two remarkable people were partly supporting themselves by establishing web pages and offering themselves as speakers on their daunting experiences.

"Thomas Drake's story is tragic, as is Jesselyn Radack's. They have both written books about their travails. After having her career ruined at DOJ because she insisted on due process for John Walker Lind, an American captured in Afghanistan, she became Thomas Drake's lawyer and got the government to drop its most serious charges against him—violation of the Espionage Act—for which he could have spent his entire life in prison. Drake had merely tried, by going through proper channels at NSA, to end surveillance programs that eventually were determined to be illegal by federal courts. Nevertheless, Drake had had his home raided and his family broken up over the charges against him.

"At the Syracuse panel, I had to follow Tom Drake, who had those in an auditorium on the edge of their seats with his true accounts of what the government had done to him as a whistleblower. It was hopeless to match his incredible story, so I immediately told everybody to take a deep breath, sit back in their seats, and hear about a story with a happier ending. Everyone laughed and was relieved.

Oberg explained how on the Whistleblower Tour he handled the matter of his settlements, some of which required him not to single out individual defendants. "I always started out my appearances with disclaimers: I was not going to talk about current litigation with the remaining four 9.5 scheme defendants, nor would I talk about any of the defendants with which I had settlement agreements. That essentially left SLFC, with which I had no such agreement and about which my counsel said I could tell or write anything.

"But mostly audiences were interested in the retaliation whistleblowers faced for their actions. Mine was a different experience, I often said, as I didn't consider having one's job description changed to be serious retaliation. It might have been, of course, had I been in mid-career. But, over the years, I eventually learned more about attempted retaliation against me at the Department of Education, which I had not originally been aware of.

"To be sure, I knew that Grover Whitehurst had put out the word in 2004 and again in 2005 against anyone in the Institute attending my periodic 're-search brown-bag' lunches in the NCER conference room. This was a harmless get-together that I sometimes arranged with academics from out of town to give them a chance to talk about their higher-education research and to get to know people in IES.

"Neil Seftor, who along with Dr. Sarah Turner of the University of Virginia, had done a paper on student financial-aid packaging with conclusions similar to one of my own papers, once gave a presentation. Dr. Bridget Terry Long of Harvard stopped by, as did researchers from the University of Georgia and elsewhere. Our own Dr. Clifford Adelman presented his research.

"The IES employees who attended were those in offices in proximity to mine, who risked the wrath of Grover Whitehurst out of friendship to me and their own dedication to their work on behalf of taxpayers, who were paying their salaries.

"I later learned that a research round-table hosted at the American Council on Education, which I often attended and for which I even suggested speakers, was off limits to Department of Education people if I were to be present.

Among the speakers I had produced for the ACE get-togethers were Dr. Thomas Weko of GAO, economist Dr. Robert Archibald of the College of William and Mary, and Kevin Carey of The Education Trust.

"In other words, there had been retaliation against me, but in the form of taking action against other people, like Dr. Michael Wiatrowski, whose career was apparently ruined over the job-description nonsense, and against other causes and forums all across town from Union Station to Dupont Circle. For what purpose, especially if I never knew much about it or took it seriously?

"To send messages to others, of course, that federal employees are not to speak up. That's why GAP was eager to have me on its panels: to tell the story of a successful whistleblower—even if I didn't embrace the description—for whom all turned out fine, and to illustrate just how low organizations would go when faced with whistleblowers.

"GAP also developed a curriculum on issues surrounding whistle-blowing for use in colleges and universities; my case was one they were eager to include in their materials."

As some students in the GAP-tour audiences had received federal Pell Grants, they had a special interest in hearing the story behind what Oberg would call, "a quantum leap in Pell Grant funding after 2010." In fact, just a few months after Oberg's lawsuit was made public, Congress killed the FFEL program, prospectively. Then, via the use of a special congressional budget process known as reconciliation, Congress put subsequent savings into Pell Grants—with other savings directed toward funding for the Affordable Care Act, which was part of the same legislative package.

Oberg continued: "As to the who and the why behind this legislation, I am not sure. It seems to have taken everyone by surprise. It is likely that they had the blessing of Dr. Jonathan Gruber, an MIT economist who worked on the ACA for the Obama Administration. Jonathan Gruber was no stranger to the FFEL versus DL battles a dozen years earlier; he and I visited congressional offices together to compare subsidies in the competing student loan programs.

"The legislation killing FFEL likely was done on the initiative of Bob Shire-man, who had battled against FFEL subsidies for more than two decades on the Hill, at OMB and the Domestic Policy Council, and most recently, as Deputy Undersecretary of Education.

"But regardless of whoever was responsible for students receiving more grants and fewer loans, the students were most grateful."

CHAPTER THIRTEEN

"FEW BORROWERS EVER SAW RELIEF
FROM KHESLC"

For five years, between 2011 and 2016, Jon Oberg and his attorneys went back and forth with Judge Claude Hilton over the sovereign immunity of the remaining four defendants, "as if we were in a tennis match, both slugging from the baseline," Oberg said. "We appealed the judge's first ruling and prevailed. The appellate court in Richmond sent the case back to him to look at again, this time using the Fourth Circuit's four-part test for determining whether entities, such as those in our case, were arms of their respective states. This appeals court decision became known as *Oberg I*.

"Judge Hilton then ruled that he was right the first time around: all four were arms of their states. Whereupon we appealed again.

"In *Oberg II*, the appeals court ruled for us with regard to PHEAA and VSAC. They let ASLA of Arkansas out of the case as having sufficiently passed the four-part test."

Meanwhile, Kentucky Higher Education Student Loan Corporation (KHES-LC) surrendered, deciding to settle in lieu of rolling the dice with the appellate court—after a federal mediator determined that their proper settlement number should be $7.25 million.

"KHESLC, which viewed that as a good break, had been among the larger abusers of the 9.5 scheme, even though it was among the last to take advantage of the 9.5 gimmicks."

Oberg added, "But once committed to it, they used the crudest methods to move loans around among bond trusts to claim the 9.5 guaranteed return subsidy. Their rationale was that if others can get away with it, so can we.

"Being a non-profit, KHESLC actually came up with a plan that would have benefitted many of its borrowers with the 9.5 windfall, if it had only worked. In the KHESLC plan, borrowers who became special education teachers would have their loans forgiven. The loan forgiveness program, 'Best in Class,' was quickly expanded to those who became nurses. Colleges that offered special education and nursing programs started to recommend KHESLC and its affiliates to their students who needed to borrow tuition money.

"Colleges in the Direct Loan program were sorely pressed to return to FFEL lenders in order to take advantage of KHESLC's loan forgiveness program. That was one of the real purposes of the plan in any case, to drive DL out of Kentucky.

"But few borrowers ever saw relief from KHESLC. Kentucky Governor Ernest Fletcher's budget office saw that KHESLC was receiving a windfall in federal funds—about $81 million—and decided to appropriate it, to balance the governor's budgets without tax increases. Whereupon KHESLC found that it had made promises that it could not keep. Angry borrowers who had changed their careers to go back to school to take advantage of the KHESLC offer—including some two-borrower couples—felt betrayed.

"KHESLC responded by saying the borrowers should have read the fine print, which indicated the offer was contingent on funds being available. Borrowers came back at them with evidence that on many of the loan documents, there was no such fine print.

"Disgusted borrowers took up their case with Kentucky officials, but got nowhere. The chairman of the legislative committee with jurisdiction was himself an official of KHESLC. Kentucky's congressional delegation was no help, as they had long been under the influence of the lobbying of the Education Finance Council, with which KHESLC was affiliated."

Adding to the controversy over KHESLC's loan forgiveness program was an article in the *New York Times* on May 26, 2009, accompanied by unsympathetic photographs of victims of the student-loan program living in a nice home with a late-model pick-up truck in the driveway, and a large flat-screen television in their living room.[32]

The Times stated, in part:

> From Kentucky to Iowa to California, loan forgiveness programs are on the chopping block. Typically founded by their states to help students pay for college, the state agencies and nonprofit organizations that make student loans and sponsor these programs are getting less money from the federal government and are having difficulty raising money elsewhere as a result of the financial crisis.

> The organizations say the repayment programs have been hurt by a broader effort by Congress to tackle the high cost of the federal student loan program by reducing subsidies to lenders.

> Curbing the programs will make it harder to lure college graduates into high-value but often low-paying fields like teaching and nursing.

> While few schools may be hiring now in this economic climate, there may be shortages later, educators say.

---

32   Jonathan D. Glater, *New York Times*, "Recession Imperils Loan Forgiveness Program," May 26, 2009.

Writing on behalf of New America, Stephen Burd lauded the *Times* for the effort but criticized its execution of the story, which did not even mention the role of 9.5 fraud. Burd wrote:

> [U]nfortunately, the *Times* didn't tell the whole story and instead left its readers in the dark about the real reasons for the loan forgiveness program's collapse. We fear that this omission could lead policymakers and the public to learn the wrong lessons from this debacle.[33]

Oberg continued: "The U.S. Department of Education was of no help to the jilted borrowers. First, it had sent out program reviewers to KHESLC to determine if its 9.5 take was legal, setting off a round of contradictory findings. KHESLC worried that it would have to pay back some or all of its 9.5 haul from money it did not have because Governor Fletcher had discovered it and had subsequently spent it.

"Next, the federal Department of Education did nothing to investigate whether the problems at KHESLC were violations of its FFEL participation agreements. In cases of mismanagement, the Secretary of Education has the power to limit, suspend, or terminate any participating organization, be it a college, a guaranty agency, or a secondary market. Surely offering the forgiveness of loans guaranteed by the federal government with no money to back it up should have set off alarms and perhaps even sanctions against KHESLC. It did not happen.

"Finally, the ED Ombudsman was no help to the borrowers left at the altar by KHESLC. The Ombudsman is housed in the same office, OSFA, that is heavily lobbied by lender interests and seldom sides with borrowers whatever the issue. Only when the Consumer Financial Protection Bureau was established did student loan borrowers begin to get an effective voice in federal agencies."

---

33   Stephen Burd, *New America*, "*The New York Times* Misses the Story," June 1, 2009.

Oberg concluded that had anyone taken the side of borrowers, they could likely have received some relief, as promised: "When Secretary Spellings offered all 9.5 claimants an opportunity to have independent audits to determine the extent of their legal 9.5 loan eligible holdings, KHESLC declined. It simply made no more 9.5 claims rather than have auditors going through its books. I believe KHESLC, had it undergone an independent audit, would have been able to make legal claims on old loans, on loan recyclings, and perhaps on loans financed by certain bond trust re-fundings. With such revenues, it perhaps could have made good on at least a few more of its promises.

"When it started to look as if KHESLC might have to open its books, this time to discovery from my lawyers, it sought refuge in settlement. They saw what happened to other secondary markets that underwent discovery and they wanted nothing to do with it.

"I settled with KHESLC when it briefly had the upper hand, after Judge Hilton for a second time determined that KHESLC was an arm of the commonwealth of Kentucky. This was before we prevailed over PHEAA and VSAC on the same question in *Oberg II*. I had no wish to prolong things with KHES-LC and had no remaining questions as to what had happened there. It was a profoundly sad story of the avarice of KHESLC executives who liked to pose as high financiers, victimizing those they were supposed to help, and of betrayal by the governor and the Kentucky congressional delegation, who cared so little for the victims of this so-called arm of the government of Kentucky."

In *Oberg II*, the appeals court again remanded the case back to Judge Hilton to determine on a factual basis whether PHEAA and VSAC could meet the four-part arm of the state test. This time, his decision was to be based on actual discovery and depositions. Oberg's lawyers looked at PHEAA evidence as to how much business it was doing outside Pennsylvania, for example, as opposed to inside. They also took depositions from Pennsylvania elected officials on the PHEAA board of directors to determine what they knew about this supposed arm of their government. Not much, it turned out.

Oberg explained: "PHEAA had been notorious as a student loan secondary market with much money to spend on parties, dinners, travel, and bonuses. Board members were ignorant of the details of its operations.

"Pennsylvania state auditor Jack Wagner wrote a devastating comeuppance of PHEAA and its excesses in 2007, prompting the ouster of its CEO, Richard Willey, and a re-shuffling of its governing board. My counsel had much difficulty getting documents out of PHEAA. PHEAA lawyers said certain documents did not exist, but later, when PHEAA officials were put under oath, they produced at least a few of them.

"This resulted in court sanctions at one point against PHEAA, imposed by an outraged Judge Anderson. On one of the four-part tests, PHEAA was not allowed to argue its case inasmuch as it had withheld evidence. He also required PHEAA to pay us $45,000 in legal bills."

Still, Oberg and his attorneys continued having problems in the U.S. District Court for the Eastern Division of Virginia, especially with their assigned judge, Claude Hilton.

Oberg explained: "Despite what we felt was convincing evidence that PHEAA especially, and also VSAC [Vermont Student Assistance Corporation], were not arms of their states, Judge Hilton still persisted and ruled for them in what was supposed to be a fact-based determination as required by the appeals court in *Oberg II*. We appealed once again to set the stage for what was to become *Oberg III*.

"In the meantime, VSAC decided it wanted to settle. The prospect of an *Oberg III* from the federal appeals court, after which VSAC would have to submit to discovery and depositions on the merits of our case, hung over their heads."

Scott Giles, who had once lobbied Congress that the whole 9.5 scheme was illegal, was now CEO and would have to defend VSAC's having participated in the scheme. Oberg expressed his mixed emotions: "This prospect gave me no pleasure, because I knew VSAC to be among the better secondary markets in the country with real concern for its borrowers. They also ran federal programs to help to prepare students for college. One such program, GEAR UP, was one I had helped establish when I worked in OLCA at the Department of Education in Washington. In fact, Scott Giles had been on the staff of Senator James Jeffords of Vermont at the time of the creation of the program. I had spent a lot of time in Senator Jeffords's office working out his concerns to make sure entities like VSAC could participate.

"On the day of settlement, Scott Giles sat across a table from me in VSAC's lawyer's office in Washington. It had been ten years since we discussed the 9.5 scandal. He made a good pitch for a low settlement figure, explaining all the good things VSAC was doing, which he knew I cared about. My lawyers, also present, had previously told me that VSAC's officials, their lawyers, and everyone involved with VSAC had been courteous and easy to deal with, especially compared to PHEAA.

"We settled with VSAC for approximately twenty cents on the dollar. I made the point that even after settlement, VSAC profited by approximately $18 million for their decision to join the 9.5 scheme, and DOJ approved the settlement. There was no talk at any point of a supplemental settlement restricting either party as to what could be said about the scheme or VSAC's participation in it.

Not fully recovering illegal claims bothered Oberg: "In fact, every entity with which we settled, so far, had come out ahead, overall. It was as if we, and DOJ with its settlement approvals, were sending a message that fraud pays. All of these lawsuit troubles—to many 9.5 participants—were merely a cost of doing business. Maybe in the case of the for-profit entities, even tax-deductible. And what a good deal, to get taxpayers to pay to defend those who had defrauded them in the first place.

"All of which stiffened my resolve to get the last case against PHEAA right. PHEAA was not a good actor. It had had many other scrapes with the law. In 2012, it settled with the IRS, paying a $12-million fine for violating arbitrage laws. It was also one of the lowest-rated loan servicing agencies in the country, with more consumer complaints than all but one other national student loan servicer.

"I was doubly pleased when the Richmond-based appeals court came down with *Oberg III* in the fall of 2015. PHEAA would have to drop its sovereign immunity defense and submit to discovery on the merits of our case. Not only that, but in a companion case brought by Virginian Lee Pele against PHEAA under the Fair Credit Reporting Act, the appeals court ruled that PHEAA could also be sued under that act as well as the False Claims Act."

That meant borrowers could now sue PHEAA directly.

CHAPTER FOURTEEN

"WINNING THE BATTLE OVER SOVEREIGN IMMUNITY"

Jon Oberg's law firm, Wiley Rein, had scored a huge victory with the double ruling by the appellate court. It had not been easy, however. Lee Pele's litigation had been assigned to review before Oberg's, causing concern because the foundation of Pele's case was grounded too much in *Oberg II* and not enough on actual evidence that PHEAA was not an arm of the state.

Oberg explained: "In a series of motions, we got *Oberg III* ahead of *Pele,* to the benefit of both."

It was a masterful maneuver by Wiley Rein.

To be sure, PHEAA had challenges arguing *Oberg III*. So, for its oral argument before the appellate court in Richmond, the company retained one of the biggest guns in the legal corral: Paul Clement, the former Solicitor General in the Bush Administration. After PHEAA's loss, Clement asked for reconsideration by the appeals court, en banc—by all of the judges in the circuit rather than just the three-judge panel that had written *Oberg III*. The en banc petition was denied by the court with not a single vote to second-guess the panel.

Then, in February 2016, Clement, on behalf of PHEAA, filed for a writ of certiorari—which orders a lower court to deliver its record in a case so the higher court can review it—with the U.S. Supreme Court, hoping for a reversal of both *Oberg III* and *Pele*. Along with his appeal to the high court, Clement solicited *amicus curiae*, friend-of-the court briefs, from those entities which had profited from PHEAA's largess, as well as those who feared that PHEAA's fate of becoming subject to FCA and FCRA might become their own.

Oberg continued: "Neither we nor Pele sought *amicus* briefs, not wishing to make it appear that there were real issues involved that deserved the attention of the Supreme Court. Nevertheless, the Supreme Court in conference decided to ask the current U.S. Solicitor General for his views on the matter.

"To me, there was never much doubt that PHEAA and similar quasi-governmental agencies did not come under the sovereign immunity shield of the Eleventh Amendment. I had always remembered Bob Kutak's briefing and assistance for us when we set up the Nebraska Mortgage Finance Fund in the 1970s. He had been an innovator in creating quasi-governmental agencies and was perhaps the nation's leading expert on them.

"The genius of them, he explained, was that in some regards they had the characteristics of the states that created them, so they could issue tax-exempt bonds. In other regards, states would not have to take responsibility for them, as their statutory creation explicitly indicated that they did not have the full faith and credit of the state, and they could sue and be sued in their own right. They were like municipal corporations.

"I have often wondered what Bob Kutak would think of the litigation against PHEAA. Unfortunately, he died suddenly while jogging in Minneapolis in 1983, at age 50. He had just completed drafting new legal ethics requirements for lawyers on behalf of the American Bar Association. This stellar work would eventually be incorporated into state bar standards across the country.

"My guess is that he would strongly be on our side, especially after taking into consideration that PHEAA was, for all practical purposes, a national business enterprise operating under the names of American Education Services (AES) and FedLoan Servicing. It was one of the largest loan servicing operations in the country. As such, it would also impress him that PHEAA, with revenues in the billions, could afford to pay any judgment itself, without resorting to support from Pennsylvania taxpayers. Indeed, that was one of the four tests of the Fourth Circuit Court of Appeals, not to mention that the Pennsylvania statute itself did not pledge the commonwealth's full faith and credit.

"My own inclination was to pursue PHEAA to the end, over every legal hurdle it might try to throw in our way. PHEAA was one of the largest abusers of the 9.5 scheme. It was also the first, or among the first deliberately to move loans into old bond estates to increase its federal subsidy illegally. It had the political connections to try to pull it off without anyone other than a few key people being the wiser. It had tenaciously fought for years to prevent us from discovering what had gone on inside PHEAA, and from seeing what PHEAA's connection was to the U.S. Department of Education, when the FFEL program attorneys from the Office of General Counsel were taken off the job because they were doubtful of the legality of the whole scheme."

As the high-court process began, the U.S. Solicitor General requested the views from the Oberg and Pele attorneys and PHEAA's legal team about the court's request for the U.S. government's views.

Oberg recalled: "On a particularly hot day in the summer of 2016, the parties to the case met separately with SG lawyers in the ornate Solicitor General's office, just a few doors down the hall from the Attorney General at the Department of Justice. PHEAA's lawyers went first. A half-hour later, they were shown out a side door, so that we did not cross paths in person. We, along with Pele's lawyers, then met with the Solicitor General lawyers, along with lawyers for DOJ, Education, and Treasury.

"I was the only principal in attendance, and I spoke occasionally.

"I was not particularly worried that SG lawyers may have been hired at one time by Paul Clement and felt an obligation to him, as PHEAA had probably hoped in retaining Clement. We felt it was a good meeting and were not surprised when the Solicitor General gave his written views to the Supreme Court. The U.S. government's position was that the court should deny PHEAA's writ of certiorari."

In January 2017, the U.S. Supreme Court handed down its decision, denying PHEAA certiorari. With Oberg winning the battle over sovereign immunity, the case, *U.S. ex rel. Oberg v. PHEAA*, on its merits, was remanded back to Judge Hilton's court in Virginia's Eastern District.

To Oberg, the trial would be anti-climactic. He, a political scientist and retired civil servant, had taken a case to the U.S. Supreme Court over the hurdle of the Solicitor General and had won against incredible odds. And best of all, he felt it was an important cause to open the courts to thousands of beleaguered borrowers who now had their chance at justice.

CHAPTER FIFTEEN

"THE TALKS BROKE DOWN BEFORE THE DAY WAS OUT"

With the Supreme Court decision paving the way, Jon Oberg and his attorneys prepared for trial against PHEAA.

Oberg remembered: "My counsel began to collect documents from PHEAA in early 2017, and they from me. Because I had been in court for many years against other lenders, PHEAA already had the benefit of the others' experiences, documents others had collected, including depositions I had given, and arguments favorable to lenders that Judge Anderson had granted.

"We had the benefit of having taken depositions of PHEAA people previously on arm-of-the-state matters, some of which overlapped with false claims issues. Interrogatories and legal jockeying went back and forth for weeks.

"I gave a deposition to four PHEAA lawyers in April 2017, over one full day, as agreed. Matthew Regan of Kirkland and Ellis's Chicago office did the questioning.

"I was offended by many of the questions. He tried to create a case that I had read about the 9.5 scandal in the press and tried to claim it as my own discovery. He accused me of fabricating documents years after the fact to make it appear as if I had sent them earlier. He accused me of doing what I did for politically partisan reasons and to favor one loan program over another. He tried to get me to contradict statements I had made under oath seven years earlier. It was shameful.

"Through discovery, we found much of what we were looking for at PHEAA. We had suspected that PHEAA had a plan to grow its 9.5 portfolio and we found it, dated May 2002. It even included a caution not to grow the claims too much for fear of 'political ramifications.' PHEAA had denied the memo's existence for years, under oath.

"A month later, in June 2002, incoming CEO Richard Willey told his people to 'maximize' the claims to get the revenue. The revenue would be used, the Pennsylvania auditor general later determined, for 'self-reward' among PHEAA's executives as they showered themselves with increased salaries, pensions and perks.

"We also found emails that showed who, by name, PHEAA was counting on at the Department of Education as its friends to protect it: Bill Hansen and Sally Stroup."

Hansen, when he was Deputy Secretary, was the subject of a May 2002, memo from lobbyist Scott Miller of PHEAA shortly before Miller suggested a 9.5 growth scheme to new PHEAA CEO Richard Willey. Miller wrote to Willey:

> This is a fast follow-up to our conversation yesterday regarding the possibility of PHEAA increasing its holdings of loans funded with tax-exempt obligations that would be eligible for the 9.5% yield floor.... We can take some comfort that Bill Hansen (Deputy Secretary of ED) has a great deal of sympathy for tax- exempt funders of student loans. . . . [34]

Oberg explained: "This corroborated other discovery evidence showing that Hansen was vetting 9.5 schemes in 2002 and 2003, violating his recusal.

---

34   *U.S. ex rel. Oberg v. PHEAA*: (Trial exhibit PTX 001)

Even after he left the Department, Hansen was active in trying to persuade OMB and the White House not to require repayment of proceeds from any of the 9.5 schemes. In October of 2006, PHEAA included him at his new company, Chartwell, in its 9.5 strategizing emails, illustrating his primacy in the schemes.

"We also discovered that Sally Stroup passed along inside information to PHEAA from her position as Assistant Secretary." In another memo from Miller to Willey, dated August 25, 2005, Miller says this of Stroup and how they relied on her to try to keep one step ahead of the Inspector General and the Department's lawyers:

> She also told me that she had to fight very hard to clear New Mexico of the IG audit findings and that the lawyers at ED were still not happy about it. She expects every subsequent audit of 9.5% loans by the IG to be as controversial. And, she expects that we are high on the IG's list....She said the key point seems to be the need for an unimpeachable link between each loan and the specific bond issue through which it was originated or funded. NM was able to produce a comprehensive "genealogy" of its bond issues, but not enough on the linkage to specific loans. Should we get the notice from the IG, it may be worth having [CFO] Tim [Guenther] talk to Sally before the IG arrives.[35]

As to other discoveries, Oberg elaborated further: "When Stroup left the position, internal PHEAA emails lamented losing their friend, inside source, and referee and worried about what would happen without her protection.

"We found no evidence that PHEAA's 9.5 growth scheme ever had the benefit of a legal opinion, even one written by their Washington lobbyists, as other lenders like KHESLC had done with their later 9.5 schemes. We even found emails that showed PHEAA's compliance officer did not understand how the 9.5 scheme worked. We found an internal PHEAA email that advised

---

35   *U.S. ex rel. Oberg v. PHEAA*: Case 1:07-cv-00960-CMH-JFA (Document 833-3)

against asking officials at the Department of Education if the scheme was legal, because that might precipitate an answer back that it was not. We found emails recommending who among career officials to talk to 'off the record' at the Department, and strategies as to how to ask questions so that they appeared to come from others. This would keep an 'ostrich defense' intact for PHEAA, should one be needed, to allow them to argue that they never knew what they were doing was illegal.

"We even found a 2006 email from PHEAA to a Department official asking if there was some way to stop my appearance on a panel at the New America Foundation, more than a year after I had retired, out of fear that what I would say would not be good for either PHEAA or the Department.

"We took new depositions of many individuals, confronting them with discovery evidence contradicting their earlier sworn statements, evidence of perjury. We took depositions from officials at the Office of Inspector General who had audited PHEAA without the benefit of the evidence we had uncovered. PHEAA had told them falsely that the documents did not exist."

Discovery in *Oberg v. PHEAA* ended on August 4, 2017. The court set the trial date for November 28. Predictably, PHEAA filed a motion to dismiss, but Judge Hilton rejected it—and then encouraged settlement talks. Oberg agreed, but PHEAA rejected the suggestion at first—although it reconsidered a month later.

Explaining the possible motivation, Oberg said, "PHEAA stood to have to pay back $116.5 million in false claims, which would triple by law to take into account mandatory damages, for a total of nearly $350 million. . . .

"Magistrate Judge T. Rawles Jones, who had been part of the settlement talks with other lenders in 2010, convened us in early November. DOJ sent two representatives. PHEAA did not make a serious offer to settle. Its last offer was sufficient to pay attorneys' fees, leaving little to reimburse taxpayers.

"Apparently, the tactic was to hope my counsel would abandon me and bank the fees. To its credit, Wiley Rein didn't flinch at the offer and rejected it immediately.

"The talks broke down before the day was out."

According to Oberg: "PHEAA's presence at settlement talks was partly designed, apparently, to send a message to Judge Hilton, through Judge Jones. PHEAA negotiator Matthew Regan told Judge Jones, in the presence of our negotiator, that PHEAA was prepared, if it lost at trial, to appeal the verdict for years, and that former U.S. solicitor general Paul Clement was being retained to do so. It would be a very long time before PHEAA would ever pay any money, Regan promised.

"PHEAA said it would be noting all of Judge Hilton's rulings during the trial and instructions for purposes of appealing a losing verdict, if necessary. Of course, that would happen anyway, but PHEAA made a point of it in the hopes Judge Jones would pass the information to Judge Hilton, and that Judge Hilton would be especially cognizant that if PHEAA lost, Paul Clement would be all over the case on behalf of PHEAA.

"PHEAA also made certain my counsel got a message that it did not intend to go after me, personally, at the trial. Regan said PHEAA would only agree with me, using documents I wrote that were critical of how the Department of Education handled the 9.5 claims.

"That was a nice try at misdirection if not an outright lie, to get us not to prepare fully for the trial. I wasn't buying it, as I knew what was coming. Indeed, at trial, PHEAA used every opportunity to try to undermine my credibility and veracity.

"The talks broke up well before the day was out, as Judge Jones did not insist on further efforts to bring the parties closer together. For my part, I was ready to settle not far above PHEAA's last offer as I knew a trial could be difficult for us in Judge Hilton's courtroom. He had ruled for PHEAA in our three previous cases before him, and it required years of appeals to get him reversed. But we had already made a sustained effort, through depositions and discovery, to get at the truth behind PHEAA's claims, and to be able to reveal what we had found, win or lose at trial, was paramount."

Oberg continued: "In November, my counsel and I prepared for trial. Trial prep involved several hours of practice testimony for me. Counsel conducted mock jury trials. Thousands of documents were prepared to enter into evidence. *In limine* motions on the admissibility of evidence went back and forth between the litigants and the court. Expert witnesses, who had prepared papers on the details of the case earlier in the year, readied their presentations. Other witnesses were subpoenaed.

"We had five attorneys who would interrogate witnesses before the judge and jury, with two more attorneys assisting along with paralegals.

"We set up a war-room in a hotel across from the Alexandria courthouse, with a bank of seven computers. Visuals were readied to coordinate interrogations with documents projected on two large courtroom screens.

"The defense prepared even more, sparing no expense. I estimate that PHEAA spent, in total over several years, $10-15 million against us. Surely, they were second-guessing their decision not to settle for less when they had had the chance. KHESLC, in the nearly identical situation as PHEAA, had settled for $7.25 million (a figure set by the Fourth Circuit's mediator) before *Oberg II*, thus avoiding discovery and depositions. Not only were the legal bills piling up for PHEAA, but PHEAA, by not settling, had lost its sovereign immunity in the process. Now PHEAA would be desperate to win at trial or face paying nearly $350 million in restitution and penalties."

CHAPTER SIXTEEN

"I WAS TAKEN ABACK BY THE JUDGE'S OPENING"

The four-day trial, *U.S. ex rel. Oberg v. PHEAA*, began on November 28, 2017, in Judge Claude Hilton's courtroom in the U.S. District Court for the Eastern District of Virginia in Alexandria.

The courtroom was art-deco elegant with an arched ceiling with eight brass and rounded milky-white glass lights hanging from the ceiling. The rich, dark-brown wooden walls were divided by large wooden-shuttered windows, flat slabs of purple-grey-black-white marble, and panels of purple-blue-grey-orange paisley-patterned, heavy-duty cloth fabrics.

A clock with Roman numerals was above the large double doors leading in and out of the courtroom. There was another clock between the two other entrances/exits, one led to the judge's personal chambers. The other led to a holding cell for prisoners.

Hanging on the back wall was a large oil portrait of Judge Hilton, who had approved of the courtroom's design years earlier and who sits directly across the room in his elevated, boxed-in bench, flanked by the American flag on his right and the State of Virginia flag on his left. Above his head on the front wall is a bronze seal of the "U.S. District Court for the East District of Virginia."

Sitting at a small desk against the wall to the judge's front right is a friendly, gray-haired security officer, working under the U.S. Marshals Service, who directs the members of the jury, who sit in front and to the left of the judge, in and out of the courtroom.

Two large flat-screen televisions for exhibiting documents and videotaped testimony appeared in front of and on both sides of the judge. His two law clerks and the alternating court reporters sit at tables below and to his right and left, respectively. The clerk of courts was seated alone at a long table directly in front of the judge.

The plaintiff's table is just a few feet in front of the jury box. The defense table is to the judge's right, close to the security officer. A wooden podium was placed between the plaintiff and defense tables where the attorneys sat.

Positioned to face the jury, the witness chair was next to the judge.

The public section of the courtroom had three rows of wooden benches, like pews in a church, and three-armed chairs against the wall near the entrance/exit.

PHEAA had nine attorneys, along with numerous aides from three different law firms, led by the Chicago-based Kirkland & Ellis, LLP. The plaintiff had three principal attorneys from only one firm, Wiley Rein.

Inasmuch as the judge was still in his chambers and jury was still in the jury room, the entire courtroom was filled with loud chatter which was suddenly silenced at exactly 9:46 A.M. when 74-year-old, well-dressed Jon Oberg, at a brisk pace, entered the room. Not a word was spoken until Oberg took his seat at the plaintiff's table next to his attorney, Bert Rein.

After a very quick jury selection, Judge Hilton—a short and stocky man with a handsome round face and a full head of hair—explained to the all-white jury, composed of six men and two women—that they would be deciding on a case brought under the False Claims Act, in which the "relator," Jon Oberg, a private citizen who, representing the government, is the plaintiff in a *qui tam* action.

Specifically, from the bench, Judge Hilton summarized:

> Ladies and gentlemen, we have for trial a civil case wherein the United States has filed in this suit via whistleblower, John H. Oberg, under the False Claims Act against the defendant, the Pennsylvania Higher Education Assistance Agency, alleging that the defendant knowingly presented and caused to be presented false and fraudulent claims to the Government. The False Claims Act allows a whistleblower to file this kind of suit and to receive a financial reward if he is successful.

Addressing this skewed introduction, Oberg later reacted: "I was taken aback by the judge's opening. The relator's share was a matter of law, not something that a jury would determine. PHEAA was on trial for making false claims and the jury would decide matters related to those claims and nothing else. I remarked to my counsel at the first break that we got off to a very bad start if the jury thinks this is all about relator's share, and if this is going to be a trial of the whistleblower."

During the opening statement the tall and distinguished-looking Bert Rein explained his case on behalf of Oberg, stating:

> Now, Dr. Oberg, who is right there, is a relator in this case, as you've been told. And that means he's really standing in the shoes of the United States and he's seeking to recover on behalf of U.S. taxpayers more than $116,000,000 that the defendant, which is known as PHEAA, and sometimes American Education Services, falsely extracted from the U.S. Department of Education, which we call DOE for this purpose, you'll hear that term, between 2002 and 2006. Now, PHEAA is a student loan company that made or acquired federally guaranteed student loans.

Between 2002 and 2006, the Department of Education was obligated by law to provide an incentive for student lending by paying lenders like PHEAA quarterly cash subsidy money. And that was called a Special Allowance Payment or SAP, you'll hear that term, SAP, on each federally guaranteed student loan that PHEAA owned.

In that period, two separate formulas were established by the governing law, Higher Education Act, to calculate the amount of that SAP. One formula, which we call ordinary SAP, was based on prevailing commercial interest rates and it resulted in that period in very small payments because the rates were very low after 9/11 drove them down.

The other formula called 9.5 SAP or floor SAP guaranteed that SAP payments would boost the lender's total interest return to 9.5 percent in those same years to contrast with the ordinary SAP, which boosted it to about five.

That was an extraordinarily profitable return, especially when PHEAA raised money at a cost of about 1 percent. And the evidence will show that PHEAA executives schemed to grab all the 9.5 SAP they could without regard to the legal distinction between these formulas.

On behalf of PHEAA, the young, intelligent, and talented defense trial attorney, Matthew Regan, responded in his opening statement:

I represent the Pennsylvania Higher Education Assistance Agency or called PHEAA. What is the dispute in this case?

PHEAA made loans to hundreds of thousands of students over the period of time at issue and it received federal subsidies for a portion of those loans. Some of those federal subsidies were these 9.5 yield subsidies that you just heard about.

PHEAA stands behind its certifications that it made to the Department of Education, that those requests for subsidies complied with the law, complied with the regulations, and complied with the policies of the Department of Education. Those certifications were not false. They were not reckless

They were consistent with the regulation that applied at the time.

Now, Dr. Oberg doesn't challenge all of the subsidies that PHEAA received. He only challenges a portion. And even within this 9.5 percent group, he only challenges the growth of those subsidies. That's what the dispute is about.

He claims that PHEAA violated the False Claims Act by having a growing balance of these 9.5 percent minimum yield qualifying student loans. What he challenges is the growth.

After opening arguments, Oberg was the first witness in the plaintiff's case. As the trial was in the home of "The Rocket Docket," Oberg only testified for about an hour on direct examination and then a half-hour on cross-examination.

From the outset, the entire pace of the trial seemed rushed. Also, during the usual morning and afternoon breaks, jurors, in lieu of being separated from everyone else, were physically in the midst of the usual routine at the courthouse—encountering lawyers, witnesses, and anyone else in the hallways, the elevators, the bathrooms, and even in line at the small courthouse café.

No one ever alleged any attempts to influence any members of the jury, but certainly the opportunity was clear and present.

Notably, while going through his background, the jury, seemingly confused and bewildered by the lawyerly presentations of the schematics of the 9.5 subsidy, along with its taxable and tax-free bond applications, seemed to come to attention as the professorial Oberg described his naval and public service.

Explaining his experience on cross-examination, Oberg recalled: "Sure enough, PHEAA went after my credibility right away, suggesting that I had misled an audience at the New America Foundation in a panel discussion in 2006. I had told the NAF audience that I did not pursue a retaliation remedy with the federal Office of Special Counsel over having my job description changed at the Department of Education as a consequence of my discovery and my internal reporting of lenders' false claims. PHEAA's Regan asserted that was not true, as it was the Office of Special Counsel that did not pursue the matter, not me, writing in the Spring of 2004 that it considered the 9.5 matter *de minimis* and not worthy of its further time. Within a few weeks, however, the Government Accountability Office (GAO) came out with a report, as a consequence of my briefing them on the matter, in which it said *billions* of taxpayer dollars were at stake. I could have sent the GAO report to the OSC (with great satisfaction) and appealed the OSC decision that the matter was *de minimis*, but chose not to, nor to make any appeal to an agency that clearly was not up to task of looking into what I had presented it. That is what I was referring to in my remarks to the NAF audience, that I dropped the matter rather than appealing it."

Oberg later reflected: "I thought this was a cheap shot by PHEAA—the first of many. They made $116.5 million in illegal claims but were trying to impugn my integrity by twisting my completely truthful words, about how I did not appeal OSC's "*de mimimus*" conclusion, into something they hoped the jury would find untruthful, and somehow equivalent to what Regan would soon have to defend against, actual PHEAA perjury."

CHAPTER SEVENTEEN

"PHEAA HAS 'LOST SIGHT OF ITS MISSION' IN FAVOR OF 'SELF-RE-WARD'"

T he trial continued. . . .

Oberg explained: "Following my testimony, we presented two of our three experts, each of whom did a superb job on both direct and cross examination. We then called six other witnesses, including four PHEAA executives: Timothy Guenther, Richard Willey, Andrew Mehalko (by deposition videotape), and James Preston. We presented evidence from discovery, including the May 2002 memo from Guenther to Willey which laid out the 9.5 growth scheme, the existence of which Guenther had previously sworn under oath did not exist."

Oberg continued: "We showed the [Andrew] Mehalko deposition in which he was uncertain as to what provisions in law or regulation allowed 9.5 portfolio growth. There was no such law or regulation. Such growth was, in fact, a violation of law and regulation, a determination that Secretary Margaret

Spellings finally made, albeit well after PHEAA had pocketed $116.5 million illegally.

"We questioned Richard Willey about what PHEAA did with the money, especially how PHEAA, under his direction, started paying huge bonuses to executives, including himself, who had come up with the 9.5 growth scheme. Willey tried to change the subject to how PHEAA used the money to further its millions of helping students pay for college."

Refuting Willey's claim that PHEAA was just trying to do the right thing by helping students, Oberg said: "This was not true: a 2008 audit of PHEAA by the Pennsylvania auditor general found that PHEAA had 'lost sight of its mission' in favor of 'self-reward.' However, when our counsel Michael Sturm tried to put the audit into the record as evidence, PHEAA objected and Judge Hilton sustained the objection. We subsequently asked the judge for a sidebar discussion, arguing strenuously that PHEAA had brought up its mission and we only wanted to show that PHEAA had lost sight of its mission. The judge said he would not allow the evidence."

Oberg continued: "This was a second major setback for our case. First, the jury had been told by the judge that the case dealt with relator's share and, now, evidence from Pennsylvania's auditor general, no less, about what PHEAA did with its ill-gotten gains would be kept from the jury.

"Before resting our case, we also put on the stand our third and final expert, an accountant and fraud investigator who pored over PHEAA's records obtained through discovery to make the determination that the amount at issue in the case was $116.5 million."

Oberg continued: "We also put an official on the stand from the Department of Education's Office of Inspector General, Jeffrey Nekrasz, to testify about how PHEAA had not produced all relevant 9.5 documents when the IG audited PHEAA in 2007. These were documents absolutely essential to the audit, which PHEAA had said under penalty of perjury did not exist, only to turn up in 2017 through discovery."

As the plaintiff's attorneys wrapped up their case, Oberg noted: "Finally, Howard Sorensen, IG's legal counsel, testified by videotape about the IG's audits of 9.5 growth at several lenders, including PHEAA. One of these audits had been given the prestigious Alexander Hamilton award by the Council on Excellence and Efficiency as the best audit in all of the federal government for 2006.

"It was on seeing this audit that Margaret Spellings finally confronted the illegality of 9.5 growth and issued the letter confirming the illegality and shutting it off for good, as I had recommended four years earlier."

But would the prosecution's case convince a jury? That was the question.

CHAPTER EIGHTEEN

"THE EXCHANGES WERE HEATED"

O n day three of the trial, PHEAA launched its defense, surprisingly calling as its first witness the plaintiff, Jon Oberg, who said: "Their goal was to get me to concede that my effort at the Department of Education to stop 9.5 growth had been rejected by numerous Department officials, that the GAO report indicated 9.5 growth was legal, and that a review of 9.5 growth at Iowa, by regional officials in Dallas who concluded it was illegal, had been overruled.

"I would not agree to any of the assertions. My efforts at the Department were ultimately successful, although the Department was asleep as to what was going on for a long period.

"The GAO report did not conclude that 9.5 growth was legal, because one of the options GAO gave for cutting it off was simply to *clarify* current law and regulation that it was illegal, which Secretary Spellings actually did in 2007. As to the Dallas office being overruled, it was but the overruling was *itself* overruled in time."

Although Oberg, new to courtroom battles, occasionally fought back while under cross-examination during his earlier testimony, he quickly evolved into an absolute street fighter while on direct for PHEAA's case. He simply refused to allow any false allegations, such as those earlier used against him, to pass without a forceful response.

"The exchanges between us were heated," Oberg said. "Everyone in the courtroom seemed surprised that I protested as vigorously as I did to the questioning, raising my voice and coming out of my chair on occasion. I was not taking PHEAA's half-truths sitting down. . . . On cross examination from Bert Rein, I also got a chance to make my speech about the purpose of the False Claims Act being deterrence, that this case presented an opportunity to send a message to the government that it should not set up moral hazards in which contractors suffer no consequences when caught making illegal claims, other than having to stop making them going forward.

"When we returned to the war-room at the end of the day, my legal team gave me an ovation, to my embarrassment. Our feeling at the end of the previous day—halftime, so to speak—had been that the case was a toss-up with the jury. At the end of the third day, we felt we were ahead and wondered why PHEAA would put me on as their witness for an hour, allowing me to dispute virtually everything they said."

In effect, plaintiff Oberg, in his role as PHEAA's contrived witness for the defense, became the star witness for his prosecution of the student-loan lender.

CHAPTER NINETEEN

"'IT'S ALL LEGAL' – FORMER PHEAA EMPLOYEE SALLY STROUP"

O ther witnesses called by PHEAA were Andrew Mehalko; Terri Shaw, the CEO of FSA, on videotape; Sheila Ryan-Macie of Navient; Steven McCullough of Iowa Student Loan Liquidity Corporation; and Sally Stroup, Assistant Secretary, also on videotape.

Later, Oberg remembered his impressions of these witnesses: "Under PHEAA questioning of its own person, Mehalko, the carefully scripted testimony seemed for a moment to go off track. It was an awkward moment, and we did not know if PHEAA's script called for it or if Mehalko started to freelance on the witness stand. Earlier, we had introduced evidence from discovery that PHEAA considered the Department of Education, from which PHEAA got its money, to be 'pathetic' and 'weak-minded.'

"Now, on the stand, Mehalko doubled-down and said in response to a question from his own counsel as to what PHEAA thought of Secretary Spellings' determination that PHEAA's claims had been illegal, that 'we got the joke.' In other words, PHEAA was taking it all as a joke. We thought the jury would not take kindly to PHEAA's cavalier attitude toward taxpayer money." Questioned on direct by defense attorney Michael Glick, here was that exchange with Mehalko:

Q. So, Mr. Mehalko, did PHEAA challenge this 2007 Dear Colleague Letter?

A. No.

Q. Why not?

A. We got the joke.

Q. . . . . Well, let me ask you to follow up on that. What do you mean by "we got the joke"?

A. There was a lot of noise around 9.5 percent floor loans. TTPA was enacted. HERA was enacted. There continued to be noise with news articles. And that this was a way for the Department to get an out and get rid of 9.5 percent floor loans.

Oberg, who has had a long career in government fiscal administration at both state and federal levels, was surprised at the admission that a federal contractor would say in open court that it took the legal interpretations of the Secretary of Education as a joke. "I would worry that it could lead to debarment."

Recalling other trial testimony during the defense case, Oberg said: "The Ryan-Macie and McCullough testimonies were not all that helpful to PHEAA. Although each, under direct examination, expressed their views that 9.5 growth was legal, under cross-examination, they did not do as well. McCullough had to admit that Iowa's 9.5 growth was a function of using PHEAA's software and not a policy choice of the Iowa Student Loan Liquidity

Corporation. He also acknowledged that Iowa immediately complied and did not resist Secretary Spellings' determination that 9.5 growth was illegal and made subsequent downward adjustments to its billings."

McCullough apparently did not take the Secretary's ruling as a joke.

Continuing with his view of the defense case, Oberg added: "Ryan-Macie did not do well in cross-examination and left the stand visibly shaken. Apparently, she did not think that we knew her history of having formed a consulting group, Aurora Consulting, through which she marketed a way that for-profit lenders could make extraordinary money from her 9.5 growth scheme. She and Lawrence O'Toole had sold the for-profit South Dakota secondary market SLFC on the idea for a two-percent share of the extra claims. She was reluctant to admit any of it, feigning ignorance of the fact that she was the managing director of Aurora, even purporting not to recognize the name of the South Dakota secondary market through which she made ill-gotten gains."

Indeed, in its own special way, the testimony of Sheila Ryan-Macie was one of the most memorable moments of the trial. With Bert Rein cross-examining her, defense counsel Tracie Bryant did a desperate, though unsuccessful, job, of trying to protect her witness.

Q. All right. So, when did you start working for Aurora Consulting?

A. I would say 2001-ish, 2002.

Q. And what was your position there?

A. I was a consultant.

Q. Weren't you a managing director?

A. That might have been my title. I just don't -- I don't recall.

Q. You don't remember. Did you -- when you testified previously, did you tell me that you were a manager director at Aurora?

A. I don't recall what my title was, so...

Q. Okay. And you don't recall, sitting here, what your title was?

A. No, I don't recall.

Q. And you received compensation, did you not, bonus compensation based on the earnings of Aurora?

MS. BRYANT: Objection, outside the scope.

MR. REIN: It's not -- Your Honor, this is going to show the bias of this witness. She has --

THE COURT: Objection overruled.

BY MR. REIN:

Q. You did, didn't you?

A. I'm sorry, what was the question?

Q. You received compensation based on the earnings of Aurora, did you not?

A. I received compensation based on Aurora's performance, yeah.

Q. Okay. And did Aurora propose a strategy for the growth of 9.5 percent loans to a company called Ed-Link?

A. I don't know that company's name. So, do they go by a different name too?

Q. Well, it would be South Dakota —

A. Okay. We did work for South Dakota, yes.

Q. And were they paid a percentage of the additional SAP income that could be generated by their consulting advice?

A. I -- I'm not -- I think that's how we were paid. I'm not sure.

Q. You're not sure. You want to look back at your deposition? I'll give you a copy.

MS. BRYANT: Your Honor, this is improper impeachment. The witness has already answered the question.

MR. REIN: Your Honor, I just asked her a completely different question. I don't know what she's already answered. She's uncertain.

THE COURT: The objection is overruled. Give her the deposition.

BY MR. REIN:

Q. Now, I will explain to you, Ms. Ryan-Macie, that is a copy of the deposition you gave under oath. It was dated June 16th, 2010. Do you see that? Do you recall that when you were giving this deposition, you were employed as an expert by a prior defendant in this case?

A. I was.

Q. And were you compensated by that defendant for your testimony as an expert?

A. I was.

Q. Yes. And are you being compensated for your testimony today?

A. No.

Q. Okay. Turn to page -- the pages are numbered, and they are a little bit small, but you can see that each one is numbered there. You might want to look at page 34, numbered at the top on the right. Okay. And it's referring at this point to a memorandum that was given to Ed-Link or South Dakota by Aurora. Do you see that? You can go back and look at 33.

A. 33?

MS. BRYANT: Your Honor, I don't believe there's a question pending. I'm not sure what we're doing with the deposition transcript.

THE COURT: Objection overruled.

MR. REIN: I'm just letting her see the reference, Your Honor. I have a question.

BY MR. REIN:

Q. Have you had a chance to look at that?

A. So what do you want me to look at?

Q. Okay. Just look at pages 33 and 34 to refresh your recollection. And this question says -- and this is on 34 -- in this memorandum, this is a memorandum that Aurora, on which you were a managing director, gave to Ed-Link. We will address how Student Loan Finance Corporation can manage its tax-exempt financing and related student loans in the context of these regulations promulgated by the U.S. Department of Education that govern how holders of student loans assets made or acquired with tax-exempt sources may bill for special allowance. Do you remember that now?

MS. BRYANT: Your Honor, this is an improper refreshment of the recollection.

THE COURT: Objection. You've got to read the question and answer and ask if she said it.

MR. REIN: And all I'm asking is: Do you now recall that Aurora was –

THE COURT: Did you read the question and answer? I couldn't tell.

MR. REIN: Okay. I can restate the question.

THE COURT: When you read the question and answer, ask her if she said it.

MR. REIN: Okay. By memory, my question was whether she said she had a hazy recollection. I'm asking her: Does reading this refresh your recollection that this is what Aurora proposed to do for Ed-Link?

THE COURT: Oh, I misunderstood your question. Objection overruled. She can answer that. It either refreshes her recollection or it doesn't.

THE WITNESS: Right.

MR. REIN: And that's all I asked her.

THE WITNESS: So, South Dakota was a client, and Aurora did work on 9.5 for South Dakota.

BY MR. REIN:

Q. Okay. And did you not propose -- Aurora not propose to South Dakota that they could transfer loans out of pre-existing 9.5 status, retain that status, transfer loans in, and claim that status? Isn't that what Aurora proposed?

A. If that's what the report says, yes.

Q. Okay. So, you don't have any personal recollection that that was the proposal made by Aurora?

A. So my involvement in the project was pretty limited.

Q. Okay. And Aurora was paid for the extra money that Ed-Link got by these transfer techniques. Correct?

MS. BRYANT: Objection, asked and answered.

THE COURT: I don't remember. Objection overruled.

BY MR. REIN:

Q. Correct?

A. I assume so.

Q. So basically Aurora sold to Ed-Link for profit the concept that you're testifying today, that loan -- lenders could switch loans and increase the volume of 9.5. Isn't that right?

A. I would have provided information about the Department's guidance to the community.

Q. You were part of Aurora. And so I just asked you: Isn't it true that Aurora sold this concept and -- through a consulting arrangement through Ed-Link, and took a 2 percent share of the extra money Ed-Link got by switching these loans? Correct?

MS. BRYANT: Objection.

THE COURT: Objection sustained.

MR. REIN: I think I made that point, Your Honor.

Speaking of other key witnesses, Oberg said: "Shaw's videotaped testimony, from a 2010 deposition, helped PHEAA in that she confirmed that she had been sitting next to Sally Stroup, the Assistant Secretary for Postsecondary

Education, in November of 2003 when Stroup said, in an apparent reference to 9.5 growth, 'It's all legal.'

"Stroup's videotaped testimony, also from a 2010 deposition, was so disjointed it is hard to say which side it helped, although she was PHEAA's witness. She confirmed that she had said 'it's all legal' at a student financial-aid conference, but also acknowledged that she did not have clearance from the Department of Education to make such a statement on her own. PHEAA's point was that she made it, so how were they supposed to know what they were doing was illegal? Our point was not only that she did not have authority to make the statement, it came a year and a half after PHEAA's hidden memo outlining its 9.5 growth scheme.

"Stroup was supposed to testify in person but could not because of a death in the family. This disadvantaged us greatly, because when she gave the deposition in 2010, PHEAA was not a defendant, so she was not interrogated from the standpoint of having been a long-time PHEAA employee and, as discovery had shown, that she maintained a close relationship to PHEAA while she was assistant secretary. When she left that position, PHEAA's internal emails showed that they were concerned that they had lost a friend and referee and that they were in for very difficult times without her protection."

CHAPTER TWENTY

"WHAT A GOOD CITIZEN DOES"

After PHEAA rested, Oberg felt confident, saying: "Despite this disadvantage [of losing Sally Stroup as a live witness], we felt relatively good that our third-quarter lead had held up as PHEAA's witnesses on the fourth day did not perform well and two of them were downright embarrassing."

On Monday, December 4, already a long day with much testimony, both sides delivered their closing arguments. From his front-row seat, Oberg saw it this way:

"If PHEAA was to prevail with the jury, Regan would have to pull it out with rhetoric, not evidence. I was immediately offended by PHEAA's closing assertions of half-truths and outright mischaracterizations of evidence. For example, both the GAO report and the Shireman and Kvaal policy paper "Money for Nothing" were written to cut off 9.5 growth as soon as possible. But Regan described them to the jury as supporting its position that the growth was legal, a total twisting of their purpose and intent, as neither work was an analysis of the legality issue.

"Also, although I knew it was coming, Regan leveled a personal attack against me in his closing. Regan told the jury that my motivation was greed, and that—because I had not shared in any proceeds from Congress's 2004 and

2005 legislation, or from Secretary Spellings' actions in 2007 to declare once and for all that 9.5 growth schemes were illegal—I had to file a False Claims suit to get any money for myself in order to cash in on my work.

"We had made clear that my actions were only taken as a last resort, but PHEAA wanted to leave the jury with the impression that the whistleblower should be the one on trial, not PHEAA. Unfortunately, this echoed Judge Hilton's opening comment to the jury, that they would be deciding a False Claims case in which the relator gets a share of the proceeds."

In his closing argument, Matthew Regan, on behalf of PHEAA, stated, in part:

> When Congress changed the law in 2004 and 2006, that prospective legal change was what Dr. Oberg was asking for in his many written complaints that you have before you. He was part of a chorus of voices of people that needed to modernize DOE policy because of a historic change in interest rates. But, of course, Dr. Oberg didn't share in any recovery based on the actions of Congress. And he did not benefit from the DOE's decision in 2007 to create a new policy and to tell lenders it would not try to look at their past special allowance payments so long as lenders in 2007 adopted this new rule. He didn't share that either.

> Indeed, it is only when he seeks to share in the potential recovery of the money that Dr. Oberg embraces his role as the government's proxy.

"Regan closed with a razzle-dazzle, large-screen animated graphic with arrows and colored lines to try to show the jury that many attorneys in the Department of Education, by name, had looked at my allegations of false claims and concluded I was wrong. The names were lifted off procedural, not substantive, communications. It reality, the individuals had made no such determination and, as we had previously shown, when the Department finally acted on my allegations in 2007, both the Office of Inspector General and the Office of General Counsel (including some of the same attorneys) agreed with my analysis. That was of course omitted by Regan, but the animated graphics were showy. Our side had no such display of video graphics with flashing arrows."

Under the rules of the court, Oberg's counsel Bert Rein had the opportunity to give a rebuttal to PHEAA's closing argument, as well as his final defense of Oberg, saying:

> So, when you come to the end of this, they want to criticize Dr. Oberg… He saw that the taxpayers' money was being taken improperly. He understood from his own experience that you couldn't use unqualified funds to buy 9.5 loans… And guess what? Jon Oberg was right. Jon Oberg carried this crusade on for your benefit, my benefit, every taxpayer's benefit, and Jon Oberg should be validated for doing what a good citizen does, continue to press it even after his supervisors said, lay off, you know. This is okay; these are our friends. He said, no, I am going to insist.

Judge Hilton then gave the jury its instructions. The jurors—who had been bombarded by complex evidence and conflicting testimony of high finance and subtle corruption involving hundreds of millions of dollars—were not permitted to take notes either during the complicated four-day trial or on the judge's instructions. Soon after retiring from the courtroom, the jury sent a message to the court asking for the judge to repeat "the five conditions that must be met in order to find for the relator." Obviously, members were confused about what they were supposed to do.

The jury was brought back into the courtroom.

> THE COURT: All right. You all may have a seat. I gather from your note you want me to read you again the five essential elements that the plaintiff must prove beyond a reasonable doubt.

MR. REGAN: Your Honor, preponderance.

MR. REIN: No, preponderance.

THE COURT: I mean preponderance of the evidence, excuse me, trying a criminal case. Preponderance of the evidence.

First, that the defendant presented a claim against the United States.

Two, that the claim presented was false or fraudulent.

Three, the defendant knew the claim was false or fraudulent at the time it was made.

Four, the false claim was material to the government's decision to pay the claim.

And five, that the government sustained damages because of the defendant's false statements.

Okay. All right, you all may retire to continue your deliberations.

Oberg was dismayed with the jury instructions: "Judge Hilton's third condition actually omitted an essential part of the False Claims Act, a provision regarding what the relator did *not* have to show for conviction; that is, 'specific intent to defraud.' That provision of the law had always been important to me from the very beginning of the litigation, in 2007. It had been added to the FCA in 1986 so as to preclude ostrich defenses, which PHEAA was using. Had it not been there, likely I never would have filed lawsuits.

"So, in spite of our finding a smoking gun in PHEAA's 2002 plan to increase 9.5 holdings, without the judge's instruction to a jury that such evidence, for conviction, did not have to include 'specific intent to defraud,' the jury could discount our hard-won discoveries. PHEAA essentially was allowed to use an ostrich defense, that it didn't know what it was doing was illegal, in spite of its attempt to cover it up for years."

In other words, by his omission, the judge left the impression that Oberg had to show specific intent to defraud, when actually the False Claims Act provided the opposite. It was another blow against the relator, perhaps fatal to his case.

On Tuesday, December 5, the federal jury, after fewer than two hours of deliberation, returned with its verdict, ruling for the defendant PHEAA.

The relator reflected: "My own guess is that although PHEAA's disingenuous closing took its toll on our case, the Stroup statement that 'it's all legal'— whatever 'it' referred to – was probably as important. Indeed, the Department of Education paid PHEAA's claims for years while she was assistant secretary. Unfortunately, we were not able to put Stroup on the stand to confront her with what we had learned in discovery. And, in the absence of clear instructions to the jury as to their choices, the vote in the jury was likely just an impatient decision to go home after having already spent five days on the case.

"I was disappointed at the outcome, especially for all the Wiley Rein attorneys who had done remarkable work on PHEAA and other cases over the years, especially Christopher Mills and Stephen Obermeier, as well as Michael Sturm and Bert Rein. Although we had many victories together and, with TELG, had re-shaped the student loan landscape significantly to help borrowers and taxpayers, the last defendant got away without a settlement or a conviction. The consolation was that there was not much we could have done about it, given what we were not allowed to enter as evidence, who we could not put on the stand, and the judge's intransigence on jury instructions. Taking a longer view, it was hardly a loss for us in that the defendant lost its sovereign immunity in the process and would be paying a price in future cases for years untold, if not in this one."

CHAPTER TWENTY-ONE

"ONE MORE CHANCE IN THE FOURTH CIRCUIT"

The case still had another year to run. The relator, with three victories behind him already in the Fourth Circuit federal court of appeals, would try for one more.

Oberg explained: "A few days after the verdict, I sought advice about whether to appeal, especially from my original counsel on the case, Jason Zuckerman. He was now heading his own firm, Zuckerman Law, after leaving TELG and after working at the federal Office of Special Counsel, where he had helped restore credibility to that agency and reduced its backlog of cases.

"Eric Bachman of Zuckerman Law wrote the appeal briefs, focusing on two errors that might give us a chance of a remand. One was Judge Hilton's decision not to allow us to enter into evidence the Pennsylvania Auditor General's devastating findings ('self-reward') on PHEAA. Another was Judge Hilton's failure to tell the jury that the relator did not need to show that PHEAA had specific intent to defraud. That is right out of the statute, and Judge Hilton omitted it."

Oberg explained why he thought he could prevail in a fair trial, with proper jury instructions, which was also in the minds of the several defendants that settled earlier rather than risk a trial. "There are two parts to the False Claims statute that deal with what is necessary to establish a false claim. Part A requires only a "reckless disregard" by the defendant in making the claim. This is not a terribly high bar. And part B makes clear that the relator does not have to show specific intent to defraud in order for there to be reckless disregard, another advantage for *qui tam* relators. Our appeal was based on the likelihood, if not the certainty, that the jury decided that because specific intent to defraud was not established, they could go home without even think-ing about whether PHEAA had acted with reckless disregard. Judge Hilton certainly left them that option by not making sure they knew about part B of the statute. He actually withheld that provision from them.

"But the Fourth Circuit did not agree that the errors were enough for a remand. It is a high bar to overrule a trial judge on what evidence is admissible. As to the jury instructions, the appeals court thought we should have objected more when the judge issued them, and because we did not, its decision had to be made on a higher standard, so-called 'plain error,' which is much harder to reach. In hindsight, perhaps we should have objected when the appeals court thought it would have been appropriate, but certainly it did not seem that way at the time. Judge Hilton had just said, moments before, after we had already engaged him on the jury instructions, that he would be making no changes. Had we raised further objections, the jury likely would have thought we were being unnecessarily quarrelsome, and it would have been counterproductive. One had to be in the courtroom to know what was appropriate and what not. I was there, and the appeals court judges were not.

"So, we lost the appeal. I was not disappointed in the outcome from a personal standpoint, in that had we won a remand, I would have had to give up another year or two of my life in discovery and depositions, and likely suffer more personal attacks from PHEAA's lawyers if the case were remanded back to the district court once again. I had to pay a bill of costs to PHEAA because we did not prevail on appeal, but I had been reserving my share of the SLFC settlement (Aurora Consulting) for such an eventuality, so it was not as if this was a personal setback from a financial standpoint. Who better to pay the bills than other 9.5 schemers?

"Moreover, we had already accomplished much of what we set out to do. By going to trial, we entered into the public record a mountain of evidence detailing both the internal machinations of the defendant and the sheltered relationship it enjoyed with the Department of Education. We showed that cheating taxpayers comes with risk, for which the reward may not be worth it. At least two lenders shook up their governing boards as a result, one at the insistence of a governor.

"We also demonstrated how political appointees with primary allegiances to their industry lobbying groups can—and do—interfere with enforcement of the rule of law, and that the Inspector General's and Department of Justice's remedies were weak and ineffectual in response.

Oberg showed his frustration over the fact that PHEAA committed perjury and got away with it: "Under questioning by PHEAA at trial as to whether the IG would be revisiting any issues in light of perjury brought to light by discovery, the IG witness simply said no. In other words, when a lender was required to provide documents under penalty of perjury if it did not, there was actually no penalty. This is ripe for congressional oversight as to whether IGs need more enforcement powers or need to have more law enforcement backup."

The whistleblower was likewise perplexed by decisions at the Department of Justice: "As to DOJ, its priorities are inscrutable. When two Department of Education high officials held stock in lenders the department was regulating, DOJ acted to remove them from the government and levied monetary penalties against them. The potential for conflict of interest in those cases was obvious. But when other officials whose actions were far more damaging to the rule of law, suggestive of corruption and racketeering and costing taxpayers hundreds of millions, DOJ gave them a pass."

Oberg also noted his displeasure with Secretary Margaret Spellings: "Her decision not to recover illegally claimed funds, over the objections of the Inspector General, was disastrous in that it signaled the Department of Education was not up to the job of policing the lenders and servicers.[36] PHEAA took the Department as a 'joke' after the Spellings decision, still brazenly describing its contempt in open court ten years later. PHEAA is the sole servicer of the scandal plagued TEACH and PSLF programs. It's no wonder tens of thousands of borrowers are victims of poor servicing. That is the legacy of the Spellings era: not the 'Spellings Commission', but the 'Spellings Omission.'"

---

36   Lieber, Ron. *New York Times*, "Your Student Loan Servicer Will Call You Back in a Year. Sorry." April 12, 2019. FedLoan, the servicer at issue, is an arm of PHEAA.

CHAPTER TWENTY-TWO

"A LOOK TO THE FUTURE"

After years of work on student loans, Jon Oberg looked forward: "All does not end with the conclusion of the 9.5 litigation. Several of the same defendants are also defendants in new class actions and state attorneys general lawsuits. Our victory on sovereign immunity has made some of these possible. I'm looking forward to borrowers getting their day in court, so they can get their lives back on track. There are huge numbers of borrowers, hundreds of thousands, who have been wronged by poor and sometimes fraudulent student-loan servicing.

"Congress can and should exercise its oversight responsibility to see what lessons can be learned from the 9.5 scandal cases. Much of the discovery and deposition record is already public, no subpoenas required. Many of the individuals in the lobbying iron triangle are still employed in higher education finance, involved in new schemes that undermine the programs of the Department of Education. The abject failure of the Public Service Loan Forgiveness (PSLF) program, for example, is not a surprise to those of us who saw such programs fail as part of 9.5 loan schemes.

"Congress may well conclude that it needs a major reform in student loans, to collect repayments through the tax system as is done in other countries.

The savings from eliminating the servicers (many of them the defendants in these cases) could be substantial, up to $1.5 billion per year, and passed along to needy students in the form of grants, or to the underfunded IRS. There is a precedent, when Congress eliminated FFEL middlemen in loan origination in 2010.

"GAO, the Inspector General, and DOJ should reflect on what went right and what went wrong on these cases from their perspectives. They need to ask themselves whether in the end, they aided in upholding the rule of law or whether other contractors in the future may consider that getting caught in fraudulent schemes at the Department of Education is just a part of the cost of doing business with the government."

CHAPTER TWENTY-THREE

"IT WAS ALL WORTH IT, AND MORE"

No interview with a whistleblower would be complete without the mandatory question: Was it all worth it? For Jon Oberg, the effort had taken many years of work and there must have been a personal toll from all the contentious litigation.

Oberg answered: "Of course, it was worth it. A lot was accomplished in the first four years, before going to court. My initial complaint took root first with GAO, which wrote a report upon which Congress acted to save taxpayer money, in the billions of dollars. My analyses were a help to the Inspector General, which produced one award-winning audit and several others that convinced the Secretary of Education to act as I had recommended: to restate law and regulation that 9.5 growth schemes were illegal and always had been.

"Our litigation against ten lenders, filed in 2007, was made public in 2009. It detailed charges against the lenders and explained how they were bilking taxpayers. Some people took notice, at least in higher education circles and on Capitol Hill, as it was only a few months later that Congress killed the bank-based, corruption-riddled FFEL loan program entirely. This was a move I had recommended when I testified before the Senate HELP Committee in 2007.

The budget savings from this move was channeled back into grants for needy students over the ensuing years, in an amount of approximately $30 billion.

"The litigation resulted in discovery at six lenders and produced settlements with seven lenders. The settlements returned over $70 million to the U.S. Treasury.

"Although the total of the settlements was much less than the total of the unrecovered illegal claims, the litigation put a dent in the moral hazard created by either incompetence or corruption, or both, of individuals at the Department of Education. Making illegal claims carries risk under the False Claims Act. Contractors should be on notice that they are risking money and reputation, even the viability of their enterprises, when they are tempted to make false claims.

"The victory over PHEAA at the Supreme Court, stripping away its sovereign immunity, should have salutary effects at many loan servicers that have been brushing off borrowers for years, giving them not only unsatisfactory servicing, but in some cases ruining lives when borrowers are caught in loan hell and cannot get out due to the indifference of servicers, schools, and the Department of Education itself.

"Many charities that have benefited from the fund created with settlement proceeds would likely agree that the effort was worth it. Most know only that they are recipients of a charity, not the story behind it. I have publicly acknowledged my connection to only one charity, Veterans Education Success, which protects veterans from predatory colleges and lending practices. VES does great work, as do all the assisted charities, whatever their endeavors."

Oberg concluded by saying the story of the charities was perhaps another chapter for another time. "I am giving you the information about my case only with the hope that it will make a difference in the fight against corruption, especially at the highest levels of government."

He would not budge from anonymity regarding the charities. "That chapter is years off, maybe never."

PART TWO

FOR-PROFIT COLLEGES

CHAPTER TWENTY-FOUR

"WE WON, SETTLING WITH THE TERMS STILL SEALED"

Attorney, policy advocate, and investigative journalist David Halperin, a respected and talented crusader for social justice, was born on November 28, 1962. He received his undergraduate degree from Yale College in 1984. Fresh out of undergraduate school, he was hired as a research analyst with the Arms Control Association, preparing reports on nuclear-weapons issues. In 1985-1986, he also worked as a research assistant for former Secretary of Defense Robert McNamara, helping him draft and edit his best-selling book, *Blundering into Disaster*, which warned of a future catastrophic nuclear war.

After graduating from Yale Law School in 1989, Halperin served as a law clerk for U.S. District Judge Gerhard Gesell for two years during which time he assisted the judge on the Iran-Contra criminal cases, among many other matters. Following his work for Judge Gesell, Halperin worked on litigation matters with Harvard law professor Laurence Tribe before becoming counsel for the U.S. Select Committee on Intelligence, working with committee chairs Senator David Boren (D-Oklahoma) and Dennis DeConcini (D-Arizona), as well as committee staff director George Tenet, who later became the director of the CIA. Tenet referred to Halperin and a junior colleague, Zach Messitte, as "Woodward and Bernstein" after their diligence uncovered part of a scandal involving the CIA, Iraq, and an Italian bank. In addition to his counsel duties, Halperin was eventually given staff oversight of FBI counterintelligence and counterterrorism budgets.

Halperin left government service in 1993 when he co-founded Progressive Networks with Rob Glaser, a former vice president of Microsoft. The enterprise aimed to create an interactive online video network that would offer progressive content and promote activism. Coming in the era before Fox News and before the widespread use of the worldwide web, it was an ambitious project. The company later shifted to developing streaming audio and video and changed its name to RealNetworks. Halperin left in 1994.

"I knew it would be successful," he said. "But I wanted to focus on political and social change."

Halperin returned to working with Tribe and others on constitutional law cases, including civil rights and consumer protection matters in the U.S. Supreme Court. He also served as a fellow of the Harvard Law School's Berkman Center for Internet & Society, writing a paper on the implications of the Internet for U.S. security. Simultaneously, Halperin was a legal and policy advisor to Ralph Nader from 1995 to 1997.

Earlier, after law school, Halperin had met Robert Shireman whose wife worked with Halperin's then-wife at the U.S. Public Interest Research Group (PIRG). The two couples became friends.

In 1995, Shireman, who was then working at the Office of Management and Budget, asked Halperin to file a lawsuit in response to an ad published in major newspapers by Haley Barbour, the chairman of the Republican National Committee.

Halperin explained: "Barbour held up a check for a million dollars like Ed McMahon on behalf of American Family Publishers, saying, 'I'll give you a million dollars if you can prove this statement false.' Barbour claimed that the Republicans' Medicare plan increased Medicare spending between 1995 and 2001. The statement was false.

"Bob submitted an entry. Then, he wanted me to sue, because they sent him a letter back saying he was wrong. I looked at this thing. It sat on my desk for a while. I decided he was entitled to the money.

"We sued in D.C. Superior Court. I didn't have a press conference. Nothing. I didn't want to make it seem like a publicity stunt, because it wasn't. We wanted the million dollars. So, we went to court. They had a motion to dismiss.

"I had very little litigation experience at that point. I think I was thirty-two, and I had really not practiced law that much. But I won the motion. The judge refused to grant their motion and ordered a trial.

"They countersued us in Jackson, Mississippi, under the federal interpleader statute, saying that people all over the country might be trying to win. They can only have one winner, if any. They sued everybody else who entered the contest, including Carl Levin, a senator from Michigan, Gene Taylor, a congressman from Mississippi, and a bunch of really pissed-off people who were crazy enough to enter the contest. Suddenly, there's this circus proceeding.

"I got Jimmy Robertson, who was a former Supreme Court justice in Mississippi to be my co-counsel. We went in, filed a hundred-page motion to transfer it back to DC, and the judge was like, 'I don't want this.' But it got transferred to the federal court in D.C., where it dragged on for several years.

"In the end, we resolved the case—with the terms still sealed."

By then, Halperin had become a speechwriter and foreign-policy aide to President Bill Clinton, remaining at the White House until near the end of Clinton's term, appointed as Special Assistant to the President for National Security Affairs. He also served as a staff member of the National Security Council, working on such major issues, such as the Kosovo conflict, the Middle East peace talks, nuclear weapons, terrorism, cyber-security, human rights, and global economics.

CHAPTER TWENTY-FIVE

"TELL US ABOUT YOUR EXPERIENCE WITH FOR-PROFIT EDUCATION"

In early 2001, Halperin joined the board of a new organization, the American Constitution Society (ACS), and soon the other board members convinced him to become the group's first executive director. The group sought to counter the Federalist Society, which had engaged conservative lawyers, professors, students, and judges across the country. Halperin wrote that the ACS's mission was "aimed at moving national law and policy debates in a progressive direction."

Under Halperin, the group quickly built chapters on scores of law schools across the country; hosted major events with major speakers. including Hillary Clinton, Janet Reno, Eric Holder, and Sonia Sotomayor; received attention from the national media; and raised millions from charitable foundations to pay for staff and programming.

Halperin left the ACS in 2003 and joined the presidential campaign of former Vermont Democratic governor Howard Dean as a senior policy advisor and speechwriter, temporarily moving to the campaign's Burlington, Vermont, headquarters.

In this period, Greenpeace hired Halperin to help with strategy and mes-saging, surrounding an unprecedented indictment of the organization by the Justice Department over a protest by Greenpeace activists aboard a ship smug-gling mahogany from the Amazon rainforest into the Port of Miami. The case, with Halperin serving as one of two defense lawyers, resulted in an acquittal.

After Dean ended his campaign, Halperin went to the new progressive think tank, the Center for American Progress (CAP), where he served as senior vice president and founded Campus Progress—now called Generation Progress—a project to engage young people in policy, politics, and journalism while working with young activists for progressive victories. CAP was run by former Clinton chief of staff John Podesta and Clinton's former deputy director of his National Economic Council, Sarah Wartell, who later became the president of the Urban Institute.

As he had with the American Constitution Society, Halperin built a thriving operation from scratch. Over eight years, Campus Progress became one of the country's leading youth advocacy groups. It helped achieve federal and local policy wins on issues from college access to civil rights to clean energy; supported more than 100 student journalism outlets and 60 local activism campaigns; created a website with investigative reporting and innovative mul-timedia content and featured writers including Chris Hayes, Matthew Yglesias, Ezra Klein, Shani Hilton, and Dana Goldstein; held over 800 speaking events; ran national conferences with speakers including Barack Obama and Bill Clin-ton; and reached over 800 campuses and communities. Campus Progress's budget, with support from leading U.S. foundations, reached $2.7 million and the staff grew to twenty.

Halperin explained: "The original idea of Campus Progress was we would do a lot of the same things that conservative youth organizations were doing. Funding youth and college journalism and sending speakers to college cam-puses and to youth-oriented events to have them speak. We weren't really thinking about engaging in policy issues as lobbyists or advocates. We only had a small budget. We thought we wanted a focus.

"Pretty quickly—because we were part of Center for American Progress and because we were starting to get attention—we were being asked by others to get involved in issues. We were asked by students at Princeton to support their filibuster effort to protest the Republican strategy on judicial nominees.

"Then, we started helping local student activists. We also got called in by Congressman George Miller who was then the ranking member of the House Education Committee and asked if we would play a role on some student-aid issues, relating to Pell grants and student loans. That's when we started to get engaged on these college-access issues.

"Even then, I didn't really even know what for-profit education was. It wasn't on my radar. Amazingly still, I talk with educated, intelligent people all the time. They still haven't heard of it, even though it's been on the front page of the *New York Times* over and over again.

"It wasn't until Barack Obama became President, and Bob Shireman, the former head of The Institute for College Access & Success, was named the Deputy Under Secretary of Education in 2009 that the department decided to undertake reforms, particularly the gainful employment rule.

"This became a fight, and I got involved in it. I was basically asked by TICAS, the group that Bob got started and had left to go work in the government. Pauline Abernathy, who was a vice president there, started talking with me about this and getting me engaged in it.

"Campus Progress worked on climate change. We were working on LGBT issues. We were still doing all our journalism work, supporting local activism. There were a lot of things we were doing. Very quickly, I realized how serious this for-profit college issue was, because I started reading about it. I started talking with people. We started engaging more organizations, and we started building a coalition."

On August 4, 2010, the Government Accounting Office released a report, "For-Profit Colleges: Undercover Testing Finds Colleges Encouraged Fraud and Engaged in Deceptive and Questionable Marketing Practices." It was extremely critical of for-profit colleges, documenting numerous instances of false advertising and even outright fraud.

Specifically, the GAO report said in summary:

Undercover tests at 15 for-profit colleges found that 4 colleges encouraged fraudulent practices and that all 15 made deceptive or otherwise questionable statements to GAO's undercover applicants. Four undercover applicants were encouraged by college personnel to falsify their financial aid forms to qualify for federal aid--for example, one admissions representative told an applicant to fraudulently remove $250,000 in savings.

Other college representatives exaggerated undercover applicants' potential salary after graduation and failed to provide clear information about the college's program duration, costs, or graduation rate despite federal regulations requiring them to do so. For example, staff commonly told GAO's applicants they would attend classes for 12 months a year but stated the annual cost of attendance for 9 months of classes, misleading applicants about the total cost of tuition.

Admissions staff used other deceptive practices, such as pressuring applicants to sign a contract for enrollment before allowing them to speak to a financial advisor about program cost and financing options. However, in some instances, undercover applicants were provided accurate and helpful information by college personnel, such as not to borrow more money than necessary.

In addition, GAO's four fictitious prospective students received numerous, repetitive calls from for-profit colleges attempting to recruit the students when they registered with Web sites designed to link for-profit colleges with prospective students. Once registered, GAO's prospective students began receiving calls within 5 minutes. One fictitious prospective student received more than 180 phone calls in a month. Calls were received at all hours of the day, as late as 11 p.m. . . . .

Programs at the for-profit colleges GAO tested cost substantially more for associate degrees and certificates than comparable degrees and certificates at public colleges nearby. A student interested in a massage therapy certificate costing $14,000 at a for-profit college was told that the program was a good value. However, the same certificate from a local community college cost $520. Costs at private nonprofit colleges were more comparable when similar degrees were offered.[37]

In the aftermath of the GAO report, Halperin became more involved in the for-profit college issue, meeting with members of Congress and with top officials in the Obama Administration, including Gene Sperling, President Obama's director of the National Economic Council, about a proposed rule called "gainful employment," which would penalize for-profit and career education programs that consistently left students with more debt than they could afford to repay.

In addition, Halperin put out an online clarion call, asking students and others to "tell us about your experience with for-profit education." He brought two of those who responded to Washington, D.C. in early 2011: Adam Gonyea, a Navy veteran, who had attended ITT Tech in Virginia, and Rashida Smallwood who worked at ITT Tech in Texas.

Halperin explained: "Adam had a terrible experience with an overpriced, low-quality education. Rashida had worked in financial aid and had been basically told to lie, to say people were independent when they weren't, and to misstate their financial status so that this school could get the maximum financial aid."

---

37   For the complete GAO report, see: https://www.gao.gov/products/GAO-10-948T

Halperin and Campus Progress hosted a Capitol Hill press event with Gonyea and Smallwood and put a video of the event on YouTube. No members of Congress attended, so Halperin took Smallwood to visit the members of Congress in their offices. But, still, no one wanted to meet with them.

In the midst of the campaign, Halperin also became the target of a malicious smear campaign, apparently launched by for-profit college insiders. It falsely claimed that he was taking money from short sellers on Wall Street in a cynical effort to make money by undercutting the for-profit schools.

Defamatory letters about Halperin were sent to groups in his coalition, such as the National Association for the Advancement of Colored People and the National Center for Lesbian Rights.

Halperin responded: "They said that I was taking money from Steve Eisman, the Wall Street short seller. I had no connection to Steve Eisman whatsoever. We weren't taking any money from him. That's when I realized how serious the fraud was and how determined the people behind the fraud were to maintain their privileged position and keep the money coming in. It really woke me up to how serious this was."

The for-profit college industry had made a major television ad buy to oppose the Obama gainful-employment rule. So Halperin and Campus Progress made their own ad supporting the rule. An intern prepared the spot, and they spent just $3,000 to run it about ten times on *Morning Joe* and *Fox & Friends* on the Washington D.C. cable system.

A group of conservative bloggers attacked Campus Progress over the ads, all using the same talking points. Perhaps surprisingly, they were joined in their attacks by Melanie Sloan, the executive director of Citizens for Responsibility and Ethics, a non-partisan, public-watchdog operation. It was revealed a few years later that CREW [Citizens for Responsibility and Ethics in Washington] was receiving grants from a foundation tied to billionaire John Sperling, the founder of the University of Phoenix, the largest for-profit college and an aggressive opponent of the gainful-employment rule.

Halperin said: "Sloan and various bloggers claimed that we were running a multimillion-dollar ad campaign. . . . A multimillion-dollar ad campaign? They just made it up.

"The White House was getting pressure from people like Don Graham to back off."

Graham was the owner of both the *Washington Post* and Kaplan University, a major for-profit college business.

Halperin continued: "In response, we had an amazing meeting where a lot of groups on the fence came in. Gene Sperling, a top economic advisor to both Presidents Clinton and Obama [and no relation to John Sperling], showed up and gave a really strong statement, comparing the for-profit education situation to the sub-prime mortgage crisis. It was very powerful.

"I was very heartened that Gene seemed to be on our side in that way. At the same time, lobbyists from the Association of Private Sector Colleges and Universities (APSCU), which was the for-profit trade association, came to see not only my Campus Progress people, but they also went upstairs to see the heads of the Center for American Progress. Basically, trying to get CAP to get us to back off.

Don Graham personally met with Sarah Wartell, who was number two at CAP.

"That was the kind of environment that I saw.

"Trent Lott was lobbying for APSCU. Dick Gephardt was lobbying for Corinthian Colleges, one of the worst predatory colleges. When we went into the big room in the Capitol, where people meet with lobbyists, we were meeting with staff. We could see Heather Podesta, the lobbyist for DeVry University, meeting with members of Congress.

"Heather Podesta was then married to the brother of John Podesta, Tony Podesta, a major lobbyist who also was lobbying for the industry. Everybody was.

"They also had Robert Raben, a former assistant attorney general in the Clinton Justice Department, who is one of the most influential progressive lobbyists. He represents most of the civil rights groups, and he was lobbying for Kaplan.

"So, yes, there was a lot of intensive lobbying. These groups were not just trying to co-opt members of Congress. They were also trying to buy the media and get the media to sponsor their events:

"For instance, the *Chronicle of Higher Education* had an event sponsored by Career Education Corporation. They let Career Education Corporation pick all the speakers.

"The University of Phoenix sponsored NBC's annual Education Nation conference and influenced the roster of speakers. I worried about that. They were giving money to think tanks. For example, Americans for Democratic Action took money from the industry, and they opposed the gainful employment rule."

Halperin left CAP and Campus Progress in early 2012 after almost eight years. He started his own one-man operation, doing policy advocacy, investigative reporting, legal advising, litigation, and organizational consulting. He took on a number of issues, including climate change, chemical plant security, public access to government materials, and money in politics.

But the one issue he kept pursuing from his Campus Progress days was for-profit colleges. "I was, and am, determined to keep fighting on this issue for students and taxpayers until we drive the bad actors out," he said.

CHAPTER TWENTY-SIX

"THE REPUBLICANS ON THE COMMITTEE WERE OBSTRUCTING IT"

T he year 2011 was the height of power and revenue among the for-profits colleges. Their enrollment had gone from 365,000 to 1.8 million students during the previous ten years. Their peak of federal aid totaled about $32 billion—one-quarter of all available financial aid.

When Halperin came onto the scene following the release of the August 2010 GAO report on for-profit colleges, the U.S. Senate Committee on Health, Education, Labor and Pensions (HELP), chaired by Senator Thomas Harkin (D-Iowa)—which had started on June 4, 2010—was also in the midst of exposing more abuses by for-profit colleges.

However, Senate Republicans, led by Senator Mike Enzi of Wyoming, the ranking minority member, were not cooperating. "The Republicans on the committee were obstructing it all the way," Halperin said. "They were denouncing the hearings as a 'kangaroo court' and then walking out. They wouldn't participate. They just didn't want to hear the truth. . . .

"Harkin gathered the information from these schools. The schools turned over documents. The hearings had witnesses. They were telling the truth. There wasn't any doubt about that. He wrote a comprehensive report."

Released on July 30, 2012, the Harkin report—called "For Profit Higher Education: The Failure to Safeguard the Federal Investment and Ensure Student Success"—documented egregious deceptive and abusive practices, and under-spending on instruction, across numerous for-profit schools.

The report also suggested what needed to be done.

According to its executive summary, the committee Democrats recommended :

* Enhance transparency by collecting relevant and accurate information about student outcomes.

- Require that the Department of Education collect comprehensive student outcome information and enable data retrieval by corporate ownership;

- Establish a uniform and accurate methodology for calculating job placement rates;

- Increase the regulation of private lending.

* Strengthen the oversight of Federal financial aid.

- Tie access to Federal financial aid to meeting minimum student outcome thresholds;

- Prohibit institutions from funding marketing, advertising and recruiting activities with Federal financial aid dollars;

- Improve cohort default rate tracking by expanding the default reporting rate period beyond 3 years;

- Require that for-profit colleges receive at least 15 percent of revenues from sources other than Federal funds;

- Use criteria beyond accreditation and State authorization for determining institutions' access to Federal financial aid.

* Create meaningful protections for students.

- Create an online student complaint clearinghouse, managed by the Department of Education, for the collection and referral of student complaints to appropriate overseeing agencies, organizations and divisions;

- Prohibit institutions that accept Federal financial aid from including mandatory binding arbitration clauses in enrollment agreements;

- Enforce minimum standards for student services that include tutoring, remediation, financial aid, and career counseling and job placement;

--Extend the ban on incentive compensation to include all employees of institutions of higher education and clarify that this ban extends to numeric threshold or quote-based termination policies.[38]

After years of lax enforcement by the Department of Education, especially under the George W. Bush administration with regard to existing regulations over for-profit colleges, the Harkin committee provoked the Obama Admin-

---

38   For the complete Harkin Report, see: https://www.help.senate.gov/imo/media/ for_profit_report/Contents.pdf

istration and its Department of Education to impose many of the needed proposed reforms.

The Harkin Report also insisted that for-profit colleges be subject to the gainful-employment rule, along with other career training programs.

According to Harkin's public statement on this matter: "The 2012 report showed that for-profit colleges accounted for approximately 12 percent of students yet consumed almost 25 percent of the federal financial aid budget and accounted for almost half of all student loan defaults. Between 2009 and 2010, more than half a million students at for-profit colleges left with debt but no diploma despite a $32 billion annual investment by taxpayers in the schools."

However, aggressive lobbying by the for-profit college industry pushed the Obama Administration to water down its gainful-employment rule, producing a final regulation that made no one happy.

Halperin and other advocates for students and veterans saw the rule as better than nothing, but, in many respects, they viewed it as a sellout, one that would penalize only the worst of the worst programs. The industry, having enjoyed decades of unimpeded access to billions in taxpayer dollars, continued to push back against any regulation. When the industry trade association sued in federal court, a federal judge upheld the power of the Department of Education to issue the rule but found the agency had failed to provide an adequate justification for alternative measures that schools could use to show compliance with the rule.

Halperin explained: "After the first gainful-employment rule was struck down by a federal judge, the Obama Administration had choices: They could appeal. They could drop the whole thing. They could issue a weaker rule, or they could try to issue a rule that was compliant with the ruling, but nevertheless was stronger. That last option—the best one from our perspective—is what they did. We pushed very hard on that, helping to shape the rule; I participated in all that."

Halperin said that Department of Education procedures require a complicated process for issuing new regulations: "Most agencies just issue a proposed rule. Then people submit comments and have meetings. Then, they issue a final rule.

"The Department of Education has a process called 'negotiated rulemaking' where all the stakeholders get nominated, representatives of for-profit schools, nonprofit schools, students, veterans, consumers, whatever, lenders, and accreditors. Everybody sits around a table and they debate these issues. The department has three sessions. They'll have three days of meetings. Then a month later, they'll have three more days. Then a month later, have three more days. They'll keep on submitting new proposals that get debated. They have an effort to build consensus. And then, they go ahead and issue a draft rule.

"I was involved in going to every one of those sessions, passing notes up to the negotiators, writing about what was going on, and then attending meetings, meetings with the agencies, meeting with the White House. You have a chance to argue about these rules."

Halperin played that role throughout the process for creating a revised gainful-employment rule. Then, he did it again for a second Obama rule called "defense to repayment."

Halperin explained that the latter rule is "about the procedures and standards by which students who claim they were defrauded by their schools can ask for their federal loans to be forgiven. It also includes more obligations for schools to post letters of credit in case they misbehave, and in case the school collapses.

"It deals with the issue that all for-profit colleges, or most, have been forcing their students into mandatory arbitration. It's going to say that schools can no longer do that. It's either going to modify or ban them from doing that, so the students will be able to go to court with their claims."

In the final year of the Obama administration, the collapses of two predatory college giants, Corinthian and ITT Tech, and the mounting revelations in the media of fraud in the industry, finally pushed the Department of Education to get tough, with a strong borrower defense rule, a termination of accreditor ACICS, which had failed to monitor abuses at numerous schools, and a rejection of the supposed conversion of the CollegeAmerica chain of schools from for-profit to non-profit.

Halperin played a key role not only in pressing for the reforms, but also in exposing the abuses, delivering key stories to major media outlets.

Halperin recalled: "When I was at the Center for American Progress, I did occasionally write something on our blog about these issues. When I left in January 2012, one of the things I did was to create my own blog, *Republic Report*, and to start cross-posting on the *Huffington Post* blog."

Gaining immediate respect for Halperin's authoritative work, *Republic Report* focused on cases of special-interest money corrupting democracy and sound-policy outcomes. The publication was launched out of a start-up non-profit dealing with money and politics and also featured reporting by Lee Fang and Zaid Jilani (both now with *The Intercept*), Matt Stoller, and Suzanne Merkelson.

The non-profit soon jettisoned the blog, in part because its hard-hitting money in politics reports ruffled feathers among well-heeled supporters of the group. So Halperin made the blog his own, with occasional contributions over the years from Fang and others.

"I started writing regularly about these issues, recognizing that it is unusual for someone to write investigative pieces while participating as an advocate. My position was, 'I'm writing up opinion pieces just like the head of the for-profit college trade association, Steve Gunderson, is writing opinion pieces.' But mine are more useful, because I have new information. I've called people to check out whether the information is accurate. I behave as a reporter, but in service of my advocacy.

"If you take an organization like the Public Interest Research Groups, the PIRGs, they do investigative reports as well, and they advocate. It's not unprecedented. Sometimes people think it's odd that I am functioning as a journalist and as an advocate.

"People invite me on to press calls. I'll do them. I try not to jump ahead of the queue and ask questions. I'll let the people from Bloomberg and AP go ahead of me.

"I've always had the dual focus in the writing on both the underlying abuses at the schools and the corruption of Washington that makes it possible from the beginning."

In 2013, Halperin wrote an article, "A Nation of Trump Universities," after Donald Trump's unlicensed for-profit real-estate school was sued New York Attorney General Eric Schneiderman.

In his article, Halperin wrote:

> Because the media loves discussing Donald Trump, it wasn't surprising to see heavy press coverage of a lawsuit brought by New York Attorney General Eric Schneiderman accusing the unlicensed Trump University of "persistent fraudulent, illegal and deceptive conduct." Trump responded by harshly attacking Schneiderman, whose suit demands that Trump pay back at least $40 million to the 5,000 people who were enticed into paying $10,000 to $35,000 for real estate investment courses "that did not deliver on their promises." Trump University's sad broken promises included telling some students they would get a photo-op with the Donald, when all they got was a picture with a cardboard cutout. But the real fraud was convincing enrollees that the Trump-owned for-profit "university" would get them on the path to a successful career, which apparently didn't happen for many of them.

Halperin compared the bad behavior at Trump's school to the actions of the federally subsidized for-profit colleges. "My point was that these things are all over the place," Halperin noted, adding: "Basically, it said, 'This is going on all over the place with our tax dollars on a much larger scale.'"[39]

---

39   David Halperin, *Huffington Post*, "A Nation of Trump Universities: The Abuses of For-Profit Colleges," August 28, 2013.

"At the same time, I was getting so many calls and so much information from whistleblowers at the schools themselves."

Halperin also viewed the for-profit-college situation as conducive for political corruption—even among those in government and politics that seemingly had solid records and sterling reputations.

"Truthfully," Halperin explained, "if you add up the campaign contributions, they're not really that big. One of the things that's so shocking to me is how little money you can give to the late John McCain, a Roy Blunt, or an Alcee Hastings, to get them to become your attack dog.

"We don't know about all the dark money out there. McCain got the Pentagon to back off the University of Phoenix, along with former DOJ attorney Jamie Gorelick, a Democrat, secretly serving as their lawyer inside.

"For those people, you could say, it's more consistent with the Republican philosophy. 'It's private sector,' they say. But it's not private sector. Ninety percent of it is government money. It's a welfare program for those who run these for-profit schools.

"The issue should be about waste, fraud and abuse of federal dollars. I thought Republicans were against that.

"Look at the Congressional races. There are many, many races where the issue of who's in bed with for-profit colleges comes up. No one is jumping up to say, 'Yes, I'm for for-profit colleges.'

"In 2012, Mitt Romney was praising a for-profit college, and it turned out that that particular college was among his donors. . . . Romney was in the business, just like Donald Trump.

"Romney was an investor in the company that owned Full Sail University in Winter Park, Florida, as well as the nationwide Vatterott Colleges, terrible, terrible predatory schools. That was the school that Michael Brown, the student who was killed by a police officer in Ferguson, was attending when he was killed.

"Do you know what Romney did in 2012? . . . He had his donor conference and all his donors there. On the same site, on the same day, he had an investor conference for Solamere Capital LLC, which was started with his ten million dollars. It was run by his son, and the finance manager of his campaign.

"Basically, if you wanted to suck up to Romney at this donor conference, you could put money into his investment company.

"To make it even worse, Karl Rove was not permitted to speak at the donor conference. He was running a Super PAC and wasn't allowed to coordinate. But he did speak at the investor conference. That's how corrupt the whole thing was. Solamere was invested in both Vatterott and Full Sail University.

"The former Republican Governor John McKernan of Maine—who was the husband of former Republican Senator Olympia Snowe—was the CEO of Education Management Corporation (EDMC) during the period when it behaved the very worst.

"And it's not just Republicans. There's California Democratic Senator Dianne Feinstein's husband, investment banker Richard Blum, who was the biggest investor in two of the seven biggest for-profit colleges. . . .

"It's free money. It's 90% dependent on taxpayers. They need to invest in Washington. That's why you see so much overlap between the politicians and this industry. . . .

"Ed Rendell, a Democrat and the former governor of Pennsylvania, stood as a beard for this industry, because he joined the Coalition for Educational Success, which was started to lobby on behalf of the for-profit colleges. They had Ed Rendell and Republican Tom Kean, the former governor of New Jersey, chair a committee that was going to create a code of conduct for the industry. They wrote an op-ed, explaining why this was a wonderful idea and why there shouldn't be regulation.

"But the op-ed never identified Kean as a partner in a private equity firm, Quad Partners, which was invested in for-profit education, specifically Marinello Schools of Beauty, a cosmetology-school chain with as many as fifty-six locations in six states.

"Quad was the owner of that. . . .

"The Washington attorney, Lanny Davis, was hired to work for this entity. They got the former Attorney General of Rhode Island, Patrick Lynch, another Democrat, to be the guy who supposedly was to help create these standards of quality and compliance for this industry.

"Well, at some point, that was their argument—that they should have 'standards' instead of regulation. That just disappeared without any announcements. Suddenly, there was no more Ed Rendell, Tom Kean, Patrick Lynch, or Coalition for Educational Success. They just went away.

CHAPTER TWENTY-SEVEN

"THESE FOR-PROFIT SCHOOLS ARE RUINING PEOPLE'S LIVES"

S ome who have seen Halperin's detailed work have been struck by his position, questioning whether the government should continue to give money to students . . . whether it's good for the students or not.

Halperin insisted, "Many of these for-profit schools are ruining people's lives. They use deceptive marketing to sell programs that were defective in three ways. One, they're too expensive. Two, the quality generally was too low. And, three, they're admitting all kinds of students.

"I wouldn't say at all that these students don't have the capacity to go to college. I would say many for-profit schools admit students whom their programs are not designed to help. Certainly, any person could be improved by some kind of educational program. But ITT, the Art Institutes, Corinthian Colleges, and all these for-profit colleges admitted a lot of students knowing their program really wasn't designed to help them.

"What that meant was that student would be completely ripped off, because they'd be lost. They'd given the money. They'd probably drop out the first semester, or they'd stay and keep accruing more and more student-loan debt. In cases where there actually is quality instruction, such as in some Art Institutes programs, it's also bad for the other students in the class who are qualified, who could succeed in that program, being held back by students with a more remedial situation. The professors and teachers are trying to teach a class and have students who just can't possibly succeed in that class.

"The school knows if and when their program is not helping students. The school shouldn't admit them, but that's what they are doing.

"Steve Gunderson, the former Republican congressman from Wisconsin who is the chief for-profit college lobbyist, had the nerve to say, essentially, 'Yes, we made a mistake. We were thinking with our hearts and not our heads.' In other words, they admitted the students, because they felt bad for them. They really wanted to help them.

"But that's complete bullshit.

"Gunderson is the head of what used to be called APSCU. Now, it's called Career Education Colleges and Universities (CECU). CECU is the trade association of for-profit colleges.

"Most of the big for-profit colleges were members at one point. They basically turned the thing into a beast that lobbied as hard as it could against any kind of reforms, and then, when the Obama rules were issued, all the big schools quit. But there are still some regional companies in it.

"When the 2010 GAO report came out, I didn't really know what University of Phoenix was. Very quickly, I heard people say, 'Kaplan, that must be one of the good ones, because Don Graham, the publisher of the *Washington Post*, owns it.'

"Don Graham and his company also owned ten percent of Corinthian. That's forgotten all the time.

"Clearly, Kaplan was not one of the good ones. It had poor outcomes and had been investigated and taken to court by federal and state law-enforcement agencies."

"Kaplan's hallmark," Halperin said, "is not telling students that the program doesn't have the necessary programmatic accreditation," also known as specialized or professional accreditation.

"Just an example is their Concord Law School, unaccredited by the American Bar Association. Just so you know, the only state you could sit for the Bar was in California. They would say, 'We told all they students that.' But, when you ask the students, they didn't know that.

"Clearly they were not making that clear to students. It might have been in the fine print somewhere. That's a pretty big detail. It was the same with their massage-therapy students and their nursing students. Over and over people would say, 'I didn't know that I couldn't be a massage therapist in Florida. That was my dream. That's why I enrolled here.' And the school would then say, 'Well, it was in the fine print.' They didn't make it clear. . . .

"The biggest thing I reported at Kaplan was creating the fake scholarships for dreamers.

"The dreamers are the children of immigrants who came here as young people. They weren't born here in the United States and aren't entitled to citizenship, but they don't really have any connection to their birth nations. They're the ones that Obama and others have argued ought to be able to have an approved immigration status. It's not their fault that they were brought here. They have no connection to their original home.

"Don Graham has become a hero in that community by creating the dreamers' scholarship for those students who can't get federal financial aid. He raised money from Bill Gates of Microsoft, Mark Zuckerberg of Facebook, Bill Ackman, and assorted wealthy donors to create the scholarship.

"Then, under the radar, he put his own person in charge of which schools would participate. One was his own Kaplan school.

"Here's how it works: You create a charity. You staff the charity. Then, you raise money from people. And then, you have the charity send money to your own for-profit company."

"But there was an even more suspicious angle.

"These Kaplan units have a problem with the federal 90-10 rule in that they're not raising enough money from non-federal sources."

The 90-10 rule is a federal regulation that governs for-profit colleges, capping the percentage of revenue that a school may receive from federal financial aid sources at ninety percent. The other ten percent must come from non-federal sources.

Halperin continued: "These dreamers are categorically ineligible for federal aid. It's a sneaky plan to be praised at a dinner as a hero of these young immigrants. In fact, what you're doing is propping up your scam college by sending private money to them. It's astounding. And I called them out for it.

"I wasn't going to write about it, because the dreamers are my friends. Indeed, the dreamer that Don Graham hired to assist with the program was somebody I'd worked with. I was just like, 'This is horrible. But I don't want to hurt this program.'

"Then, Michelle Celarier, a reporter with the *New York Post*, questioned me about this. She asked, 'This dreamer scholarship, does any of the money go to Don Graham's schools?' I replied, 'Yes, it does.'

"When she published her article, I had my story ready. The *New York Post* is only going to get six-hundred words, so I did a long investigative piece that came out two minutes after the *Post* piece.

"What Graham was doing was an absolute travesty. Of course, the IRS is not in the business of actually enforcing the nonprofit laws at all. This thing is just going on. . . .

"I've regularly criticized Kaplan for being just as bad as some of these other schools and for abusing students and for deceiving students.

"*TheWashington Post* used to always disclose when they wrote editorials about for-profit education that they owned Kaplan. But then they'd also run editorials by people like Marc Morial, the president of the National Urban League, who joined the board of Corinthian. The *Washington Post* didn't disclose that the writer had this connection.

"After Don Graham sold the *Post* to Jeff Bezos, Katharine Weymouth, his niece, was still the publisher. . . . They said in their editorial, 'We used to have a conflict. Now, we don't anymore, but we still think for-profit education is awesome and unfairly maligned by the Obama administration.'

"I wrote an article that said: 'Your publisher is still on the board of Graham Holdings, which owns Kaplan and a piece of Corinthian. You really have the same conflict.'

"After I wrote that piece, Weymouth was dismissed from the *Post*. According to an article in the *New York Times*, it was for reasons unrelated to her performance. I have no idea what the reasons were.

"The idea that Donald Graham walks around—now praised as a hero of college students, of the dreamers, that he's a hero champion of students in DC schools—is fine. The key reason that he's rich, besides an inheritance in the TV stations, is that he's presided over a scam college.

"But we haven't won that fight. Kaplan is still getting nearly a billion dollars a year from taxpayers."

In 2017, in the permissive regulatory environment of Donald Trump and Betsy DeVos, Kaplan was sold to Purdue University, a state school in Indiana, in a troubling transaction that allowed the school, now called Purdue Global, to advertise itself as part of a well-regarded public university, while programs were still run by, and profits still flowed to, Graham's Kaplan operation.

Continuing with his research of the conflicts among high-profile people who were and are still involved with the for-profit college industry, Halperin insisted: "You have Colin Powell paid to serve on the advisory board of Leeds Equity Partners, one of the main investors in Education Management Corporation, which is one of the worst predatory college companies. Powell spoke at the for-profit college industry convention and praised their schools. Former Republican Senator Bob Dole was a lobbyist for Bridgepoint, another terrible predatory college company.

"All these people—like Don Graham, Anita Dunn, who advised Graham's Kaplan, Heather Podesta, and Lanny Davis—are pillars of the Washington establishment.

"They were walking around, claiming they were the only ones helping poor students. And that's absurd."

CHAPTER TWENTY-EIGHT

"DEVOS HAS TRASHED NEARLY EVERY REFORM MEANT TO PROTECT STUDENTS"

David Halperin and his colleagues in the war against corruption within the for-profit-college crowd started working closely with the new Democratic majority in the U.S. House of Representatives in the aftermath of their big win during the 2018 midterm elections. With his deep knowledge of the industry and of Betsy DeVos and her aides, Halperin was a natural choice to take a leadership role.

On May 22, 2019, Halperin appeared before the U.S. House Oversight Subcommittee on Economic and Consumer Policy, now controlled by the Democrats in the aftermath of their big win during 2018 midterms. With his aggressive and authoritative defense of the Obama Administration's gainful-employment rule and other reforms, Halperin dominated the hearing as even Republicans on the committee were seen at times nodding in agreement with him, both during his prepared statement and during his responses to questions from members of the panel.

In part, Halperin—who had never appeared as a witness before a congressional panel but had attended many hearings and worked with committees on Capitol Hill throughout his career—testified:

> Secretary DeVos, guided by Acting Under Secretary Diane Auer Jones, has now cancelled all these pro-student, pro-taxpayer reforms and more.

> As evinced by the regulatory pronouncements of her Department, and her own remarks, the Secretary seems to believe, without evidence, that the real danger is not fraud by colleges, but fraud by students.

> The DeVos Department has eliminated protections for students and taxpayers even as state attorneys general, state oversight agencies, state legislatures, and accreditors are all moving in the direction of stronger accountability.

> The DeVos Department's abandonment of oversight of the for-profit college industry has been carried out with clear disregard for the law. Courts have repeatedly declared illegal the Department's efforts to repeal Obama-era regulations. In justifying the reinstatement of ACICS, Acting Under Secretary Jones cited demonstrably false information. Deputy Secretary Mick Zais then blatantly disregarded his duties in pressuring the Department's acting inspector general, Sandra Bruce, to curb an investigation of Jones's restoration of ACICS, and then acted to replace Bruce with a Department of Education lawyer, before that firing was reversed. . . .

> The for-profit college industry claims there's no need for the Department to increase oversight because there are no bad schools anymore—all that's left are honest mom and pop operations. That's false. They claimed about the same 10 years ago.

This very hour, across our country, for-profit schools are using deceptive and coercive tactics to persuade Americans to enroll in high-priced,
low-quality career education programs that will ruin their financial futures.

Some of the bad for-profit schools have shut down in recent years, but
many continue with a business model focused on signing up as many students as possible, getting as many taxpayer dollars as possible, spending as
little on education as possible. The money goes to lead generators, land-
lords, and lawyers, plus, of course, executive salaries and investors. When
the operators realize have sucked all the money out, or their programs
are cut off from federal aid due to violations, they shut down overnight,
students are locked out, and taxpayers have to finance another bailout.

For-profit chains also are closing physical campuses and shifting their
emphasis heavily to online instruction. Online programs are cheaper to
run, and schools often spend far less on online instruction , but schools
rarely pass the savings on to students. And the evidence, including recent
research suggests that, despite the immense promise of technology for
learning, online higher education often doesn't deliver for students, especially the kinds of students, inexperienced students, heavily recruited
by online colleges. . . .

Secretary DeVos's top two higher education aides, Diane Auer Jones and
Robert Eitel, both worked as senior executives at Career Education Corp.
through 2015. Carlos Muniz, who was until recently the Department's
general counsel, represented Career Education Corp. in the fraud case
pursued by the state AGs, even after the Senate HELP committee approved
his nomination.

Diane Auer Jones also was previously an expert witness hired by CollegeAmerica in its Colorado fraud case, and a consultant to the main for-profit college trade association, APSCU (now called CECU). Robert Eitel previously worked at Bridgepoint Education (now called Zovio), operator of Ashford University.

Other top DeVos higher education officials also previously worked at or for poorly performing for-profit education companies.

Congress should be asking whether these former for-profit college executives who are now Department of Education officials have recused themselves from matters as required by applicable law. More broadly, Congress should be asking whether these officials, along with Secretary DeVos, have been acting in the best interests of students and taxpayers in carrying out their duties. In my view, their actions have only aided predatory schools.

Explaining how he came to appear before the subcommittee, Halperin said: "After the Democrats took over the House of Representatives in 2019, the oversight committee launched an investigation of the Trump administration and its policies naturally included a review of Betsy DeVos's abandonment of accountability for the for-profit college industry.

"I was fortunate to have the opportunity to present conclusions from work I have done for nearly a decade. I appreciated that members of the committee, including some of the Republicans, seemed to be listening carefully."

Typically, at a congressional hearing, the majority party selects the witnesses, and the minority is entitled to add one witness. At the hearing where Halperin testified, the other witnesses selected by the Democrats were Maryland Assistant Attorney General Christopher Madaio, an expert on the for-profit college industry, and former Art Institutes student R.J. Infusino, who had experienced the Dream Center collapse firsthand. The Republicans chose as their witness Dr. Lindsey Burke of the conservative Heritage Foundation.

Testifying alone on a separate panel was Diane Auer Jones, Principal Deputy Under Secretary, Department of Education, who defended DeVos and the Trump Administration's policies. Halperin noted, "Diane Auer Jones appeared after our panel and continued her run of false statements to Congress, regarding the Dream Center, the controversial accreditor ACICS, and other matters."[40]

In his evaluation of the subcommittee members, Halperin said: "There's only so much detail you can address in five-minute rounds at a hearing. There's much more to discuss about the abuses in the for-profit college industry and the corruption at the DeVos Department of Education. There was much more to ask Diane Jones, to pin her down on the obvious inconsistencies in her testimony. I appreciate that the oversight committee and the House Education and Labor Committee are continuing their investigations."

Returning to the matter of Steve Gunderson, the head of the Association of Private Sector Colleges and Universities (APSCU), Halperin explained in his *Republic Report* column: "Regarding the recent epidemic of for-profit college closures, Steve Gunderson, the chief lobbyist for that industry, has taken his shamelessness to new heights—brazenly suggesting that the shuttered schools have no connection to his lobby group, CECU, when he knows full well that they used to be members and had mischaracterized industry critics' views on the closings.

"In his seven years at the helm of CECU, former Republican Congressman Gunderson has tried to defend the indefensible record of his sector through a

---

40   David Halperin broke the first big story and numerous additional stories about the Dream Center Education Holdings debacle. Relying on whistleblower reports, documents, recordings, and other insider sources, Halperin revealed that Dream Center executives were improperly mixing the newly non-profit schools with for-profit companies they owned, that the company was accelerating predatory practices, that the operation was lying to students about the lapsed accreditation of some campuses, that DeVos aide Diane Jones was changing and bending rules to assist the operation, and that Jones pushed for a private equity operation, Colbeck Capital Management, to take over many of the schools on terms obscured from public view.

The New York Times has subsequently produced its own scoops on Dream Center, and its coverage has repeatedly linked to and credited Halperin's extraordinary work.

combination of bombastic pronouncements—e.g. that critics are opposed to 'the very existence' of his industry—and complete distortions.

"Now, with a Democratic-controlled House of Representatives stepping up to hold accountable the predatory colleges that DeVos has sought to protect, Gunderson has again ratcheted up his falsehoods and distortions.

"Gunderson's most recent focus is the widely publicized closings of most schools in three career college chains, those operated by Education Corporation of America (ECA), Vatterott Educational Centers, and, most recently, Dream Center Education Holdings, which acquired its schools last year from Education Management Corporation (EDMC). In all three cases, closures were sudden, came after the schools had run into trouble because of predatory behavior, and left many students with only bad options for continuing their career training.

"On March 11, Gunderson issued a press release regarding the closures. 'Once again,' Gunderson said, 'schools that are not members of CECU are abruptly closing causing untold, and unacceptable damage to their students. In doing so, these schools just disappear. But all the multi-generation family-owned schools in our sector are left with a bad reputation created by somebody else.'

"Gunderson's statement was remarkably deceptive—and simply appalling. In fact, all three chains—ECA, Vatterott, and EDMC—had been members of CECU (formerly called APSCU) during Gunderson's tenure there. So were Corinthian Colleges and ITT Tech, two other large, awful predatory chains that abruptly shuttered near the end of the Obama Administration, as well as ATI, FastTrain, and Alta/Westwood, three smaller chains that closed after being exposed for flagrant fraud.

"Other past CECU/APSCU members include the still-operating giant predatory chain operations Career Education Corporation, DeVry, Bridgepoint, and Kaplan (now Purdue Global).

"The CECU members that remain include the Center for Excellence in Higher Education (CEHE), operators of CollegeAmerica, Independence University, and other schools, a company with a disgraceful record of predatory abuses against students and resulting law enforcement actions.

"Other current CECU members that have been the subject of law enforcement actions for abuses against students include Education Affiliates, Daymar College, and Lincoln Educational Services.

"As far as I can find, Gunderson and CECU have never once publicly criticized any of these chains while they were operating, and certainly not while they were members of his organization. Yet now that some of these operations have disgraced themselves completely and shut down, Gunderson wants us to believe he's never had anything to do with them.

"Moreover, none of the current or past CECU members I've listed could fairly be described, as Gunderson suggests, as 'multi-generation family owned.' They're publicly traded corporations, or private equity-owned, or large companies passed from one owner to another, or, at least technically, are now non-profit organizations.

"Family-owned schools, by the way, also have engaged in serious abuses— take Globe University, another former CECU member, owned by Gunderson friends the Myhre family.

"In short, Gunderson's ongoing effort to suggest that CECU is and has been made up entirely of ethical mom-and-pop operations is a lie and a disgrace.

"As for the genuinely honest, effective career education schools out there, Gunderson has done them an extraordinary disservice over seven years by fighting rules that penalize bad actors—rules that would give a competitive advantage to the good schools.

"Later, Gunderson compounded his disgrace in a letter to Representative Susan Davis (D-CA), Chair of the House Higher Education Subcommittee. Gunderson's letter offered an array of misleading statistics and again accuses critics of 'declaring war on the one sector in higher education most engaged in providing underserved students with career skills,' that is, his sector.

"Gunderson also writes to Davis, 'For reasons I don't understand, our sector continues to be criticized for its marketing.' But surely he understands that for-profit colleges have repeatedly been caught engaging in *deceptive* market-ing—lying to students about job placement, starting salaries, selectivity and urgency of enrolling, costs and financial aid, and many other matters.

"Gunderson then ratchets up his deceptions when he returns to the issue of closing college chains:

> I cannot begin to share with you my deep frustration with our opponents who have spent years seeking to destroy our sector. Now that they have succeeded in closing many schools, they raise the very issue of "too many school closures!" One cannot have it both ways.

Halperin continued: "Critics didn't cause the closures of these chains—al-though the public exposure of abuses in the for-profit college industry may well have influenced the choices of some prospective students to avoid enrolling in for-profits entirely. The chains that have closed fell as the result of their own particular predatory practices and financial and operational mismanagement.

"More importantly, critics aren't faulting these predatory schools *for closing*; many of them should not have been operating, enrolling students, and taking millions and billions in taxpayer dollars in the first place. What these schools deserve blame for is *how they closed* –shutting down abruptly, sometimes mid-semester, without giving students fair notice or taking adequate steps to guide students toward quality transfer schools or loan forgiveness options.

"The schools, knowing they were in deep trouble with accreditors or gov-ernment overseers, also continued enrolling new students and banking their federal financial checks, so they could gather in as much cash as possible—even as, in the case of Dream Center, they diverted from students the federal-aid sti-pends, the basic living expenses, to which the students were legally entitled.

"The way these institutions closed affirmed what we already knew: the own-ers of these schools, to put it mildly, never prioritized the interests of students.

"Surely Gunderson, a former congressman and member of that same House Education Committee, is smart enough to understand this distinction. But in the world of lies in which he's lived for seven years, all that matters is maintaining the pressure on government to keep the taxpayer dollars flowing to his members. The rhetoric is a sideshow, though; what really keeps CECU members in the money are their campaign contributions to politicians, mostly Republicans but also some Democrats, who then do their bidding.

"After Gunderson and an army of for-profit college lobbyists failed to halt the Obama reforms, CECU's membership and revenue dwindled. But Gunderson got extra lucky with Trump's surprise victory. He had long ago hired hometown girl Callista Bisek for his congressional office, where she met Speaker Gingrich and eventually become his wife. At CECU, Gunderson hired Gingrich to promote his industry, and then Gingrich became an early and ardent Trump supporter.

"All the crony connections were in place for a return to government complicity in predatory abuses by for-profit colleges, and that is exactly what happened. DeVos, who has barely concealed her contempt for students and Department career staff, stocked her senior team with former for-profit college lobbyists, dumped the Obama gainful employment and borrower defense rules, revived the industry's worst accreditor, dismantled the Department's enforcement unit, and stuffed the debt relief claims of defrauded students in a file cabinet. Soon after, the Department managed to get a panel of stakeholders to achieve consensus on rules that will further enable privatization of and decreased accountability for higher education—a "success" achieved by stacking the deck of negotiators, and making threats that, in the absence of consensus, the Trump-DeVos operation would write even more pro-industry rules.

"Fortunately, all the DeVos cancellations of accountability rules have been managed poorly. She has repeatedly lost in court when her actions have been challenged, and her regulatory abandonment will not survive in the long term. Moreover, the actions of conscientious state attorneys general and other non-federal officials, as well as media scrutiny and the efforts of student advocates, will continue to squeeze bad actors and help increase protections for students.

"Some scam colleges, though. will continue to operate, ripping-off tax-payers and ruining students' lives. Steve Gunderson and his fellow for-profit college lobbyists, and the owners they serve, will own the immense harm they've done to countless veterans, single mothers, and others abused by predatory schools."[41]

Speaking of the DeVos reign at the Department of Education and her role in alleviating protections against predatory for-profit colleges, Halperin said: "DeVos has trashed nearly every reform meant to protect students against tax-payers against predatory colleges—the cancellation of the gainful employment rule, the gutting of the borrower defense rule, the refusal to process borrower relief claims, the issuance of new rules further weakening accountability of schools and accreditors, the restoration of discredited accreditor ACICS, the approval of troubling conversions of poor-performing for-profit schools to non-profit status, the effective shut-down of the Department's enforcement unit, and the ending of cooperation with other enforcement agencies.

It's a brazen handover of policy to the worst actors in higher education, those that have used deception to sell low-quality, over-priced higher education programs to unsuspecting victims.

"DeVos's top higher education aide, Diane Auer Jones, worked at CEC from 2010 to 2015 as senior vice president and chief external affairs officer, a job in which, according to Jones's LinkedIn profile, she was "the senior executive responsible for company-wide regulatory operations, licensure and accreditation, corporate communications, public relations, government affairs and centralized academic services."

"CEC in 2019 paid to settle claims with 49 state attorneys general and with the Federal Trade Commission that it engaged in deceptive practices, including while Jones worked there."

—⚎—

---

41   David Halperin, *Republic Report*, "On For-Profit College Shutdowns, Lobbyist Gunderson Has No Shame," April 8, 2019.

PART TWO

In addition to his widely read blog, *Republic Report*, David Halperin has published two books about the for-profit college situation *Stealing America's Future: How For-Profit Colleges Scam Taxpayers and Ruin Students' Lives)* in 2014 and, in 2016, *Friends in High Places: Who Endorses America's Troubled For-Profit Colleges?*

– 209 –

CHAPTER TWENTY-NINE

ROD LIPSCOMB
"I KNEW I HAD NO CHOICE BUT TO FIGHT FOR THE STUDENTS"

Rod Lipscomb, a former dean at the for-profit ITT Technical Institute in Tallahassee, is one of the most celebrated whistleblowers in the world of for-profit colleges. In a major article about the downfall of ITT Tech, Lipscomb told the *New York Times*: "I really believed at that time, I could fix it if I got to the right folks. . . . But the higher I reported up the chain, the worse the environment got for me."[42]

That was the beginning of the mind-numbing consequences that Lipscomb would face, trying to right the wrongs that he discovered at this for-profit college. But his follow-up work demonstrated his commitment to service, as well as his courage as scholar, citizen, and whistleblower.

And after receiving his Bachelor of Science degree from the Virginia Polytechnic Institute and State University in 1993, Lipscomb earned his master's

---

42   Patricia Cohen, *New York Times*, "Downfall of ITT Technical Institutes Was a Long Time in the Making," September 7, 2016.

degree from Florida State University in 1995 and began his work towards a Ph.D. in Higher Education Administration.

While working on his doctorate, Lipscomb served as the assistant to the president at Florida State University from 1999-2003. Upon completing his doctorate coursework, Lipscomb was selected as the campus dean of the New York Institute of Technology where he served for three years. In 2006-2007, he spent a year as a doctoral fellow with the State University System of Florida. From 2007-2010, Lipscomb was the director for Campus Life, as well as the chief judicial officer at Tallahassee Community College.

After that position, he became the Dean of Academic Affairs for ITT Tech, and that's where this drama began.

Lipscomb explained: "I had never even heard of ITT Tech. I actually applied for a part-time instructor position, but according to the college director, he stated that after reviewing my resume, he thought I would be better qualified for another vacant administrative position.

"I was appointed as Chief Academic and Student Affairs Officer, providing leadership and oversight for the college's six schools—nursing, business administration, criminal forensics technology, electronics technology, information technology, and drafting and design. I also had oversight and management of the academic chairs, academic programs, the learning-resource center, the library, and faculty governance. In addition, I served as the substance-abuse coordinator for the campus, as well as doing oversight for student conduct, student retention, Title IX, academic integrity, academic and student-affairs policies, student activities and co-curricular learning."

In other words, Lipscomb was a very busy man with tremendous responsibilities to juggle.

All seemed well at ITT Tech for Lipscomb until students started to approach him with problems. Lipscomb recalled: "The first time I became aware of any issues is when criminal-justice students began to complain to me about the tuition and student loans.

"What raised immediate concern for me were the students who indicated they came to the college for a different program, such as graphic design, but were coerced through the admissions team into, for example, criminal justice.

"Unfortunately, in many cases, the program the student enrolled in at the college was never offered—or cost significantly more in tuition to switch into the academic program for which the student had originally enrolled in at the college.

"Also, an ITT recruiter and financial-aid representative met with me to report their concerns about the practices of the college regarding admission and financial aid. It was at that time I realized these were not isolated cases. Staff were being trained and threatened with the loss of their jobs if they did not engage in illegal, aggressive, predatory, and questionable practices.

"It was also at this time that I contacted other academic deans, only to discover this behavior was happening at their campuses, too, and it was among the unwritten rules on how to conduct business at these colleges."

Recognizing the seriousness of these problems, Lipscomb stepped up and notified the ITT Tech high command of provable high-pressure recruiting tactics, bait-and-switch enrollment strategies, financial-aid deceptions, job-placement-rate manipulation, and retaliatory devices, as well as:

* Concerns that students were being coerced into academic programs in which they had no interest in that major or career field or could not succeed based on previous academic evaluations.

* Students, without the appropriate academic experience or training, were knowingly placed in majors and classes where it was impossible for the student to pass or succeed.

* Staff members completed financial-aid forms for students; students did not understand the financial obligations being created on their behalf.

* Students were promised certain jobs and/or pay if they graduated from ITT. This promise was often fabricated and did not match the actual data.

* For students who left or dropped out of their academic programs, they were threatened that if they did not return their student-loan debts would be sent to collections, and this would negatively impact their lives.

* If students failed one academic program or did not make satisfactory progress for financial-aid purposes, they were coerced to switch to different academic majors to keep their financial support at the college, even if they had no interest in that major or career field. Financial-aid support and postponement of collections was often used to coerce or frighten the student into re-enrolling.

The ITT Tech director who hired Lipscomb supported him. However, another director and ITT Tech's district administrator were critical of him, warning that he would lose his job if he filed a formal complaint about the problems he outlined.

Lipscomb also received a visit from one of the college's corporate attorneys, who completed the bad news. Lipscomb lamented: "This was saddening and disappointing. I thought they would take action to correct the illegal and inappropriate behaviors and actions, but instead I was threatened to stay quiet or lose my job. They said that I would be terminated for insubordination and hindering other employees from doing as directed by executive administration.

"And I was actually told by the college attorney that whistleblowers have difficulty finding jobs in the future."

Lipscomb viewed this as real intimidation. And he felt fear.

"I was terrified of losing my job and being blacklisted. I knew this would make it difficult to find employment in the future, even though I was right for reporting violations of federal law."

And, through his due diligence, he continued to discover more problems in the ITT community. He explained, "Several recruiters and financial aid staff verbally raised concerns at staff meetings, but would be threatened with their jobs, terminated, or would leave on their own because of the practices.

"They even barred me from being able to attend college meetings where recruitment, enrollment, and financial-aid matters for each student or potential student would be discussed.

"Simultaneously, I informed them that I would be submitting a complaint to the Department of Education."

After Lipscomb notified ITT Tech executives about the unethical practices of the college—in defiance of their admonition not to file any more complaints—the hammer fell on him.

"Almost immediately, I was terminated from the college for insubordination—since I had been warned that I could no longer file any more complaints.

Seeing how the unfair and unjust practices had and would continue to hurt the students and their families, Lipscomb decided to go public, saying: "I heard the numerous voices of the students, firsthand, who were taken advantage of by school administrators. College students, single parents, adult learners, and many others shared their story about the college and the negative impact it had on them and their families both financially and mentally.

"Once I admitted I was part of the problem by saying nothing, and the fact the practices went against everything I learned from my mentors and university professors, I knew I had no choice but to fight for the students."

In a story about Rod Lipscomb, Patricia Cohen wrote in the *New York Times*:

> Hired in the spring of 2011, he was disturbed by the aggressive recruitment, something he had never seen during his two decades at public educational institutions. Former students returned to the school, stunned by letters demanding payment for high-interest loans they knew nothing about. Worst of all, he said, staff members would then persuade those same students to re-enroll in unrelated programs and take on even more debt as a way of deferring the loans that were already due.
>
> He started filing reports, detailing his concerns.

Finally, he was told a lawyer from the company's headquarters in Indiana and the district manager were coming to Florida to meet with him. "I was very happy," he said. "I thought they were going to take action."

Instead, Mr. Lipscomb said, they told him that if he continued to report his complaints, he would be fired.

In 2015, he was.[43]

---

43   Ibid.

Another important ITT whistleblower was Dan Graves who, along with a colleague, had earlier filed suit against the company, alleging that it had "systematically violated the law governing compensation of sales representatives." See: Gretchen Morgenson, *New York Times*, "A Whistle Was Blown on ITT; 17 Years Later, It Collapsed," October 21, 2016.

The *Times* also noted that in or about the fall of 2002, top officials at the Department of Education s relaxed restrictions on incentive compensation. According to the story:

> In another action that seemed to protect the schools from liability, William D. Hansen, then the deputy secretary of education, published guidance changing the way the government should measure damages resulting from violations of the incentive rules.

> "I have concluded that the preferable approach is to view a violation of the incentive compensation prohibition as not resulting in monetary loss to the department," Mr. Hansen wrote in an October 2002 letter to the head of federal student aid at the time. This was a major change; the Education Department had previously calculated damages resulting from a violation as the total amount of student aid provided to each improperly recruited student.

> Mr. Hansen left the Education Department in 2003 for the private sector. Now chief executive of Strada Education Network, a provider of student financial aid, Mr. Hansen was until recently on the boards of Argosy University and South University, two for-profit colleges owned by the beleaguered Education Management Corporation.

> Through a spokesman, Mr. Hansen declined to comment on the guidance, which was formally rescinded only in 2015.

—⋙—

Rod Lipscomb didn't know how to go about becoming a whistleblower, saying: "I spent numerous late nights and early mornings at home reading, studying and researching federal and state laws, as well as the procedures for reporting violations.

"Then I contacted various senators' offices and federal agents in the Department of Education and also sent in my concerns about the illegal actions of the school, but I never received a response or follow-up. However, I did receive a phone call from an investigator from the department. He specifically stated he was making the recommendation in confidence, suggesting that I might want to contact a lawyer about the matter.

"That person gave me the name of a law firm, The Employment Law Group."

Lipscomb contacted the firm and showed a lawyer his documentation. After a review of these materials, the attorney, David Scher, agreed to represent him.

"Since I was unemployed at the time," Lipscomb recalled, "and living off savings and early retirement funds, the law firm indicated they would only receive payment if they were successful with the lawsuit." When asked if he felt like he was entering the battle, feeling like David against Goliath, Lipscomb replied: "Absolutely, yes! This was not the first complaint or lawsuit involving ITT Tech, but based on my research at the time, ITT Tech always seemed to come out on top."

According to a UPI wire story:

A Florida campus of the for-profit ITT Technical Institute routinely used deceptive practices to enroll and keep students, including enrolling a blind student for a computer repair program, and coerced students into racking up huge debt, a whistleblower lawsuit said.

The lawsuit, filed in U.S. District Court, alleges ITT Tallahassee pressured students into taking out huge student loans by misrepresenting programs, lying about graduation and placement rates, all part of a larger scheme to defraud the federal government out of financial aid payments. The suit states the whistleblower, Rodney Lipscomb, a former dean of academic affairs at ITT's Tallahassee campus, was fired after raising concerns about the school's practices.

Lipscomb alleged the pattern of abuses stretched through his four-year tenure at the school, from 2011 to 2015.[44]

After Lipscomb's suit was filed against ITT Tech—which denied the allegations—he faced serious problems which he detailed: "Losing my job placed negative blight on my professional career. It made it difficult to find other employment in the beginning because ITT officials gave poor evaluations to potential employers.

"In addition, I was actually informed by an administrator from one college I applied to that I was a high-risk hire since the college was concerned that I would file a lawsuit against them if I discovered improprieties.

"As a result, I used up all of my savings and emergency funds. Unfortunately, I had to use some of my retirement funds with significant penalties to be able to live day-to-day. Due to this incident with ITT, I spent nearly $40,000 out of pocket that would not have been spent if this had not occurred.

"Also, the stress endured as a result of major medical and mental health issues due to this incident has caused me suffering to this day, both physical and mentally."

On the upside, Lipscomb was surprised by the overwhelmingly positive reaction to his disclosures. He said: "Once the lawsuit was released to news media, unbelievably, I was overwhelmed with support and positive remarks from past and present ITT students, faculty, staff and the parents of students.

---

44   Amy R. Connolly, United Press International, "Whistleblower lawsuit claims for-profit college ITT defrauding students," January 21, 2016.

I actually had administrators from other ITT campuses who contacted me and gave me accolades for doing what they should have done years ago.

"Also, the media coverage was very fair."

Lipscomb also went through a "daunting and exhaustive" period of discovery in midst of his litigation. But, with his experience as a conduct officer and Title IX investigator for over twenty years, he had been through difficult legal battles before.

When asked if he expected to win at the outset, Lipscomb said: "Actually, I never ever asked that question, nor focused on an outcome of 'winning.' Throughout the entire process, start to finish, I always shared with my attorneys that it was not about winning for me, it was about the students suffering from the illegal actions of—and being taken advantage—by ITT.

"Many of these students came from very low-income backgrounds but were racking up major debt through tuition—$50,000, even $100,000—where it was most likely the starting job obtained would be making $25,000, assuming that they were able to obtain a job in their fields of study."

"The final result? ITT closed its doors and the students were afforded numerous remedies through both state and federal governments. It was a big win for the students!"

When asked whether ITT Tech was contrite, he replied: "Never! That is the sad part of all of this. ITT Tech executives never admitted to their illegal activities and their impact on thousands of students."

Speaking of his victory, Lipscomb said: "I actually cried. I was so happy for the students, abused and misused by ITT Tech for monetary gain and greed.

"Unfortunately, once ITT Tech filed bankruptcy after it closed, I was unable to recoup any of my losses."

Lipscomb continued: "I was very pleased with the performance and representation by my attorneys. They went above and beyond, and were highly supportive, honest, and transparent about the process and their representation. There was never a week that I didn't receive a phone call or email updating me on the progress of the case."

When asked if he has inspired or encouraged other whistleblowers to come forward, Lipscomb candidly replied: "This may sound cowardly, but no. For me, it was the right thing to do. But I wouldn't want any person to go through what I went through during the complaint-and-litigation process. The actions of that time are still negatively impacting me today, both mentally and financially.

"However, during this same process, I had numerous ITT students and employees thank me for what I was doing, and that, if they were needed to testify or provide information, they would be willing to do so given my actions and bravery."

Asked for his message about for-profit colleges in general, Lipscomb replied: "Like any other industry, for-profit colleges are not 'evil' or 'bad.' I'm certain there are for-profit colleges that are ethical and caring and follow the law and put the education of students first.

"In the case of ITT Tech, most of the faculty and staff were honest people committed to the education and success of its students. It was the executive administrators who lost sight of education, focusing on making the highest profit necessary for themselves and investors.

"My message is this: Creating an educational environment which supports, promotes, and fosters student success—academically, mentally, and socially— through honest and transparent policies and practices is paramount.

"When profit becomes the measure of success in education, we all lose— consumers, taxpayers, employers, families, and most of all, the student."

Thinking back on his accomplishments, which carried tremendous consequences and sacrifices, Lipscomb reflected: "Would I do it again? . . . I sometimes ask myself whether it was worth the mental, physical, and financial anguish and burden it has caused me. But I remember the numbers of awesome students that were positively impacted and 'saved from the action of greed.' And that outweighs any burden I suffered through today as a result of this incident.

"I will leave this earth knowing I did the right thing."

PART THREE

ACADEMIC CORRUPTION IN THE WORLD OF ANI-MAL RESEARCH

CHAPTER THIRTY

"CONCEPTION TO CONSUMPTION"

D r. James Keen was born in Minneapolis, Minnesota, on December 9, 1957. His father worked as a research chemist for General Mills. His mother was a homemaker who raised young James, along with his seven brothers and four sisters. Among the twelve children, James was the second oldest. The family lived in New Brighton, just north of the Twin Cities.

While James was in junior high school, his family moved to Riverside, a wealthy suburb of Chicago, where his father, who became his role model, changed jobs and went to work for Corn Products, aka CPC International, which made and distributed Skippy Peanut Butter, among other foods.

James attended and graduated from Riverside Brookfield, an exclusive high school, in 1976. "We were middle class," James said, "but we were surrounded by really wealthy people."

James received a grant-and-aid for track and cross country to Eastern Kentucky University in Richmond, Kentucky, in the midst of coal and tobacco country in the foothills of the Appalachians. At school, he ran the steeplechase and the 5,000 meters. However, during his second year of competition, he was injured. By then, though, he had earned an academic scholarship, so his college career remained on course, uninterrupted.

Inspired by his father, he studied science, majoring in biology. He received his Bachelor of Science degree in 1980.

After graduation and his decision to postpone medical school—with three of his siblings becoming MDs—James joined the Peace Corps, assigned to go to West Africa. Fluent in French, he taught high school for two years and then traveled the world before returning to school in 1984.

After his travels, James Keen briefly moved in with his parents in Illinois, and, while living in their neighborhood, he met the woman who would become his wife, Connie, a registered nurse.

The Keens would later have five children—four daughters and a son.

In lieu of becoming a practicing MD, Keen went to veterinary school, receiving his degree from the University of Illinois in Champaign-Urbana in 1988.

After graduation, Keen saw an ad for a one-year fellowship with the United States Meat Animal Research Center in Nebraska—aka USMARC or just MARC—offering a program in food-animal medicine.

Founded in 1964 by Congress under the umbrella of the U.S. Department of Agriculture, the Clay Center-based MARC is the largest livestock-research facility in the world: a giant 35,000-acre triangular-shaped ranch—twice the size of Manhattan. The land was formerly a Naval ammunition depot and was later transferred to the USDA.

Getting even more specific about the MARC site, Keen explained: "It's a big ranch. They have about 30,000 acres of pasture just primarily for their cattle. They also have about 5,000 acres that they grow corn on, which they use to feed the animals, and they also grow some alfalfa."

Upon receiving the grant, Keen moved his family to south-central Nebraska—even though his wife totally opposed the move. She didn't want to leave Illinois.

They settled in Hastings, Nebraska, which, with a population of 25,000, was the largest town near MARC. "They didn't have a lot of outsiders in there," Keen noted. "For my wife it mattered because she is very social. She is a city girl, a city woman."

Keen recalled his first impression of south-central Nebraska, adding: "It's flat and very, very empty. I never saw anything like it.

"Coming from Illinois or Minnesota in suburbia, you're used to seeing development things. . . . My wife, Connie, commented, 'It's not the end of the earth . . . but you can see it from here.'"

Keen continued, "Actually I thought it was interesting. I worked for the University of Nebraska at Lincoln (UNL). MARC is run cooperatively between the USDA and the University of Nebraska, although the USDA really has all the political and decision-making power.

"I was a UNL employee and my job was to take care of the animals. It was clinical care, and I was a clinical veterinarian.

"They have a campus in the center, which is like a small university campus. That's where the USDA employees work. Most of them are animal scientists, geneticists, physiologists, meat scientist and nutritionists. Most research effort is on cattle, with a much lesser amount on swine and sheep."

Keen explained the financing that supports MARC: "Although it varies a little bit by year, USDA at MARC receives $22 million a year in appropriations from Congress.

"Also, MARC sells the excess animals every year, because you can't just keep every animal, right? You'd run out of pasture, labor, and space. MARC generates about $5 million per year from livestock sales. But the amounts varied, based on how many cows, sheep, or swine were sold and their market prices. . . .

"Basically, how the USDA MARC budget works is they are appropriated about $500,000 per year, per scientist. This is about $22 million that MARC gets per year from Congress. And from the sale of breeding stock and the sale of animals that go to slaughter, they make another $5 million. But that number varies, depending on what the price of livestock is.

"Most excess MARC livestock stock are fattened and sold to buyers who bring them to slaughter, just like private farms. A smaller number are sold to private companies as breeding stock, bulls, replacement cows and things like that. They have an electronic sale. You bid online for animals. Every year there are excess livestock totaling about 6,000 cattle, 14,000 pigs, and 5,000 lambs that are sold

"Sometimes cattle are priced high, and they make a lot of money. Like the last couple of years, cattle prices were high. Sheep are usually pretty low. Swine vary a lot, so I'm saying that's probably an average figure of $5 million a year, about $27 million total per year.

"UNL employees work in the field as shepherds, as herdsmen. They take care of the animals, and they also have a farm crew who grow the crops. There are maybe eighty federal employees and about a hundred University of Nebraska employees."

Keen noted that MARC's motto is, "Conception to consumption."

"They have cows out in these pastures, along with the sheep and the pigs, and they get bred and then they are raised there. Most of them will be fattened up in a feed lot.

"There's a ranking system there, a caste system so to speak. Cattle are number one, pigs are number two, and sheep are number three.

"Sheep are very low-rated on the system. Some of the cowboys call them 'prairie maggots.' They have a very low status at the center. They get the least amount of resources and probably the poorest care.

"Cattle, however, are sacred. They have high status, and they're treated better than any of the species there. Most of the resources—I'm guessing here, probably seventy percent or more—go toward cattle. It's probably because John Pollak [the former director of MARC]and most previously directors actually were beef-cattle geneticists, and MARC was founded basically to do beef cattle genetics. That's why cattle are number one."

Keen worked for a year as a clinical veterinarian for the University of Nebraska. At the end of that year, MARC supported his return to the University of Illinois in Champagne-Urbana to work towards a PhD in livestock infectious diseases.

Keen explained: "I was at Champaign from 1989 to 1990. Then I came back to MARC to do my research from 1991 through 1993. MARC paid for my research and my salary while I was there. I worked on sheep viruses."

CHAPTER THIRTY-ONE

"MARC IS JUST KNOWN TO HAVE VERY WILD ANIMALS"

In 1994, Dr. Keen went to work with MARC's Animal Health Unit.

Keen continued: "Typically, before 1964, all of the cattle in the U.S. were basically small breeds originally from Britain. I'm thinking of Angus, Hereford, and Shorthorn. . . .

"Then, in about 1964, the meat industry received permission to import semen from cattle breeds in Europe (called "Continental breeds"), which were much bigger than British breeds, to the U.S.

"Just to be clear: The reason MARC was brought into existence was to cross these big Continental cattle with the smaller British breeds. Traditionally, when you raised cattle in the U.S.—and it's still true today—most people use a cow breed called Angus, which are black cattle. Then they breed these British cows with a European bull, often in this part of the country it's a Charolais. They are big, white cattle. When you cross different breeds, you get a beneficial genetic effect called 'hybrid vigor.'

"Outbreeding is generally good. Outbreeding maximizes the genetic diversity. If you cross an Angus with a Charolais, you get a lot of genetic diversity. By breeding crosses of multiple British and Continental breeds of cattle, MARC created a new 'composite' breed, new cattle breeds formed by combining traits from multiple other breeds. That's usually the way most new breeds are made."

With regard to livestock welfare, Keen described himself "somewhere between an agnostic and an atheist." During his early days with the MARC, he, in hindsight, viewed himself as an enabler because he witnessed activities he felt were wrong, but he believed that they were being done for "a higher purpose."

Keen explained: "When I came out of Illinois, I saw dairy cattle and swine. You didn't have any beef cattle there. One reason I wanted to come to Nebraska in the first place was because I wanted to learn about beef cattle. I had no experience with that.

"What MARC would do, because they're doing genetics, they would want to wait until say the bulls got bigger to see what they were like before they decided which ones they wanted to keep.

"I castrated a lot of larger cattle. Normally, you castrate the calves when they're young. And I castrated many hundreds of larger cattle without any anesthesia, for example. That's just how it's done, and I didn't see anything wrong with it.

"You restrain them in this big metal chute. You put a rope around their necks and pull their heads to the side so they can't move. Then, you have to go under their belly. And, while they're trying to kick you, you take a big knife and cut off their testes. That's routine.

"I never got hurt severely.

"I was working with a federal vet, a really great guy named Gary Ross, one of the best vets I've ever met. He showed me around.

"There was a sick heifer, which is a female calf, and she was running around in this pen. When I was in Illinois, and there was an animal, I'd just hop in the pen and go to work on the animal because they were fairly tame. I remember I jumped into a pen and Gary told me, 'I wouldn't do that.' I hopped in anyway and that animal just tried to take me. It just chased me. I had to high jump out of the pen.

"That's just an example of the kind of things that I did when I was a clinical veterinarian. And I did that for a year.

"I would say it's much less painful, and it's much safer to castrate a younger animal because sometimes if you do it on a large animal, they may bleed out because they've got much bigger blood vessels.

"De-horning means you take a saw, you cut off their horns, or you take a big tree branch pruner or a wire saw to de-horn.

"I would de-horn in that same way—without anesthesia. That's just how it was done. That's the way I was taught, and that's what I did. . . .

"The animals at MARC are wild. They are very, very wild animals.

"If you're a regular farmer or a rancher and you have an animal that's wild, you get rid of it because it's not worth getting hurt over. But at MARC, what happens is they kept animals based on production, which is somebody sitting in an office, like a scientist at MARC, and saying, 'This animal is growing really well and so they keep it.' So, the poor cowboys have to work with these really, really bad-tempered animals that are outright dangerous.

"In one case, a guy bought a bull from MARC. As he was unloading the bull, the animal killed him. Bulls can be very dangerous.

At MARC, you rarely see people on foot. People either ride a pickup, or they're on horseback. If you're on foot, the animals just don't respect you. They don't know what you are. And they're dangerous.

"The same thing with sheep. People would buy sheep from MARC at a sale, and the sheep were wild, too. You put MARC sheep in with a regular herd, and the MARC sheep will run, and the other sheep think something's wrong, so they run too.

"MARC is just known to have very wild animals."

CHAPTER THIRTY-TWO

"THAT'S WHEN I STARTED KEEPING A LOG"

B y 2007, Dr. Keen decided that he wanted out of MARC.

"Now, you have to remember that at this point I was pissed at MARC," he said. "My research was going really well, and then I got transferred from Animal Health—my natural home as a vet— to the Meats Unit, which is all about dead animals, against my will. "The move killed all my live-animal research that I was doing at MARC. At that time, I had a big $1.1 million grant which ended because of that.

"There's a saying. 'With a good boss, there's no bad job; with a bad boss, there's no good job.' I had a bad boss, so I wanted to get out. I wasn't happy. When I was working in the Animal Health Unit at MARC for USDA with my old boss, Will Laegreid, things were going really well. Then, I got transferred to another unit and that ruined all my research. So, I had a bitter taste in my mouth about MARC from that experience."

Shortly thereafter, Keen joined the Great Plains Veterinary Education Center (GPVEC), which was part of the University of Nebraska at Lincoln's veterinary school, located on the MARC campus—although it was independent of MARC.

He started to work there on November 1, 2007.

Keen said: "Great Plains was set up in the early 1990s staffed mostly with clinical veterinarians who worked for UNL. Their job is primarily to train veterinary students who come there. Then, the students go out in the field, and they learn experientially, because they help treat the animals at MARC.

"Each spring, MARC has about 35,000 animals. After those animals are weaned, there would be fewer animals later in the year, because some get fattened and sold in the summer. . . .

"Anyway, the job at GPVEC opened up there, so I went over. This was a hundred yards from my old MARC office, and I went to join that unit. So, for the University of Nebraska, I basically did three things: I did some continuing education for veterinarians; I taught clinical veterinary medicine to students at MARC; and I taught formal courses to veterinary students at Lincoln. Plus, I did research, too. It was a very different job than my full-time research position had been when I worked for USDA.

"When I was with USDA at MARC from 1994 to 2007, I tried to do research, but the problem was that there were about 8,000 adult cows at the center. And most of those have calves every year. Of those 8,000 cows, about 7,500 are tied up in long-term genetics experiments, which means they're 'sacred cows,' and nobody can do anything to them.

"Essentially, there are five-hundred cows for other people (about non-geneticist 40 scientists) to work on and that just wouldn't work for me, because my PhD was in epidemiology, which is doing work on groups of animals. So, I did almost all my work off-center—on farmers' and ranchers' herds."

With Keen's return to academia—with all the benefits of tenure—he began to reconnect with some of his former veterinary colleagues, who then began telling him more horror stories, which he chronicled and memorialized.

Keen continued: "At Great Plains, there were three clinical veterinarians. They would tell me disturbing things that they saw at MARC.

"That's when I started keeping a log of things that I saw and things that my colleagues saw. I wrote down the dates, who it was that told me, and what had happened.

However, the log no longer exists.[45]

Keen explained: "Hearing these stories from my colleagues, I realized that there was something wrong . You have to remember, most of my colleagues were untenured faculty.

"I came in as tenured faculty, so I was safer. For example, one of my colleagues took pictures of some things. I asked him for the pictures, but he wouldn't give them to me. They were of poor animal welfare events that he saw, such as bulls that starved to death or pigs that were eviscerated due to improper surgery.

"I don't blame my colleagues for not sticking their necks out by sharing what they had discovered because they were at risk, professional risk.

"There are two separate types of poor animal welfare at MARC. One is what I call just terrible experimental design. If there would have been an IACUC [Institutional Animal Care and Use Committee] there, these experiments would never have been approved because of the severe pain, suffering and death they caused to the animals.

"The second issue, a welfare issue, is just the way the animals were treated at MARC. Cattle were generally treated pretty well. Pigs and sheep got the raw end of the stick.

"I'll give a couple of examples with the sheep, which have a chronic problem with rectal prolapse, which is where the rectum everts. You see the sheep and, of course, they have the white wool, and you see this foot-long or foot

---

45   With regard to the fate of his log, Keen explained: "After outed as a whistleblower in May 2014, I was permanently banned from MARC without warning, so my log was left in my office. When I was allowed to return to my GPVEC office fifteen months later in September 2015 for one hour (with Nebraska State Patrol escort) to retrieve my personal belongings from my office, I was unable to find my log. So, I do not know what happened to it. My guess is that my office was searched, and the log taken—although I obviously cannot prove this."

and a half-long swollen red thing that looks like a sausage hanging out from their rear ends.

"This just happened routinely, and they were typically ignored for a long time. Sometimes the area would become maggot infested. This was one thing one of my colleagues brought to my attention. Actually, it's easy to fix, but MARC shepherds often ignored them.

"But here goes another issue that I'm going to bring up: The Great Plains Vet Educational Center always had at least three clinical vets who each had twenty to thirty years of clinical experience. I'm not a clinician. I would teach students, but mostly I'm a researcher.

"The way the memorandum of understanding was between GPVEC and MARC, UNL GPVEC vets could not treat any animal at MARC unless they got permission from MARC first.

"If I went out and I saw a sheep with a rectal prolapse—and this happened to me—I would not be allowed to treat that sheep unless I first talked to MARC, and they said, 'Yes, you have permission to do it.' Usually MARC declined.

"That was a strange deal, so the veterinarians basically had no authority to do anything.

"That's always been the case with Great Plains. Great Plains was put there for political reasons. You have to remember, MARC is a genetics center, and it's run by animal scientists. There's a traditional animosity between veterinarians and animal scientists pretty much everywhere. I don't know why that is. They just didn't like veterinarians at MARC."

CHAPTER THIRTY-THREE

"I WAS AFRAID TO TAKE FURTHER STEPS FOR FEAR OF RETRIBUTION"

I n 2010, Jim Keen began working on an important project on the *E. coli* bacteria. Most strains of *E. coli* are harmless, but some strains of *E. coli* I can be deadly. This is the nasty intestinal bacteria that is often transmitted to people through meat contaminated by livestock feces. It is a challenge to scientific investigators, especially to epidemiologists like Dr. Keen. He was the lead investigator on a competitively awarded USDA-funded grant of $24.8 million. The project was funded in 2010, but it didn't begin for two years—on January 23, 2012. The proposal submitted to win the grant was hundreds of pages long.

Keen explained: "It was exhausting to write the grant. Although there were other people involved, I wrote most of it myself, and it was mostly based on ideas and field data that I had generated.

"We won the award, but one of the groups that lost the competition filed a lawsuit. That took a year to get that resolved. It was supposed to have started in 2010, but it got delayed.

"There was a two-step process. They had maybe twenty-five research teams that had applied the first round. They got it down to four, and you had to make an oral presentation. So, we were in the top four. And in the second round, we won it.

"Texas Tech was one of those in the top four. But because Texas Tech didn't get the award, they filed a lawsuit, which basically sucked up a year of my life fighting that lawsuit. I worked with UNL lawyers all of 2011."

Keen worked on the *E. coli* project from April 2010 to June 2012 when he resigned from the project. He noted: "The reason I resigned was the University of Nebraska at this point had unilaterally changed four or five of the conditions that were written in the grant protocols. The biggest one was that I was out in Clay Center a hundred and five miles away from Lincoln. I had written in the grant that I needed to have two support staff with me at Clay Center—one to do budget, and one to do project management. The University of Nebraska research administration insisted that those two positions be based in Lincoln instead of in Clay Center, which would have made it impossible for me to execute the grant.

"They told me that I had to commute to Lincoln, which I didn't really have much stomach to do.

"The distance from my home in Hastings to Lincoln was a hundred and five miles each way. I had been doing that previously, the summer of 2011, meeting with the UNL lawyers."

With a two-hour drive each way, Keen was spending four hours a day in his car.

"What made me mad was that the university changed the stated conditions of the grant after we won the award. It was like moving the goalposts. There was no way that I could run the grant under those circumstances. So, I resigned from the *E. coli* project. It was not easy to let go of $25 million in research dollars."

The time that Keen spent on the project and the time he spent away from home—during which he never took a vacation—caused problems in his personal life.

"This took a huge toll on my marriage. I can tell you that. My wife was really upset. I was never there, because I was at work on the *E. coli* grant all the time. This caused a tremendous stress on our relationship. I was an absentee husband and father for more than two years. In retrospect, writing and winning that $25M grant was by far the worst experience of my entire professional career and the most damaging to my personal life.

"Be careful what you wish for."

Despite all this on his mind, Keen reported his animal welfare concerns to his three supervisors at Great Plains at the university from 2008 through 2014.

The response?

Keen said: "To my knowledge, there was no response from my supervisors. In fairness, Great Plains has no direct power to influence MARC and the vets were marginalized, as I stated previously. Furthermore, as believers in Big Ag, I suspect my GPVEC supervisors looked at poor animal welfare as a cost of doing business in production livestock research."

Frustrated with all of the inaction, Keen then went outside the university and MARC. He recalled: "I contacted an animal-protection group in early 2013 for two reasons: First, I realized UNL would not—or perhaps could not—take action. Second, I was afraid to take further steps for fear of retribution."

Speaking about his decision to go outside his bureaucracy for reform, Keen said: "I told my immediate supervisor specifically what I saw and what my concerns were. The first was Dr. Gary Rupp. He retired, and then I told Dr. Dave Hardin. He was the interim director at Great Plains and also the Director of the Veterinary School in Lincoln. Then we got a final GPVEC director Dale Grotelueschen. They were my in-house, direct supervisors, and I spoke to them at least once a year, sometimes more, about my specific animal-welfare concerns at MARC. This went from 2008 to 2014. Nothing happened.

"They could've gone to talk to the MARC director. As far as I know, they didn't even try.

"There was a case where they had—and this was really sad—I think it was eight or nine bulls that starved to death. . . .

"MARC is broken up into what are called pole sheds, basically herds of five-hundred animals. The woman who runs this pole shed, I've known her for many years and she's a great cowgirl. This was in the wintertime in 2011 or 2012, and there was nothing to eat in the pastures. And she said: 'My bulls are starving. They need more feed.' And the cattle manager said, 'No, you don't.'

"And, then, eight of the bulls starved to death. Then, he said, 'Oh, I guess you need some more feed.'

"That was just terribly poor management. She did what she was supposed to do and yet nothing happened. My friend, my former vet colleague, got photographs of the animals that starved to death. That's not a research issue. That's actually an animal-management issue. Cruelty from terrible research design and execution and cruelty from terrible animal management.

"Poor welfare outcomes were even more common in sheep than cattle, because they were out on the fields on their own—and they got the really short end of the stick.

"At that point in 2013, I contacted the director of an animal-protection group. Just to be clear, the state of Nebraska hates animal-protection organizations. One of our previous governors said, 'I'm going to kick them out of the state.' They're just really not liked by the state.

"I told everything to the animal-protection director: what was on my list, and what was going on at MARC—just to inform her and ask if there anything that she could do. She said she would see if she could do anything. She didn't commit to anything, but I remember I said to her, 'If you want to send anybody undercover, I could tell you when and where to go.'

"Anyway, it turned out that, as I recall, she told me that for whatever reason, her organization couldn't do anything."

CHAPTER THIRTY-FOUR

"INSTEAD OF ME CONVERTING MY DAUGHTER, SHE CONVERTED ME"

B etween July 2012 and January 2014, Jim Keen found himself at a cross-roads, deciding that he was no longer interested in doing the food-safety research which he had performed for several years.

Keen recalled: "This actually goes back to part of my transformation. . . . Let me step back for a second.

"From 1994 until the time I left USDA in 2007, most of that time I spent on *E. coli* and *Salmonella*. And what I worked on mostly was: How do you get rid of *E. coli* O157 (a dangerous strain of *E. coli* that causes sometime fatal bloody diarrhea and kidney failure in people) in feed lot cattle? In Nebraska, commercial feed lots are all around, you should see one some time. They're scattered around.

"Basically, how it works is that beef cattle are usually born in the spring. They'll be with their moms on grass through the summer. In the fall, they get weaned, which means they're taken away from the mothers. They're put in what's called a feed lot.

"In the feed lot, they're herded into pens, and each pen holds about two-hundred animals. Let's say that they are five-hundred pounds each. That's about how big they are when they're weaned. They're going to stay in their pens until they're twelve-hundred to fourteen-hundred pounds.

"Now, a cow is really designed to eat grass. What they do in a feedlot is slowly increase the cattle from being on basically zero-percent grain to ninety-five percent grain within a month's time.

"The reason they do that is there are tons of cheap grains. That's part of what growing all the grain, corn and soybeans in Nebraska is about. A lot of it is going to feed lots. It's actually subsidized by the USDA.

"And the reason they feed them grain is that it's energy dense, so they can reach slaughter weigh in, let's say, in a year and a half. If they're on grass, it's going to take them more than two years. It's a time-versus-money thing. I've seen a hundred-thousand animals in one feed lot. You can imagine how many pens that would be. And how much corn. And how much manure.

"The cattle are standing in or walking in or lying down in a foot of their own manure and urine; a thousand-pound steer produces about sixty-five pounds of manure per day.

"Ninety-nine percent of every feed-lot cow in the U.S. in the summertime has *E. coli* O157 on it, covering its hide, in its mouth, in its GI tract, by the billions.

"My research job was how do I get rid of *E. coli* O157 in live feed-lot cattle so that it would not contaminate the meat at slaughter.

"When you think about it, if people were living in houses and defecated everywhere, they would all probably have *Salmonella* just because of the environment. I tried a whole bunch of experiments with this system and basically nothing worked."

Keen further noted that, because they were living in their own waste, the cows had to receive antibiotics. He explained: "If they didn't get antibiotics, this system wouldn't work, because it's such a filthy environment. Without antibiotics a lot of them would die.

"But these antibiotics lead to antibiotic resistance and that results in manure run-off into the environment. This generates more antibiotic resistance in the environment. The other thing I realized then was that this whole system—this production system, industrial-animal agriculture—is bad for the animals.

"Also, it's bad for the workers. In terms of their health, in terms of their welfare, and as a result of the contamination of the environment, a lot of the workers aren't treated very well, many of whom are undocumented Hispanics who do all the work.

"So, it's the whole system. Animal welfare is just part of the problem in the pathological animal-factory-farming system.

"There is a famous phrase by a Dutch ecologist, Lourens Baas Becking. His hypothesis is: "Everything is everywhere the environment selects." Basically, that means given this horrible feed-lot environment, it would be impossible to get *E. coli* O157 out of there. That's what I realized.

"The whole system is insane. It's against nature. That's one of the things I realized. That's when I realized that I'm never, by research alone, going to solve this problem. I realized I was trying to divide by zero.

"That's when I also realized that, first, this whole feed-lot system is abnormal. Secondly, there are a lot of human public-health issues related to this abnormal system, especially with *E. coli* and *Salmonella*. There're also a whole bunch of animal-health and animal-welfare issues.

"This was one of the big moments for me. The other moment was when I realized that this production of agriculture system—which I'll call 'Industrial Ag'—is a screwy system and it's anti-nature.

"This stuff with the feed lot was not in my log. My log was only about animal-welfare issues, livestock welfare issues. This was my own thinking."

At the same time in about 2008, Keen's daughter, Hannah, started what's called a CSA.

He explained: "CSA is 'community-supported agriculture.' They're all over the country. People buy subscriptions. At the beginning of the spring, people give money to small farmers of their choice in the CSA program. The farmers use that money to grow the food for the subscriber.

"So, my daughter has one. She's up to around eighty customers who each receive a basket of food every week for twenty-two weeks beginning in the spring and lasting into the fall. Where I used to live, it's called an acreage. They've got about eight acres. Of that land, my daughter farms about three acres."

Keen's daughter, Hannah, who was twenty-five when she started her CSA, inspired her father who remembered: "When our kids were growing up, I saw nothing wrong with production agriculture. I'd say: 'You guys have to eat meat. I'm making my living off of meat.' We used to eat the typical Nebraska meal: a big steak with a baked potato and a little bit of salad. It tastes good, and that's the system here. That's what people like to eat."

Keen's daughter attended a local college for two years, but she did not receive a degree. Instead, she moved to the west coast to participate in a year-long internship, working on several organic farms.

With admiration for his daughter, Keen said: "She wanted to learn the business, hands on. When she left college, she told me, 'This isn't good enough for me. This isn't helping me.'

"When she returned to Nebraska, she said, 'I'm going to try it here.' So, she tried it on our property, the eight acres that we own, just to make it easier for her. And she did it.

"I didn't think it would work, because we're surrounded by gigantic fields of genetically raised corn. But, it's a weird thing: genetically modified organisms [GMOs] are Round-Up ready."

Continuing his thoughts about corn, Keen described the scene in Nebraska, saying: "Basically for corn fields in Nebraska, and most of the country, forty-five percent is going to be used for animal feed, forty-five percent will be used for ethanol, bio-ethanol, and five percent will probably go to feed people in the form of high-fructose corn syrup. That's essentially what makes Coca-Cola sweet.

"Also, there's a huge subsidy for this corn. My daughter who runs the CSA, the organic CSA, said organic food isn't more expensive. Instead, it's the real cost of food. It doesn't have the subsidy. If you raise corn, for example, you get a subsidy. You can accept direct payments if the price gets too low. You get crop insurance which covers two-thirds of the cost of the insurance. That cheap food is what feeds the livestock. It's incredibly subsidized.

"My daughter showed me that there are alternatives."

"I have four daughters, and they were all vegetarians at some point. Some still are. My daughter, Hannah, raised some heritage pigs one year, called Berkshires, which I helped her raise. The meat is just delicious. The pork is red, not white, with a lot of fat. It tastes fantastic.

"In the end, she didn't like taking the pigs to slaughter, so she didn't want to raise animals anymore. . . .

"With CSA, she doesn't use any fertilizers. She uses no pesticides. As I said, she's fed up to eighty families. When she started with the program, she was the only CSA between Lincoln and Denver.

"Right here, this is the middle of Big Ag country. I think if she can do it here, she can do it anywhere.

"She also grows about an acre of flowers that she uses for a cut-flower business, and she has about fourteen beehives for honey. The flowers support the bees, which pollinate her vegetable crops, and then she uses the flowers as another source of income. Basically, she has a sustainable system.

"I realized from seeing what she did that there are alternative ways that do not do damage to people or to the environment.

"I wouldn't say that my daughter radicalized me, but she did help to convert me. All these years, I would have these dinner-table arguments. I would try to convince my family that we needed to feed the world by growing animals and crops this way. Hannah said, 'No you don't.'

"Instead of me converting daughter, she converted me."

Ultimately, there were two additional reasons for Keen's conversion.

Keen explained: "My research was trying to enable an industrial system that shouldn't be. When you're with USDA, you're assigned the research that you do. I had no choice on the research. But I realized that trying to fix that *E. coli* problem in feedlot cattle was impossible given their filthy environment.

"The other thing is that if you go into a GMO, genetically modified corn field, it's lifeless. It's sterile. There are no weeds, no insects. There's nothing in there due to high herbicide and pesticide use which is in huge contrast to when you go into a beef-feed lot where it's the filthiest place in the world—where methane gas is produced."

Keen continued: "Basically, cattle burp out methane. An animal will get bloat—which basically means the rumen gets blocked—and so all this gas and the bacteria just blow up like a balloon. You look at their sides, and they're actually blown up like a balloon.

"The treatment is you use a trocar or a needle, a sharp hollow piece of metal, that you stick in the cow to let the gas out. If you put a little lighter on that when you let the gas out, there will be a blue flame. You can imagine the volatility. Basically, it's a form of natural gas.

"At that point—after talking to my different supervisors and directors, as well as to the animal protection group without success—I was at a dead end."

As Keen approached his dramatic point of no return, he turned to his family, his wife and five children to discuss their future.

Keen said: "I told my wife about animal welfare problems that I saw at MARC or heard about at MARC. And she told me: 'You need to do something. You need to speak up.'

"Truth be told, I was always afraid to that, because I knew how it worked out there."

Even though his wife encouraged him to step forward and go further than he had previously gone to report the animal-welfare issues, Keen said that she was also concerned about putting his family and job at risk, adding, "She was afraid someone might burn our house down."

In his effort to protect his family, he didn't reveal his plan.

CHAPTER THIRTY-FIVE

"I REALLY THOUGHT I WAS GOING TO BE ARRESTED"

S eeing that working within the system was not really working at all, Keen decided to reach out to reporter Michael Moss of the *New York Times*.

"*The New York Times*, I figured, was the best one. I did a Google search and I don't recall the search terms I used; but Michael's name popped up first. He had won a Pulitzer Prize in an area that I knew something about: *E. coli* O157. I had done a lot of research on that.

"He won his Pulitzer for following up on a woman who had gotten sick from eating hamburger that was contaminated with *E. coli* O157 and suffered a lot of really bad things from it.

"I contacted Moss in November 2013. I sent him a cryptic email via my Gmail account. I said that I had some animal-welfare issues. I gave my name and a number and simply told him, 'If you're interested, contact me.'

"I think he looked me up, and then he called back and wanted some more detail. So, I told him a little bit. Of course, I'm nervous here, talking to him. I didn't know him or how it was going to go, but then he told me, yeah, he'd seen some of my work on *E. coli*."

When Keen and Moss first spoke to each other, Moss asked Keen what he wanted to happen. Why had he reached out to the *New York Times?*

"I can't remember exactly what I said, but basically, I said I want the animal welfare of the livestock at MARC to get better—the poor production practices and the research malpractice. Those are two separate things that act in tandem. . . ."

"We had a few more conversations, and slowly, I started feeding information to him, suggesting that he file Freedom of Information Act requests. I knew these documents existed, so I said, 'Request this set of documents, it might be experiment outlines.' He started doing that.

"By getting some documents, he also was able to FOIA other documents that I didn't know about. In the end, he got about ten-thousand pages."

In an unofficial memorandum he wrote to himself in or about March 2014—but shared with Moss—Keen stated:

Pre-2013 -All 30K animals at MARC owned by UNL
(8000 brood cows (most have one calf each year), 3000 breeding ewes (most have twins or triplets annually) ~500 breeding gilts (2 litters of ~10 piglets/yr)

Sometime in 2013, ownership of cattle & sheep (& pigs?) as they were born as calves & lambs began to be transferred from UNL to USDA MARC. With sheep and cattle breeding stock replacement rates of about 20% per year, it will take about 5 years for all cattle & sheep at USMARC to be Federally owned. I am unsure if MARC assumed ownership of pigs; if so, this would take only about a year since there are only gilts kept at MARC (*i.e.* the female pigs are sold after giving birth for the first time)

I was told (I believe by my former USDA boss Will Laegreid; now Univ of Wyoming Vet Sci dept head) that UNL technically owned the animals at USMARC so that receipts from sales of excess live animals as well as

animals sold for slaughter would remain at USMARC in a revolving fund
e.g. to pay UNL employees at USMARC. Supposedly if USDA owned the
animals then sales receipts would return to the US Treasury.

I was told in early April 2014 by Kelly Heath, UNL Institutional vet in
Lincoln, that he (Dr Heath) had received notification (letter, or email)
that he was now responsible for animal welfare of UNL-owned animals at
USMARC. Kelly told me the message came to him from Dr David Jackson
(then a UNL research dean) (or Archie [Clutter], the UNL Ag research
dean). I asked for a copy of the letter but he declined. He said that UNL
was taking control of UNL-owned animals at USMARC b/c of a State of
Nebraska (Mike Foley's office) audit of UNL that found that animals at
MARC owned by UNL had to be under UNL control and UNL IACUC.

GPVEC veterinarian faculty (Dale Grotelueschen, Jeff Ondrak, Kathy
Whitman and Brad Jones) had a meeting with MARC Director John Pollack in March or April 2014. (I did not attend this meeting as I believe I
was teaching in Lincoln that day.) Based on my memory, Dr Brad Jones
told me that MARC Director John Pollack told the GPVEC vets that
MARC was taking ownership of all livestock at MARC to avoid UNL
IACUC protocols.

"Moss came out to visit me in Nebraska, I think, three times. He wanted
to see the Easy Care Sheep project at MARC for himself, because that was
still going on. It was a big deal. He had talked to one of my former students
from Brazil, who had actually worked on that project for a few months. And
he had heard about it directly from somebody who worked there.

"I had seen it, but I hadn't actually worked on it. I knew where it was, and I
knew that they started lambing in May. I also knew that they had a lot of lamb
deaths. Lambs are most vulnerable when they're newborns.

"I respected Michael Moss because he wanted to see it. And when he wrote, he wouldn't put anything in his article that was hearsay. He had to talk to the person directly.

"I introduced him to a lot of people who had seen things, but a lot of them refused to talk to him, so he couldn't mention them in the article.

"I suspect UNL employees at MARC were given a, 'Don't talk to anybody or you'll be fired' kind of an ultimatum.

"Moss came to Nebraska on the Saturday before Mother's Day, May 10, 2014.

"Michael basically worked on this project full-time, and he had one person just dealing with the FOIA requests full-time.

"He also had a videographer working part-time. It cost a ton of money.

Keen continued: "Michael and I went out there at MARC to see the Easy Care Sheep. This is an especially egregious MARC research project that ran from about 2002 until 2017 where domestic sheep, dependent on human care and protection, were placed on isolated pastures to fare for themselves as if they were wild sheep. Predictably, domestic sheep managed as wild sheep, but they didn't do very well. It's a coyote buffet, lamb starvation, and disease convention. Animals that die out there, many hundreds per year, get necropsied or autopsied to see the cause of death. I had arranged to necropsy the dead lambs with one of the clinical vets out there that Sunday, and I wanted Michael to see it.

"Michael and I got there at like ten o'clock, and I was showing him the dead lambs. Then, another vet showed up early, an hour and a half early.

"It was a woman." Keen asked that she not be identified.

In the end, it was this woman—who was on a year-to-year contract—who outed Keen with his superiors.

Did she do it intentionally or unintentionally? Maliciously or not?

Keen replied: "Well, I don't know. I think she felt obligated to do it, probably. If she didn't, she likely would have been fired. . . . I don't blame her.

"I had brought Moss there. I think she had met him. She knew who he was. He may have even said at that time, 'I'm from the *Times*.' I think I introduced her.

"Anyway, I didn't say anything when she arrived. We just necropsied all the sheep. There were probably thirty or forty. We looked at what they died of. You can tell if an animal died from hypoxia—from lack of assistance at birth. You can tell if a coyote ate it, because its brain is open. You can tell if it froze to death from hyperthermia."

While Moss was at the facility, a severe hailstorm killed 120 lambs.

Keen remembered: "Michael saw it. He saw a bunch of dead lambs that had died the day before. He had seen the actual live lambs, and then he saw the storm. He took his own pictures, and I think I took some too, just from my cell phone."

Explaining the details of what happened, Keen continued: "That afternoon. We necropsied about fifty sheep. Michael wanted to see where these sheep were, so we drove about two or three miles away where the Easy Care Sheep are. They're basically on these giant pastures, maybe a mile by a mile. There are about four of them. They're huge. But there's zero shelter from the weather—wind, rain, snow, heat, hail. It's just grass. It's just a simple woven-wire fence. A lamb could get out through the fence, and a predator could easily get in through the fence.

"Normally, baby lambs stay right next to their mothers. We had some lambs that were hundreds of yards from the mothers. A young lamb that strays from its mother on pasture has a near 100% death probability.

"I went back to work on Monday, May 12th. The other vet said nothing to me. I was hoping she wouldn't say anything. Obviously, she said something, because later that week, three SWAT officers from U.S. Immigration and Customs Enforcement showed up.

"They were dressed in all black with black baseball caps and sidearms. One was standing at right where you drive into the center. I said, 'Boy, that is really weird, what's going on here?'"

Notably, the immigration police were the only federal law-enforcement agency that was nearby.

"I didn't really put two and two together. Then, I happened to ask our custodian. He's the kind of guy that knows everything. I knew he would know. I asked what are those guys doing there? 'Well they're federal immigration police,' he said, 'There was a big security breach here, and that's why they're here.'

"At that point, I knew that they were there because of me. I knew that the other vet had said something.

"In other words, I was in a big shitload of trouble. That's what I knew."

Nothing happened to Keen for the next seventeen days. Then, on the night of May 29th, Keen saw his boss, Dale Grotelueschen, who was then the director of Great Plains.

Keen recalled: "He came to my office in a very serious way that evening around five o'clock on Thursday. He said, 'You need to report to Lincoln to see the director of the school at ten o'clock tomorrow morning.' I asked, 'Well what's it about?' He said, 'It's a very serious matter.' That's all he would tell me.

"I wasn't sure what was going to happen. I didn't know if my boss was going to give me a warning or what. But I did suspect that something bad was going to happen, so I figured I better try to protect myself.

"The state of Nebraska has a whistleblower protection law for state employees. I made an online application for whistleblower protection.

"The way the law in Nebraska works is that the application itself isn't any good. But, if you're granted whistleblower protection, it protects you from retaliation from the point that you're granted whistleblower protection onward. I didn't know anything about this. I was just frantic about what could I do.

"The next morning, I showed up at the director office, and he read me a letter, saying, 'You can take notes, but you can't have a copy of it.' I still don't have a copy. And I was later told no copy exists.

"I wanted to take a picture of the letter on my cell phone, but they wouldn't allow that either.

"The letter was from the USDA's Northern Plains division. Its headquarters is in Fort Collins. Specifically, the letter was from the USDA ARS director in Fort Collins, through the MARC Director who was John Pollak, to the director of the UNL veterinary school, who was another boss. His name was Don Beerman.

"Don read the letter to me. Basically, it said, words to the effect: 'On May 11, 2014, Jim Keen brought an unauthorized person with the press onto the MARC premises, which is a violation of USDA policy.' It also said that I took a university vehicle and had driven it about a mile to where we do the sheep necropsies.

"Again, the reason I went on a Sunday was because nobody's there on a Sunday. They didn't know where I went, but they knew I had taken him beyond just the necropsy center. . . .

"When Michael Moss was here during that same trip, he wanted to talk to some other people, so I took him to visit the former Great Plains director, Gary Rupp, whom I had known for 25 years .

"We went to visit Gary at his house. I called him first, 'Can we visit you?' I said that I was with a reporter from the *New York Times*. Mr. Moss wanted to get information from Rupp about animal welfare at MARC.

"And when we arrived, Gary made some comments to him.

"I also went to visit the former sheep manager whose name is Mike Wallace. He had retired a couple years before, too. I knew that Mike didn't like the Easy Care Sheep project. Mike actually raised sheep, too. You could see how a well-run sheep operation is at his farm, as compared to MARC. Mike would not allow himself to be quoted, so there was nothing about Mike Wallace in the story.

"I bring this up, because in the USDA letter, it said that I also took Michael Moss to visit two former employees, Gary Rupp and Mike Wallace. . . . Why would MARC complain about me visiting two retired people? I thought it was just kind of weird.

"I think that's kind of how it ended. Don Beerman, my director of the vet school, said that I was as of that moment, banned from the MARC premises, and I was put on administrative leave."

Notably, Keen had allegedly violated USDA rules, but he had not violated the university's rules.

"After I was put on administrative leave, I looked for a lawyer. Actually, Michael Moss helped me. He gave me some leads that he had. It was hard to find somebody who was comfortable doing this kind of work. It's kind of unusual, trying to protect somebody with a university job. It turned out that John Recknor had successfully represented two other former UNL tenured faculty members whom the university tried to fire."

Keen retained Recknor, who had also been recommended to him by other attorneys. Also, notably, while on administrative leave, Keen continued to receive his salary.

Michael Moss returned to Nebraska in July 2014 to join Keen at a meeting at the state capitol with the state official who granted whistleblower protections. Keen wanted a witness present.

"I asked the official if Michael, who had also brought along a videographer, could come in, and he said yes. So, Michael came into the meeting. It lasted about an hour during which time I explained what had happened at MARC.

"His response was, 'Well, this is kind of big for our office. I'm not sure what we can do, but we'll see what happens.'

Keen sensed that Moss had nearly completed his story for the *New York Times*. But Moss still wanted to see more.

"While he was in town, Michael also wanted to see a feed lot, so the videographer took film of a nearby feed lot. Also, we went to a cattle auction which they also filmed. Michael had never seen one of those before. And then, Michael and his colleague did a two-hour interview with me.

"After that, while I was still on suspension, I received numerous calls from the University of Nebraska police. They were telling me to come in, 'Just come on into the office. We just want to talk to you.'

"I refused to do it. At this time, I was living in the middle of nowhere on my friend's ranch house, and I would shut my cell phone off when I got within two or three miles of where I was living, because I didn't want anybody to trace me.

"As silly as it sounds, this isolated farmhouse was basically my hideout from the police. I really thought I was going to be arrested. That's what I really thought. I had several calls where the police said, 'Oh, just come in. We just want talk to you.'

"The police were calling me. That's actually when I thought I was going to be arrested."

Meantime, on the home front, Keen and his wife, who hadn't lived together since June 2013, were having more serious problems.

Keen explained: "At that time, my wife and I were not in a good way. She was really angry with me. That why I was living at my friend's farmhouse in the middle of nowhere.

"Here's the background story: Because of that big grant I had worked on for those two years, 2010 to 2012, I ignored my family while writing that grant. That made my wife really, really upset with me. We weren't formally separated, but we were living apart. I would only see her once in a while. . . .

"I didn't disagree with her. Probably my biggest professional regret is ever getting involved in that big grant. I had no idea what I was getting myself into. Basically, I did all that work. Of course, the university took its thirty percent, so I made the university (and other collaborating universities) about seven-million dollars out of that twenty-five-million-dollar grant.

"I didn't get a cent out of it. I just worked my butt off. And I didn't like how UNL treated me on that grant.

"It was the grant that caused problems with my marriage. I ignored my family for two years, so my wife had legitimate gripes."

With all of the overwhelming problems that Keen faced at home and at work, his health became a major concern.

"I'll say here that this is when I had a nervous breakdown. . . . It'd never happened to me before.

"I'll make a long story short. I was hospitalized for major recurring depression from July 2014 to January 2015—about six months. During that time, I was in four different hospitals."

But, mercifully, from mid-July 2014 to January 2015, Keen was also on paid leave. He never missed a paycheck from the university.

CHAPTER THIRTY-SIX

"THE FBI DOESN'T JUST SHOW UP AT YOUR HOUSE UNANNOUNCED"

D r. Keen was released from the hospital on January 15. 2015. Four days later, he received a call from Michael Moss at the *New York Times*, saying that his story would be published online in an hour. Per *Times* protocol, Moss did not give Keen his story in advance. He didn't read Keen's quotes back to him in advance of publication.

Keen recalled: "He said that's their policy at the *Times*. My attorney, John Recknor, had warned me, saying: 'You don't know what that story's going to look like. He could make you look really bad. You don't know.'

After first going online on January 19, the Moss story, "U.S. Research Lab Lets Livestock Suffer in Quest for Profit," appeared as the lead story on the front page of the *New York Times* the following morning with a new headline: "In Quest for More Profits, U.S. Lab Lets Animals Suffer: Controversial Research; Lambs Left to Die."

In the lead to his remarkable piece of investigative journalism, Moss wrote:

These experiments are not the work of a meat processor or rogue opera-tion. They are conducted by a taxpayer-financed federal institution called the U.S. Meat Animal Research Center, a complex of laboratories and pastures that sprawls over 55 square miles in Clay Center, Neb. Little known outside the world of big agriculture, the center has one overarching mission: helping producers of beef, pork and lamb turn a higher profit as diets shift toward poultry, fish and produce. . . .

"They pay tons of attention to increasing animal production, and just a pebble sized concern to animal welfare," said James Keen, a scientist and veterinarian who worked at the center for 24 years. "And it probably looks fine to them because they're not thinking about it, and they're not being held accountable. But most Americans and even livestock producers would be hard pressed to support some of the things that the center has done."

Keen was relieved to see that everything in Moss's story—his quotes and all—were completely accurate.

Keen, who had just been released from the hospital four days earlier, con-ceded, "I was still pretty fried, mentally.

"I went to a hospital in Texas, and to one in Maryland where they just treated mental health. Otherwise, you're with people who are there for addictions, alcoholism, or drug addiction, and it just doesn't work very well. That's why I had to travel out of state to get treatment just for the mental illness, rather than substance abuse. That was another ordeal.

"Anyway, when I got out of the hospital I was living back at home with my wife and family. At this time, I was told by my lawyer, 'Don't look at any of your emails from work. You're still on administrative leave.' I hadn't looked at anything for six months. . . .

"But, after the publication of Moss's story, I looked at my emails, and I had a whole bunch of messages from UNL. I still wasn't fired, but there were clear threats of termination."

How did Keen's family react to the story?

According to Keen, the support from his family, particularly from his wife, in the aftermath of the Moss story was only "lukewarm." For starters, Keen did not tell his wife, in advance, of his cooperation with Moss and the *New York Times*.

"My wife didn't approve of the way I handled it. She said it was just a stupid way to do it."

Was Keen, personally happy with the story?

"I was happy with the story, but I also knew it was going to piss a lot of people off. This is when the second round of police harassment started."

The front-page coverage of MARC's research practices drew nationwide attention. Members of Congress asked for investigations. The U.S. Secretary of Agriculture called for a thorough review.

Media offers for interviews poured in but Keen, via his attorney, turned down repeated requests, including those for Keen to appear on *Sixty Minutes* and the *Today Show*, among other news programs.

Keen simply didn't feel mentally fit enough to appear on television.

"One thing that happened was I got contacted by Christopher Quinn, a documentary maker in March 2015. He had won a Sundance Award for best documentary about the Sudanese War called *God Grew Tired of Us*. I was contacted by him, because he was making another documentary, inspired by a book called *Eating Animals*, which I highly recommend. It's a very interesting book.

"Basically, Christopher's documentary is a series of case studies. It turns out I'm one of them. He probably has forty hours of interview filming with me. He came out to Nebraska four times to visit and interview me and my daughter, Hannah, who does the CSAs. He also interviewed my wife and all my other kids.

"Christopher wanted to see MARC, what it looked like. We just drove through in my wife's car. There's a public road that goes through it. We got stopped by a security officer.

"This security officer says, 'I want to see your ID.' Christopher replied, 'I don't have to show you my ID.'

"Chris has done undercover work on factory farms, too—where he's gone onto farms and filmed secretly.

"They could see he had a camera, because he was filming out the window. I remember the security guard said, 'What are you filming?'

"Christopher said, 'A film.' That was his answer.

"He just filmed from the road, some cattle in pastures, some sheep in pastures. The security officer wrote down my wife's license plate."

"I think the next day, a local police officer drove to my home. We have a very long driveway. It's an acreage, the driveway's probably two-hundred yards long. A local Hastings police officer came down our driveway, looked at our vehicles, and saw my wife's Suburban. He made a note of it, and then he left. He didn't stop at the house.

"Then, about two or three days later, a UNL police officer came by and wanted to interview me. I wasn't home at the time.

"Later, I was chopping wood in the backyard. We have a wood stove. And an FBI agent and the head of the UNL police security showed up unannounced and said they wanted to talk to me. I remember the FBI agent said, 'Don't worry, you're not in trouble or anything.'

"I said, 'Bullshit. The FBI doesn't just show up at your house unannounced unless there's something going on.'

"The FBI agent then said, 'Okay. Yeah, yeah. You're right.'

"Then, they came in. I tried to call my lawyer, but he wasn't available. I ended up talking to the FBI agent and to the police officer from the university. My wife sat down with me, and we ended up talking, perhaps foolishly, to them for about three hours.

"The FBI agent had a file in his possession probably about an inch thick, and it had a color picture of me on the cover.

"He said that his expertise was investigating animal terrorism and eco-terrorism. Basically, he wanted to know, 'Are you hanging out with or collaborating with animal terrorists? Are you an animal terrorist?'

"That was what the line of questioning was."

The FBI special agent actually called Keen an "eco-terrorist." In addition, the FBI agent told Keen that John Pollak, the director of MARC, had supposedly used derogatory language to describe him.

"Before the FBI agent talked to me, he had visited Pollak. That's where the FBI agent told me that John Pollak had called me 'the evilest person on the planet.'

"Obviously, John Pollak doesn't like me."

Keen speculates that his detractors did not use his recent hospitalization against him—because they probably didn't know about it, adding, "I hardly told anybody."

CHAPTER THIRTY-SEVEN

"UNDISGUISED HOSTILITY FROM THE UNIVERSITY AND A USDA WHITEWASH"

Alarmed by news reports that a whistleblower, a tenured faculty member at a major university, was in trouble for calling attention to reproachable animal research practices at MARC, Louis Clark, president of the Government Accountability Project, wrote a letter of concern to the university's chancellor, Harvey Perlman.

GAP is an advocacy group in Washington, D.C., with a remarkable record of defending whistleblowers against powerful interest groups.

Perlman wrote back to Clark on April 27, 2015, in a letter that can only be described as hostile to his own faculty member:

> I am puzzled by what motivates your letter. We understand that Dr. James Keen may fall within the definition of a "whistleblower" and we have been scrupulous to treat him as legally required. I understand you have not talked to him so I am assuming there is no basis to challenge our

conduct in this regard. If you have an allegation that suggests otherwise, please let me know.

The fact that we are required to respect the whistleblower does not, of course, mean that we have to accept his allegations. First, you should understand that animal care practices at the U.S. Meat Animal Research Center are the responsibility of USDA and managed by them. Their internal investigation of the allegations could find no evidence of animal mistreatment.

We do challenge your statement that the *New York Times* article was an "independent" investigation with "credible evidence". My staff, who interacted with the reporter over a long period of time, questioned his journalistic practices. If you are looking for independent examination, you would be interested to know that the team of peer investigators who were evaluating the University's animal care protocols to determine if we qualified for accreditation, examined USMARC's practices because of our relationship with them. They found nothing wrong and we were granted accreditation.

In the last analysis, the University does not intend to address the issues raised by the *New York Times* unless and until we have credible evidence that the article was accurate. And I emphasize, again, that USMARC and its animal care practices are the responsibility of USDA, and not of the University.

The letter, contemptuous of the *New York Times* and dismissive of GAP, came at a time when Keen was trying to save his job. Since the fall of 2014 and even through all of the controversy, Keen was still on paid leave from the university, along with administrative and sick leave. Keen credits his attorneys for talking to his bosses and saving his job. It's also likely that the potential intervention of GAP weighed on the university's considerations, despite all the tough talk in the chancellor's letter.

Keen said: "During this time, my attorney and the university were negotiating a return to work. Beginning in June 2015, I was told just to work from home while an agreement was reached. I had a large research appointment, so I was writing grants.

"I actually returned to work at UNL on October 1, 2015."

The controversy did not simmer down, however. Just days earlier in September, 2015, the USDA Office of Inspector General in Washington released an interim report of its investigation of the allegations against MARC, provoked by Michael Moss's revelations in the *New York Times*.[46] With its preliminary finding that the alleged abuses of animals for profit were "in line with industry norms," the IG report sparked outrage among animal-welfare activists.

Keen describes the reaction: "Wayne Pacelle, the president and CEO of the Humane Society, condemned the IG's report, saying: 'The Inspector General's report amounts to a whitewash. The nation was appalled by the gruesome experiments conducted at a federally funded facility but somehow the government feels that the practices were customary. They were not—they were appalling.'"[47]

On October 27, 2015, Keen, in the aftermath of the IG report, sent a memorandum to Derek Morton, an official with the IG's office, saying: "Key points for discussion of animal welfare concerns at USMARC especially those not mentioned in the January 19, 2015 Michael Moss *New York Times* piece for our scheduled meeting on Wed, Oct 28, 2015 at 9:00 am at the Robert V. Denney Federal Building."

Keen added:

---

46   USDA Office of Inspector General: "ARS: U. S. Meat Animal Research Center Review" Interim Report" 02007-0001-31 (1), September 2015.

47   Nicholas Bergin, *Lincoln Journal Star*, "Animal activists condemn USDA interim report on Clay Center," October 3, 2015.

I have prepared these notes for you to the best of my recollection. I kept a log of my animal welfare concerns at USMARC from 2007 to 2014 with date and event details. Unfortunately, I am unable to locate the log. I was permanently banned from my former office at GPVEC on the USMARC campus since late May 2014. My office contents were recently profession-ally moved to my new office in Lincoln NE and I have so far been unable to locate my log. Therefore, the specific dates of some events reported below are sometimes only approximate. Also, I did not personally witness all of these events. They were often reported to me directly by my Univ of Nebraska clinical veterinarian colleagues. I have provided names of some UNL employees with knowledge of the events. You would have to speak with them directly, or with the MARC scientist who directed them, to obtain more specific details or confirmation.

Many adverse animal events have occurred at USMARC which were not mentioned in the Michael Moss *New York Times* piece in January 2015. Witnesses exist for each of these events, but they may be unwilling to provide testimony unless compelled in part because many are University of Nebraska employees. I have provided witness names in many cases in the text below.

With regard to his animal-welfare concerns, Keen continued:

There are two types of animal welfare issues in livestock at USMARC. First, there are deficiencies in animal husbandry (or outright cruelty or negligence) in the field. Second, and more important, there are animal welfare issues arising from the MARC scientific protocols and policies or the research scientists behavior themselves. Also, there is an animal value/animal welfare hierarchy at USMARC. Cattle are treated the best, pigs next, and sheep are at the bottom. For example, Sheep are some-times referred to as "prairie maggots" by MARC herdsman. Sheep and pigs are also deemed expendable for experimental surgery by untrained non-veterinarian animal scientists, their post-doc and graduate students.

It is also important to emphasize that what I report here is likely only a small fraction of the actual animal welfare violations that occur at US-MARC. I was mostly a lab-based research veterinarian from 1994 to 2007 when I was employed by USMARC, so I had little opportunity to know about animal welfare events. When I joined the UNL GPVEC in Nov 2007, I became aware again of the magnitude of the livestock welfare problems at USMARC mostly from my interactions with my UNL GPVEC clinical veterinarians. This is why I began keeping a MARC animal welfare log in 2007.

Concluding, Keen stated:

I can state and I firmly believe unequivocally that none of the events described here would be considered either good animal husbandry, acceptable livestock practice or good scientific practice, regardless of what the USDA OIG stated in its preliminary report on USMARC animal welfare. It is understandable that bad things happen everywhere occasionally. But the situation at USMARC is much different in frequency, magnitude and duration. I would describe the USMARC as a place of frequent systematic animal welfare, animal husbandry and animal science malpractice. The situation at USMARC is non "normal" in the real livestock world. For example:

* It is not normal for a livestock producer to allow non-vets to do surgery on his livestock. There is a good reason that veterinary school takes four years.

It is not normal for a reputable research institute to permit non-vets to perform surgery and questionable anesthesia on experimental animals. IACUC protocols would never approve it.

It is not normal for a livestock operation to allow newborn lambs to die from deliberate inattention from predators, starvation, mis-mothering or exposure to the elements... especially for 13+ years!

It is not normal for a livestock producer to tolerate epidemic hardware disease in his/her cattle herds or rectal prolapses in his/her sheep flock ... or to delay treatment ("chronic neglect") if illness did occur.

It is not normal for scientists to use data from health and welfare compromised animals for their studies. The results will be invalid.

But the USDA IG did not incorporate any of Keen's comments or perspectives into its final report, which was issued a year later.[48]

Instead of looking further into issues of scientific malpractice that Keen raised as an epidemiologist—or taking seriously Keen's many years of veterinary experience to determine what is "normal"—the IG doubled down on the idea that what happened at MARC was essentially business as usual.

Comparing the IG's preliminary report with its final report shows many differences. The first report, although seen by some as a whitewash, was comparatively neutral regarding the allegations made in the *New York Times*. It gave the appearance of a serious investigation. But the final report was re-written in such a way so as to put Moss's work in the worst possible light. It was as if USDA was delighted to find a long-time nemesis unexpectedly in its crosshairs and decided to try to do his reputation maximum damage.

---

48   USDA Office of Inspector General: "ARS: U. S. Meat Animal Research Center Review" Audit Report 02007-0001-31, September 2016.

The interim IG report of September 15, 2015, looked at Moss's statements. It found, by any fair reading, thirteen of the statements were confirmed, only two were not confirmed, and twelve were not yet reviewed. The analyses of five statements were redacted.

Then, a year later, when the final report was issued, a fair reading indicates the IG confirmed sixteen of Moss's statements, did not confirm three, and redacted thirteen. Again, Moss and Keen were mostly vindicated.

In other words, the majority of Moss's statements were actually confirmed in both the interim and final IG reports. Even adding what the public was not allowed to see—redactions went up between the reports from 5 to 13—would not tip the balance away from the overall veracity of Moss's work.

Enter a completely new factor to cast a totally different light on the review before publication. In the final IG report, twelve of the sixteen confirmations were labeled "lacking context." This catch-all category included simple IG dislikes of expressions Moss used to describe a burial pit.

With this transparent doctoring of its investigation, USDA put out a summary statement essentially contradicting its own work to make it falsely appear as if Michael Moss, a Pulitzer-Prize winner, had fabricated his reporting:

> After reviewing *The New York Times* article titled "U.S. Research Lab Lets Livestock Suffer in Quest for Profit," published January 19, 2015, we nonstatistically selected 33 specific statements to evaluate in an attempt to determine the veracity of the statements. . . . Of these 33 statements, we determined only 7 were materially accurate—26 were inaccurate, lacked sufficient context, or were uncorroborated.

Defenders of MARC in the meat animal industry were quick to seize on the final IG report as exoneration of the facility. The Lincoln *Journal Star* reported on December 20, 2016:

The Inspector General report looked at 33 statements made in the story and found 26 were inaccurate, lacked context or were unable to be confirmed. Nebraska Cattlemen and the Nebraska Farm Bureau cheered the report as vindication in the face of painful and unjust accusations. 'The men and women at U.S. MARC have always cared for the animals to the highest standards,' said Nebraska Cattlemen Executive Vice President Pete McClymont.

But this was too much even for defenders of MARC in the national veterinarian community who wanted the final IG report to give definitive answers, not look like a contrived cover-up that gave every indication of having been unduly influenced by those with their own agenda. University of California at Davis professor Dr. Alison Van Eenennaam, who actually wanted to see MARC exonerated, if possible, took on the IG in no uncertain terms:

[I]magine my surprise when the OIG final report was released Friday December 16, 2016.... The OIG report stated that of the 33 statements made by the *New York Times*, "we determined that only 7 were materially accurate—26 were inaccurate, lacked sufficient context or were uncorroborated." *New York Times* that is a 21% material accuracy rate—also known as an F in my classes.

So of the 26 statements in the *New York Times* article that were determined to be "inaccurate, lacked sufficient context or were uncorroborated" which was which? How many were inaccurate? There is a HUGE difference between inaccurate (i.e. fake news) and lacking sufficient context.... Only two of the statements were listed as inaccurate in the OIG report, but the OIG conclusions on several others was bizarrely redacted. So your guess is as good as mine....

And in perhaps the ultimate piece of irony, the OIG report concluded that US MARC "could make its research more transparent to the public". I might say the same to the OIG in its report! What are the privacy concerns that required the redaction of a simple conclusion of either materially accurate, inaccurate, lacked sufficient context or uncorroborated? Those sensational allegations and emotive images are out there now – right or wrong – unchallenged.[49]

In the end, both the university and the USDA passed up chances simply to commend a whistleblower for his actions, commit to making necessary changes going forward, and move on.

That is almost always the best way to handle whistleblower issues, especially those with a high profile. Instead of dealing forthrightly to address issues raised by Jim Keen, a veterinarian with decades of professional experience, both the university and the federal agency took routes that made them look vindictive and, in the case of the USDA OIG, left an indelible stain on the agency's credibility.

---

49   Dr. Alison Van Eenennaam, *Biobeef Blog*: https://biobeef.faculty.ucdavis. edu/2016/12/22/doughnuts-in-the-surgery-room/

CHAPTER THIRTY-EIGHT

"I'VE COME A LONG WAY"

Meantime, Jim Keen started having more problems with his wife and the community in which they lived, saying: "My wife was upset, as I said, because she's thinking the house was going to get burned down. It's a Big Ag community. Several people who work in town live in Hastings. And I pretty much got shut out from any contact with my former colleagues. I'd say I was pretty much shunned."

Was the university behind a smear campaign against him?

"I heard that, but I never saw it. I never experienced it myself, because again, I was just hiding out in my home. I didn't want to go out anywhere. We live on an acreage, and it's very isolated. It's on the edge of town.

"Nothing was said directly to me, but my wife knew some of the wives of other scientists who worked at MARC. She had heard from the wives that their husbands thought that this *New York Times* piece was a bunch of bullshit. That it wasn't true and things like that."

Did the animal-rights groups enter the fray after the *Times* story to defend Moss's excellent work?

"I don't know that for sure. I know that they had different groups drive through the premises at MARC after the *Times* piece came out, just to go look at it. I don't think anybody did anything other than drive through. Meanwhile, the state police put a roadblock on the entrance to MARC to screen people coming in.

Still tenured, Keen rebounded professionally, returning to work at UNL on October 1, 2015. Personally though, he and his wife started divorce proceedings shortly thereafter.

Keen reflected on the breakup of his marriage, saying: "I didn't want it at all, but my wife was very insistent on it. The big reason?. . . She told me that I had put our whole family at risk by not telling her anything about Michael Moss and the *New York Times*. She knew nothing about it until just before the story came out."

And how is Keen doing, physically and mentally?

"I'm much better now," he said. "After I got out of the hospital in January 2015, I was seeing therapists probably every week for the first few months. I was also seeing two different people, a nurse practitioner and psych people probably once a week for the first six months. And now I'm probably seeing my providers about once a month.

"I've come a long way."

"I don't regret whistleblowing. But, if I could do it over, I would do it differently to better protect myself and family from retaliation and retribution. For example, if I had read *The Whistleblower's Handbook* by Stephen Martin Kohn before rather than after whistleblowing, I would likely have come out of the shitstorm in a much better place.

"Also, Amanda Hitt, an attorney from the Government Accountability Project, tried to contact me just after the *New York Times* piece came out in January 2015. Unfortunately, I was in too dark of a place at that time to even look at my emails or even answer the phone. My guess is that if I had contacted Amanda and GAP in January 2015, things would have turned out much better for me.

"GAP provides a tremendous *pro bono* service to our society. Unfortunately, I was unable to take advantage of that expertise when I needed it most."

Keen said that GAP had sent him another book about whistleblowing, which he also found extremely valuable. That book was *The Corporate Whistle Blower's Survival Guide* by Tom Devine, GAP's general counsel.

"In the introduction to this book, Dr. J.S. Wigand, the tobacco whistleblower, gave four pieces of advice to his fellow whistleblowers: '1) Be prepared, 2) Don't quit the mainstream, 3) Be certain that you have allies, and 4) Don't quit until the truth has been fully exposed.'

"My whole career path has changed. I'm eighty-percent research appointment now. I used to be fifty percent teaching, but I'm not teaching veterinary students anymore. I taught a course for seven years, and they took that course away from me. I am banned from teaching veterinary students since I returned to work in October 2015, even though it is in my contract.

"Interestingly, because I am banned from teaching, I am not fulfilling my contract. Because I am not fulfilling my contract, the university, as of 2018, is taking steps to revoke my tenure and fire me, a classic Catch-22 situation that is not uncommon for whistleblowers.

"Sooner or later, I expect to be fired.

"Why? . . . They're afraid I'll corrupt the veterinary students."

CHAPTER THIRTY-NINE

"I WOULD DO IT AGAIN"

S adder but wiser, Jim Keen had completed his metamorphosis from company man to whistleblower to citizen activist, saying: "Nebraska is a very pro-industrial agricultural state. The University of Nebraska-Lincoln is a very pro-industrial agricultural university and so is my School of Veterinary Medicine. Much of the Nebraska economy is based on industrial crops and animal agricultural, so it is natural to defend it. I'm a sore thumb. But my experience completely changed my perspective.

"I'm now very much pro-animal protection. I do volunteer work for several animal welfare organizations. I'm on the Nebraska and National Ag advisory boards for the Humane Society of the United States. I spoke at Harvard Law School on the anniversary of the Animal Welfare Act.

"I've written letters to the editors of several publications which made UNL unhappy, I'm sure. I'm doing this as a private citizen. One thing Amanda Hitt of GAP told me was, 'Keep your activism separate from your professional work'

"Some of my colleagues said, 'You don't belong here anymore.' So, I was converting away from production agriculture. I realized I don't believe in that anymore.

"When I was in vet school, I was taught that if an animal is producing and reproducing, its welfare is fine—which is completely false. It's just not true. That's what I used to believe. I've been told, through my wife talking to her friends, the wives of MARC scientists, that MARC people believe they did nothing wrong. They believe that this is just a smear campaign."

Now a citizen activist whose big issues are animal protection and environmentalism, would Keen do it again?

"I would do it again. I certainly don't like some of the bad stuff that happened. I'm estranged from two of my daughters, including Hannah, mostly because they see my wife suffering from this. And they rightly blame me for that. As I said, my wife had reason to be upset. She really did. I was a workaholic. I used to work eighty hours a week. My whistleblowing put my family at risk."

Will Keen's story have a happy ending?

Keen replied: "Some parts. I guess maybe this had to happen. I remember my wife was really upset with this. I think my wife was okay with the whistleblowing. She just thought I did it in a stupid way.

"Again, I was in the hospital for six months. My lawyer actually advised me to go on disability, because he thought that I might not be able to work again. That's what my wife told me, too. That was part of the divorce. She said, 'You know you probably won't be able to work again, and I can't live that way.' . . . So, I'm happy I made it back to work."

Remarkably, in spite of all the trouble, Keen never lost a single paycheck—but he did have to raid his retirement fund "to pay for it," aka the legal and health cost consequences from his whistleblowing and overall activism.

He noted: "I don't know the exact number, but I probably spent fifty-to-sixty-thousand dollars on attorney's fees, and I probably spent another sixty-to-seventy-thousand dollars on my hospitalization that wasn't covered by insurance."

Keen added: "Because of my divorce, I've lost the house. And that's a problem. I'm back to renting. I feel like I'm in college again. I've got to pay alimony for many years. I don't know if I'll ever be able to retire.

"I'm happy for my wife and kids. They have a really nice house, and my daughter has her business there. So that's a good thing. . . .

"I'm looking for another job, too. I've had one job offer from a non-profit, but I will have to take a big cut in salary if I do that. It's an animal-welfare group. I'm not sure what I'm going to do.

"My intention is that I'm going to work until as long as my health holds out."

Spoken like a true whistleblower.

—∞—

But too much remains unanswered in the case of James Keen, D.V.M., Ph.D., who continues to battle both for animal-welfare and for human food-safety. Was it corruption of science that cost him so dearly in his profession and personal life?

So, it seems.

What lies behind page after page of redacted materials in the IG's final report? Who polices the IG?

Who will be held accountable for scientific malpractice that, by ignoring the dangers of *E. coli*, endangers human health, questions of animal welfare aside?

Why can't Jim Keen teach students at his university?

Who stands up for truth in higher education?

Jim Keen, for sure. Anybody else?

PART FOUR

"YOU GUYS ARE WARRIORS"

I invited Jon Oberg, David Halperin, Jim Keen, and Louis Clark to lunch, asking them to discuss their work, as well as their successes, regrets, and legacies. The lunch was recorded on July 23, 2018, at Bravo Bravo in Washington, D.C. and has been updated and edited by the five participants in anticipation of the publication of this book. For health reasons, Rod Lipscomb could not join us.

—Dan E. Moldea

CHAPTER FORTY

"WE PUSH THE POWERS THAT BE"

Dan: Gentlemen, please get whatever you want. Feel free. I've heard the food is very good. You are my guests. . . . Jim was asking David, about—go ahead.

David: I work as a lawyer, I work as an advocate, and I work as an investigative writer. Most of the work I do focuses on how money corrupts policy in Washington with an emphasis on two issues. One, for-profit higher education, about which I learned a lot from Jon [Oberg]. The other is climate change.

Jim: Those are really different.

David: Yes, but I work on a number of different issues. I've also been working on this issue of how we have to pay to read the law—that much of the law consists of standards that the government has incorporated from trade organizations or that the government has contracted with private publishers to package. And then the supposed copyright holders sue citizens, including my client, when they post their own laws online.

Jim: Wouldn't all that stuff be in the Federal Register?

David: No. Here's the thing. Many federal regulations incorporate by reference, private, technical reference standards, which I'm sure you're familiar with. Standards for motorcycle helmet safety, road safety, food safety, building safety, and so these groups that publish the standards use government officials, private individuals, people from corporations, to develop private standards, and then they lobby to make them part of the law, because they benefit from their own standards being part of the law. Then, what the federal agencies have been doing, rather than include the full text of the standard in their regulation, they say, "we hereby incorporate by reference this standard of ASTM or various other—"

Jim: Then, you've got to follow that up to see what it actually says.
David: Right, and the problem is that they want to charge for those standards. Many times, by the time they get incorporated into law, they're superseded as the standard, the private standard, but now they're the law. Some of these sell for two-hundred dollars, some of them you can't even buy anymore. But, when my client, Carl Malamud of the group Public Resource, rounded up all the thousand standards that have been incorporated by reference in the Code of Federal Regulations and posted them online, gave notice to the various groups, and said, this is the law, I'm posting it online. Eventually, we were sued by these agencies—
Jim: By the agencies?
David: By the private, non-profit agencies, which are called SDOs—standard development organizations—for copyright and trademark violation.
Jim: Is the government giving work to them, because they don't want to do it? What's the motivation?
David: Yes, the government says, it's cheaper to have private organizations do it than the government. That's correct.
Jim: Then, that's probably true.
David: It probably is true, although, again government people do participate in the formulation of the standards. But, in the end, once something is the law, citizens have a right to speak their own laws to their fellow citizens. There's a case out of Texas where the federal court of appeals said that we were correct. We posted all these standards.
Jim: That's when you got sued.

David: Yeah, that's when we got sued.

Jim: Even though the judge said you could do it?

David: Because we're not in Texas. My client was in California. Every circuit has to litigate this. We were sued in D.C., and we lost in district court, but we won in the court of appeals. We're also being sued by the state of Georgia for putting the law of Georgia online.

Jim: Why would the state sue you?

David: Because—

Jim: I could see the private companies and NGOs doing it, but why are the states doing it?

David: What Georgia does is contract out through Lexis to make a beautiful version of their state code of Georgia, which has various annotations, but it is called the only official code of Georgia. They say, if you want to know the law of Georgia, you have to buy this book. We posted it online, we said it's the only official code of Georgia, and we were sued. I mean, we're being sued by the state of Georgia, but it's really Lexis that is behind it, because Georgia feels that Lexis is codifying their code for free. . . . Our view is, tough luck.

Jim: So, the states are all doing it? It is pretty much, promiscuously applied to state and federal government then?

David: It is a practice to incorporate private standards. The problem is, it's the law. The case in Texas, a guy wanted to post the building code of his town. He found that that was based on the model building code, which is promulgated by whoever does that.

Jim: How did you find this was involved?

David: I've been working with Carl Malamud for the last seven years. I knew him before. This is his thing, putting law online, putting federal documents online, and he's being sued for it.

Jon: Did you ever have to work with PACER?

David: We've been fighting PACER.

Jim: Who is PACER?

David: PACER is the system that puts the federal court decisions and filings in federal courts online.

Jim: Kind of like the Federal Register for the courts?

David: You have to pay by the page to read the filings in cases.

Jon: You can't even know what you're buying. It's crazy. You have to pay a lot of fees in order to know what's going on in your own case.

Jim: That actually makes no sense.

Jon: Well, it's the way it is, but David also helps the whistleblowers in the for-profit colleges. That has just been great. Super.

Jim: Wasn't there some big crackdown on that recently?

David: Yeah.

Jim: Was that you?

David: We push the powers that be. There was a congressional investigation. We pushed the Obama administration hard to do more, but they were listening to people like Don Graham, who owned Kaplan, one of the worst for-profit colleges.

Jim: Is Kaplan the one that Purdue University bought?

David: Very questionable situation. Now, the scam they're doing now is, they're converting colleges to nonprofits, but they're tied to for-profit ventures that the same people own. So, they get the status of a nonprofit and get free of the stigma that they created and all the regulations that they incurred for their bad behavior.

Jim: This is Kaplan.

David: Yeah. Their new scam, Purdue Global.

Jim: What do they call it?

David: Purdue Global.

Louis: I've seen it.

Jim: There's one in Lincoln.

Jon: Yes. I've seen it. I drove by. I was in Lincoln last month, and I drove by. It says, "Purdue." It used to say "Kaplan." Now, it's "Purdue Global."

David: It's the same scam college.

Jon: Smoke and mirrors in higher education.

David: Kaplan sold it to Purdue—but with a contract to keep getting paid to provide all the services to the school.

Jim: And Purdue's getting basically a kickback from it, probably, right?

David: It's close.

Jon: That word's pretty good. Mitch Daniels is involved.

Jim: Mitch Daniels?

David: He was the governor of Indiana, now he's the president of Purdue.

Jim: Was Mitch Daniels the one who was going to be a vice presidential candidate, run for president or something like that?

Louis: He had zero charisma and that was a problem. I wanted to ask David, too: What's your experience with the Education Department's IG? I've never dealt with them.

David: While I was walking over here, I got a message. . . . Somebody asked me whether they should file a complaint with the IG about financial-aid fraud that's going on because this woman filed an anonymous complaint with the Texas Work Force Commission, and they said, "if it's about financial-aid fraud, we can't do anything." We have to refer it to the Department of Education, so she was after the IG. The IG has recently been doing some good reports, basically pushing back on things that [Betsy] DeVos is doing. I've never actually worked with them or in any way engaged with them. . . . When you were there, what was the status?

Jon: I have mixed experience with the IG. Then [to Jim], I've been reading your IG reports.

Jim: USDA?

Jon: USDA. My experience with the Education IG is I had to work with them a long time. They finally got around to producing good reports. One report that they finally produced was so good, it won the award for the best IG audit in the whole federal government in 2006.

Jim: Wow.

David: There's an award?

Jon: Yes, the Hamilton Award.

David: Who gave that?

Jon: The Alexander Hamilton Award is made by the whole group of federal IGs. The Inspectors General. It's awarded every year to the best audit in the federal government.

Jim: But you wrote it?

Jon: No, not at all, but I showed them what to look for. Then, in your case [to Jim], I've read these IG audits of the Department of Agriculture [Meat Animal Research Center]. I'm just astounded what they get by with. I'm appalled what they get by with in that [audit of MARC].

Jim: I got wind of what it was going to be like before I saw it. I don't know who told me. It was a whitewash, basically, is what it was.

Jon: Was it MARC [that whitewashed it]?

Jim: Yeah. I met with them, a couple of guys [from USDA IG] for two or three hours, but they didn't really use much. They didn't do much investigation. I told them where to look, but I don't think they did anything.

David: Are you still with USDA?

Jim: No. I haven't been with the USDA for ten years.

David: What do you do now?

Jim: I work for University of Nebraska, but they're about to fire me.

David: For this stuff?

Jim: It's okay.

Dan: In many ways, [Jim has] led a charmed life. He's really done some real important stuff.

David: I read about it.

Dan: He survived.

Jim: I survived.

David: Meaning what?

Dan: It means he still has a job. He never lost his job.

Jim: Never lost my job. I had a good lawyer, John Recknor of Lincoln. He is a really good lawyer. It was expensive, but if I wouldn't have hired that lawyer, him in particular, I would have lost my job. John had two other previous experiences protecting tenured faculty. . . . Other lawyers wouldn't have had a clue how to help me. In fact, other lawyers I talked to said "I can't do that because I don't know enough to do it."

David: Right.

CHAPTER FORTY-ONE

"JUST A CURIOUS MIND AT WORK HERE"

Jim: How does the climate change fit in? It seems like a little bit of an outlier. Is that a personal thing that you have?

David: These are all things that I'm really interested in. Years ago, I got hired to represent Greenpeace in a criminal trial in Miami where the government had put Greenpeace on trial for sailor mongering, for illegally boarding a ship.

Jim: Sailor mongering?

David: Sailor mongering was a statute passed in the 19th century. People used to board ships, get the sailors drunk, and get them so broke, so then they would then be sold into bondage to another ship, or they'd get them hooked on prostitutes. You couldn't board a ship when it was about to arrive, because people were approaching these ships and doing bad things to the sailors. Greenpeace saw a ship coming in, had intelligence that it had mahogany from the Amazon rainforest onboard, which later turned out to be true. All they wanted to do was hang a banner, that said, Stop Illegal Logging, President Bush. They didn't want to get anyone hooked on prostitutes. . . . Anyway, so the government, for the first time in history put an organization on trial for a free speech-related action.

Jim: I didn't catch the part of about the banner.

David: It said, "President Bush, Stop Illegal Logging." Normally, in these cases, the activists are prosecuted and . . .

Jim: Did they go on the ship?

David: They did.

Jim: And they put the banner up on the ship?

David: That's correct. Normally, the activists are prosecuted, they plead guilty to a misdemeanor, and that's the end of the case. . . .

Louis: Trespass.

David: Yes.

Jim: I could see that.

David: In this case, the organization was indicted, so I was hired to do a big press conference where we brought in all the civil rights leaders and said it was enough. "These people were prosecuted, don't go after an organization." It was free speech.

Jim: So, it wasn't slander or anything like that, then was it? They said what was true.

David: Correct. But they were prosecuted for the sailor-mongering offense. I ended up trying the case with a criminal lawyer from Miami. But I'm telling you this, because through working with Greenpeace, I got more focused on climate change and toxic pollution. . . . So now, I am involved with some research and advocacy regarding the fossil fuel industries. There's some media law involved that I do in addition to doing analysis—what is fair game in terms of collecting information—online, even in garbage cans.

Dan: You're such an elegant, distinguished guy. I can't imagine you doing garbology. I just can't picture that. You've done that?

David: Yes, as a lawyer, not the actual dumpster diver. Or there was a meeting in a conference room at a hotel. One of the guys left his papers behind. At seven at night, after the conference was over, a reporter went in the room, and found the papers. Is that trespass? Is that theft? Is it fair game?

Jim: Okay. Obviously, they're going to sue you if they realize you have that property, right?

David: Only if they think they have a claim, and they want to go through a trial. A lot of times, the people who are doing things are actually ashamed of what they're doing, or they don't want the bad public relations. I also represented a blogger who was sued by Bob Murray, a coal baron from Ohio. He's noted for suing John Oliver. He sued the *New York Times.*

Jim: Does he have really deep pockets then?

David: Yeah, but in this case . . . Well, my blogger posted on the *Huffington Post* and we did beat Murray. In that case, I don't know why he wanted to sue us. In my opinion, given his company's record, the trial wouldn't have been good for him. That's one reason why people usually don't sue. . . . But the real reason they don't sue my clients is because my clients tell the truth. I always ask people, "How do I avoid libel? Be accurate. It's not that hard."

Louis: Have you been involved in any case involving BPI? Beef Products Inc.? . . . Pink slime.

David: I'm trying to remember.

Louis: They sued ABC for billions.

David: No, I have not. That's right. No, I haven't.

Jim: I heard that they won-

Louis: No.

Jim: They didn't?

Jim: No? Because of the settlement.

David: Why do you ask?

Jim: Were you involved in that?

Louis: I was just curious. Oh, yes. We [GAP] were subpoenaed.

David: How so?

Louis: We represented the guy who blew the whistle on BPI.

Jim: Was he the FSIS guy?

Louis: No. He was the quality assurance guy at BPI.

Jim: He worked for BPI?

Louis: Yeah, but there were two other whistleblowers on that who were USDA. . . . And BPI sued our client for $1.1 billion or something.

Jim: Billion?

Louis: Yeah.

Jim: Wow.

Louis: And they sued ABC. We couldn't defend the case, because we were witnesses. So, we had a law firm, Loevy & Loevy, out of Chicago represent him, the whistleblower. . . . ABC threw in towel.

Jim: They settled, you mean, then?

Louis: Yeah.

David: They actually paid something?

Louis: Yeah. . . . To avoid the expense of going to trial. . . . It was a USDA whistleblower who first used the terminology, "pink slime." . . . Then, ABC went on to broadcast fourteen national shows around pink slime, using that terminology.

David: But they're in the business of settling when the other side doesn't have a good case?

Louis: It depends on who you're talking to.

Jim: Was it the terminology, Louis, that they didn't like? Or what was the issue?

Louis: It was... yeah. That was the BPI. The publicity destroyed the company.

Jim: I know they had a plant in Nebraska, and you shut 'em down.

Louis: They went down. They had five plants, and they went bankrupt, and they closed four of the five.

Jim: Did the USDA IG ever do a report on this?

Louis: No. There wasn't an issue. ABC never said there were any confirmed safety problems. The USDA said there were no safety problems. No one was there in terms of what the safety issues might be.

Jon [to Jim}: So, [the theatrically released documentary] *Eating Animals*, you're in the film. Great! A friend of mine wanted to see it. I said, "It's on Netflix." So, we tried to get it on Netflix, but it's unavailable.

Jim: I didn't know it was on Netflix.

Jon: It's on a DVD. It's not on streaming. I can't see any place to buy it. My friend desperately wants to see it, and there's no way to see it. It's left the theaters.

Jim: It's kind of moving around. It's a documentary, but they only keep it as long as people show up for it. Then, they can stop it, you know, but documentaries don't have a long lifespan. I think it's shifting all around the country in different cities. They have their website, which is called "eatinganimalsthemovie.com." It will tell you where it's going to be playing.

Jon: I thought it was good, by the way. I thought it was going to be more polemical, and it turned out to be really quite well balanced, I thought.

David: Do you know who made it?

Jim: A guy named Christopher Quinn.

David: I've heard of him.

Jim: He actually won a Sundance documentary, maybe eight or nine years ago. It's called, *God Grew Tired of Us*. It was about kids in the Sudanese Civil War who were displaced. They had to walk 800 miles . . .

David: I remember that.

Jim: . . . to escape from Sudan to get into Kenya.

David: Did those kids have a name that they were called? "The lost boys," or is that a different.

Jim: It was the lost boys. He did that?

David: I met some of them.

Jon: That was with Nigerian kids? Nigerian teenagers?

Jim: Sudanese.

David: Like Manute Bol.

Louis: What happened to him?

David: He died in 2010.

Louis: That's right, he died.

David: I saw him downtown a couple years before he died.

Jon: He had to have been pretty young, right?

David: He was young. He was like in his late forties.

Dan [to Jim]: I'm sorry, what about the mystery corporation you referenced? Jon, weren't you interested in the mystery corporation?

Jon: Yeah. About who was on your case. Some of the big meat packers or someone was really interested to see MARC come out okay on all this.

Jim: They all did. I know there was one columnist who wrote a really biting piece against me. . . . I think I told Dan this. . . . How it works there at MARC, it's a government lab. The director told me this a couple years ago. . . . If MARC wants to do a project, they can't lobby Congress themselves. They tell National Cattlemen's Beef Association what they want to do, and NCBA, in turn, lobbies Congress. The MARC gets funding typically as a congressional earmark. Then, the livestock industry usually wants something quick in return. For example, there was an important issue for the beef industry few years ago, where this a very widely used oral growth stimulant used in feedlot beef cattle for feed efficiency called Zilmax (zilpaterol, sold by Merck). It was produced by Intervet, a subsidiary of Merck & Co., and made cattle grow really, really fast, more than their skeletons could support. Several slaughter plants banned cattle that had been fed Zilmax because they collapsed when the entered the slaughter plant, and thus could not be sold. Many other cattle were made severely lame. This created a huge animal welfare, marketing, and PR problem for the beef industry. The beef industry wanted MARC to do a study on the welfare of the cattle fed zilpaterol. MARC can do a research project very quickly, because it's a federal facility. They can dedicate all their manpower to any problem. If the university did it, the project would take years. What do you call it? Quid pro quo, something like that.

David: Or pay to play.

Jim: Pay to play, yeah. Basically, they're scratching each other's backs. It's a mutually beneficial arrangement. I guess I don't blame them. Maybe I would do the same thing. Basically, the USDA is the research lab for the feedlot industry and for the meatpacking industry.

David: Does it seem like it also influences the outcomes of research?

Jim: Absolutely. I would say so. You can predict the answer. So, they did a trial with this Zilmax drug. It's a human drug, actually a failed human drug that they used to treat asthma; it's called a β_2 adrenergic agonist. It caused people to turn into Arnold Schwarzenegger. Merck had it, and said, wow, if we can't use it for people, we can use that for cattle. That's what Merck did. And it made Merck a great deal of money since the drug was fed to many millions of feedlot cattle.

David: Yeah, sure.

Jim: US MARC published their study on feeding zilpaterol to feedlot cattle at the USDA MARC feedlot in 2015, shortly after the problem with Zilmax arose. The study was sponsored by the USDA, the University of Nebraska-Lincoln, and the Nebraska Beef Council. Their paper claimed the study was about the animal welfare effects of feeding Zilmax. However, there were no recognized animal welfare metrics used in the study, and no animal welfare scientists involved in the study. To no one's surprise, the paper claimed there were no ill effects from feeding zilpaterol to cattle, just what the beef industry ordered. The paper was published in *Journal of Animal Science,* which is not an animal-welfare publication but an animal-production journal. A former MARC Director, Dr. Mohammad Koohmaraie, said many times, "MARC provides needed results for industry." Note he did not say "needed research" Of course, Dr. Koohmaraie left MARC to become an executive in the meat industry.

David: So, it's like everything else. A small investment in lobbying brings you big investments in cash, because so much of our economy is just influenced by what happens here in Washington.

Jim: Yeah. USDA MARC did a paper with the desired findings for industry, and the livestock industry will then lobby for more money for MARC. Does it always work both ways?

David: Somebody in Washington gets something out of it. Sure. Or in the government.

Jon: Well, just a curious mind at work here: I thought Pfizer Animal Health might have had some interest in that.

Louis: Wasn't that Merck?

Jim: The drug was zilpaterol sold by Merck. . . . When you publish a paper, you have to say who funded it, and it was the University of Nebraska, the Nebraska Beef Council and the USDA.

Dan: So, it was Pfizer or Merck?

Jim: There are two similar drugs fed to cattle and swine to increase their size. One is zilpaterol (Zilmax), sold by Merck. It is approved for use in only 17 countries. The other drug is ractopamine (Optaflexx® Ractopamine hydro-chloride), sold by Elanco (Eli Lilly). This drug is banned in more than 160 countries. They are very weird drugs.

CHAPTER FORTY-TWO

"IT'S ALWAYS ABOUT PRODUCTION OR REPRODUCTION."

Dan: Isn't there going to be some huge fight over lab meat or something like that coming up at the USDA?

Jim: Well, there are two phenomena happening right now that are disrupting the meat industry. One is called "plant-based protein" sources. Basically, you can figure out what proteins are in present meat or fish. Then you find all those same proteins in plants and recreate the meat with essentially the same composition but using plants instead of animals. They have these big databases of the protein compositions of thousands of plants to recreate the composition of meat. Several plant-based protein "meat" products are already on the market.

Dan: Yeah.

Jim: And the other disruptor is called "clean meat" where you actually take muscle cells from a cow, and you grow them in tissue culture, in vats. This technology is not yet mature, but there are many startups and venture capital investments. It started off being $30,000 for a hamburger. Now it's down to maybe a hundred bucks, and it's going to come down probably to the ten-dollar range in the next couple of years. It was really dismissed at first but now, even traditional meat companies like Tyson have invested in it. And Bill Gates invested in it, and . . . who's the guy who owns Virgin Airlines?

David: Richard Branson.

Jim: Richard Branson. So, a lot of smart people are investing in it, including the meat industry. It's going to be part of the future. Who knows how dominant it's going to be in the future? Scale up is the issue. That's like anything else. You start out in small scale. But the fight is: Does the FDA have the jurisdiction or does USDA? I think there was a recent meeting where FDA claimed it as their own. And USDA was not allowed at the table, and they were upset about it. . . . That's what I understand must have happened, Jon.

David: Right. That's what I heard.

Louis: And I've heard that. We favor FDA on that one, on that battle, just because FDA has the law—the Food Safety Modernization Act—that essentially allows whistleblower protection to anybody in the industry as opposed to the Department of Agriculture or meat industry which doesn't.

Dan: But you and Michael Moss [of the *New York Times*] really hit the USDA's credibility, right? I mean you really hit them hard.

Jim: Yeah. There's also another group called the White Coat Waste Project. They're here in D.C., and they just found some other USDA problems.

David: What is it? White Coat?

Jim: White Coat Waste Project.

David: I'm going to write that down.

Jim: What they do is, they're kind of a libertarian organization, but their real goal is to decrease federal funding of research involving animals. The idea is that if the research is worth doing, then private industry will do it, will fill the gap. And the truth is, the problem with a lot of federal research is the money comes in automatically. For a university to receive Federal funding, it must submit a grant proposal and compete for funding based on merit (as judged by a review panel). For intramural Federal research at USDA, FDA, or NIH, the research dollars are allocated by Congress automatically and non-competitively. This allows poor quality or marginal benefit research to be done as has happened at MARC for 50 years. In industry, of course, they've got certain money or the money of their investors. Unlike the Federal intramural research, industry cannot afford to spend money on projects with little potential value. So stupid, frankly, stupid experiments happened at MARC for thirty or forty years that never would have happened because there was never a market for their research. In fact, livestock owners didn't even want the products MARC created, e.g. cows that bore twins. So, MARC just wasted literally hundreds of millions of dollars only because they could—because money came in and basically, it's easy to spend somebody else's money.

Jon: Well, USDA's credibility is very low in my opinion, not just based on your experience. To see those audits that Dan reviewed, those IG reports—they weren't believable audits. I thought they falsified findings. And so, I think in this fight between USDA and FDA, it really hurts USDA not to have an IG who shoots straight. . . . I now see another person who is like-minded. You can't do these things as an IG. You can't say that Michael Moss's reporting was wrong because USDA disagreed with an adjective in the story. . . . He writes about "a vast excavation called the dead pit," and the USDA IG comes along and says, "Well, we disagree with that description, therefore anything he says about it is wrong." They run to the press—the Nebraska press, the national press—everybody says, "Ah! This Michael Moss and this guy Jim Keen, they don't know what they're talking about." Now I see another person noticed the same thing. I don't know if you know the name or not, but she's on the faculty at University of California Davis, Alison Van Eenennaam.

Jim: I don't know her.

Jon: Well, she tore the USDA IG apart from the opposite standpoint. She said, "This is not at all transparent. They redacted so much in the report; you can't really tell [what was going on at MARC]." And she was very critical of the report as well, but not necessarily from the same standpoint I was coming from. So, you get people on both sides saying this is really bad work. I think it's going to affect USDA credibility.

Jim: Well, one thing disappointed me. They were doing brain surgery on pigs. And I didn't see this myself, but one of my colleagues did, but he wouldn't speak to Michael Moss out of fear of retaliation if he said something. And the pig-brain research was done by a MARC scientist in collaboration with an animal scientist from the University of Georgia. And I said that the experiments were being done at [MARC], because I knew my colleague had seen it. And they said in the OIG report, "We couldn't prove that it (the pig brain research) was actually done at MARC." Which was easy to find out, I mean you could have easily proven that or not. As I said, my veterinary colleague at MARC saw the surgery. The OIG just said they couldn't find out if it was done there. It may have been done at Georgia as well, but it was absolutely done at MARC because my colleagues had seen it. I hadn't seen it, but they did. . . . MARC scientists were drilling holes in pigs' brains and injecting drugs.

David: What was the purpose?

Jim: It's always the same. To make the pigs grow faster or have more piglets. It's always about production or reproduction. That's it. It's always that. It's always the same theme. The whole thing is to maximize production, to maximize reproduction. Nothing else matters, basically.

Jon: So, I'm just trying to put two and two together as to who got to the USDA IG [to write such a bad report]? The USDA itself?

Jim: I don't know. I think it might have been [former United States Secretary of Agriculture Tom] Vilsack.

Jon: You think it was Vilsack?

Jim: Because he was involved in this. Yeah, he was really pissed off at me because I heard he got like 400,000 emails about the January 17, 2015, *New York Times* article by Michael Moss, or something like that. Some ginormous number, and he was really upset about it. I don't know that for sure. That's just a guess.

Jon: My guess is that it would not be Vilsack although it could well be. Because he probably gets hundreds of thousands of emails about a lot.

Jim: But that's for one issue. It was a lot for this one issue. I mean, I'm sure he gets lots of them. I don't know who told him. Someone told me he was really upset about it.

Jon: I'm more curious about some other players.

Jim: Actually, Ronnie Green would be a perfect. That would make sense. That would make a lot of sense.

Dan: Talk about Ronnie Green. Talk about him.

Jim: Ronnie Green actually did his Ph.D. research done at MARC. He's an animal geneticist, beef geneticist, and then went to Texas Tech for a while as a faculty member. And then he joined industry. I can't remember the name, it's somewhere in the beef industry.

Dan: Do you remember that Jon? Where Ronnie Green was? Where he was in the beef industry?

Jim: He was in, . . . I don't know which company

Jon: I think he worked for Pfizer Animal Health.

Jim: But this is before this in his career.

Jon: He was in a start-up.

Jim: Yes. He was in a start-up. He was part of a beef start-up company called Future Beef in the early 2000s, which went bankrupt about a year after start-up.

Jon: His start-up went under?

Jim: Which went broke, right. And then when the start-up went broke, he joined USDA as what's called a national program manager. He lived in Nebraska, but he worked in and commuted to D.C., going back and forth. He did that, I don't know, for seven or eight years. And then it was time to get a new director. He applied for the directorship at MARC and he didn't get it—even though the advisory board at MARC recommended him, nine-to-one. And I think, I was told because he didn't get that position that he left MARC, he left USDA, and he joined Pfizer. And at Pfizer, he was head of their global beef genetics program. And he did that for several years and then was recruited by the University of Nebraska, which has two divisions, East Campus, which is Agriculture, and the main campus which is non-agriculture.

Dan: So, he became the Chancellor of Agriculture?

Jim: Yes. He became the Vice Chancellor of the East Campus. That was probably around 2008 or 2009. He did that for six or seven years and then about two years ago, he became head of the whole university.

Dan: But he got into some trouble, no?

Jon: He got in trouble for firing an English Department grad student.

Jim: Oh, yeah.

Jon: He is trouble for putting the University of Nebraska, my alma mater, on the AAUP censor list. I mean, that was the charge that the AAUP said.

Jim: His style is very autocratic. It's just the style. He rules. Like Dr. Seuss's Yertle the Turtle, he rules all that he can see.

Jon: I know the Chancellor. I've talked to him at length on unrelated matters.

David: Since he became Chancellor?

Jon: Both. Before when he was Vice Chancellor and when he became Chancellor. We talked about other things. And, you know, actually he's a likable guy.

Jim: Well, I'll tell you this. He's extremely smart, and he's got a photographic memory.

David: When did he become Chancellor?

Jim: In or about 2016.

Dan: I'm a little unclear. How does he intersect with you? How does he affect you?

Jim: He didn't like me at all.

Dan: So, he was sabotaging you?

Jim: Well, I don't know. I can't prove that. But he'd be in a position to.

David: But he's trying to get rid of you now. . . .

Louis: So, how is he doing that?

Jim: Pardon me?

Louis: How are they moving to do that?

Jim: To get rid of me? Well, what happened was when I came back to work in October 2015. I was transferred. I used to be in this hinterland, Clay Center, where I used to work, and I was banned from the MARC facility for life by the university. So, then it was a year and a half of not working. I was paid, but not working while on administrative leave and sick leave from May 2014 until October 2015, following my outing as a whistleblower working with Michael Moss. I moved to Lincoln in about October of 2015. . . . So, what they did is, when I got back there, they didn't tell me why, but one of my major duties was to teach veterinary students two classes, and they banned me from teaching those classes. I had taught these classes for the previous eight years. So, I was banned from teaching veterinary students. I asked UNL why, and they just said, "No, you can't teach." And I asked multiple times each year in review, and they said no. They never gave me a reason why. From the last evaluation, I failed. They recommended something called "post-tenure review." . . . The rationale for post-tenure review was, if I wasn't performing my duties and I'm not teaching the classes that I'm banned from teaching. So, therefore, I'm going to have probably in six months my tenure revoked and get a one-year terminal contract. . . . I've read other stories about whistleblowers, but that's how they do it. They marginalize you and make it impossible for the whistleblower to succeed. And so, I have a research position, too, and they gave me a, literally, it's a closet for a lab. So, it is also impossible for me to do research. I understand. They don't want me there.

Dan: What is the positive impact that you have made? When the *New York Times* writes a front-page story about you—like they wrote a front-page story about Jon—I mean that's god-like status. The holy *New York Times* has written favorably about you and your contributions.

Jim: I was at this conference with people I didn't know but who knew about my story. It's good to hear that. USDA was really embarrassed. Actually, White Coat Waste Project was inspired by my story and is following up on more USDA animal abuse. USDA research was hidden and now they know that there's dirty laundry so other groups are digging. . . . When I talked to Michael Moss, he asked, "What do you want to happen?"

Dan: So, you've stayed in touch with Michael through all of this?

Jim: I have but less and less frequently. You know, I had contact with him most recently maybe two months ago, maybe three times a year.

Dan: He's a Pulitzer Prize winner, and you have total respect for him, for what he's done, right?

Jim: I do. Yeah, I really do. He left the *Times,* and he's a full-time author now.

Louis: He was the one who did the pink slime story like ten years ago.

Dan: He won the Pulitzer for that?

Jim: No, that wasn't Michael Moss. Michael Moss, I don't know who won that for that work; Michael Moss won it for work on a case where a woman from Minnesota got *E. coli O157* from eating hamburger made by Cargill. You can also find *E. coli O157* in pink slime. Mr. Moss followed her individual tragic story. A lot of horrible things happened to her just from eating a contaminated hamburger.

Louis: And it's in that story. It was the first story about the hamburger and the BPI. That was all in there.

Jim: Yeah, it was all in there. It actually is part of that bigger picture story.

Dan: So, what is your legacy, Jim? This commitment that you've made to this work you've done. What is your legacy?

Jim: Okay, I'd say my legacy is, well, Michael Moss, asked, "What do you want to happen?" . . . I want to improve the welfare at MARC and the quality of the science, too. Those two things, and I think both of those things happened. But beyond MARC, the needed changes happened throughout ARS because of the whole ripple effect. So, I think what I did helped make the agency become better actually, to better use taxpayer dollars, to do higher quality and more welfare sensitive research. I mean they're getting looked at for the first time. Before they were, I think, they basically had free range. And now they've got a little fence around them at least. So, what I wanted to happen at MARC happened.

Louis: How has PETA reacted to your work?

Jim: PETA?

Dan: Or the other animal rights organizations?

Jim: Oh, they're really, really happy with it.

David: Did they know, at the time you started speaking out, how much did the public and groups like PETA, know about what was going on inside MARC?

Jim: No, they didn't know anything about it. Nobody knew. They didn't even know it existed. No one knew it was out there.

Louis: No congressional hearing ever?

Jim: Not that I know of.

Louis: It's almost never going to be a congressional hearing around the USDA, because they just completely own the congressional oversight.

CHAPTER FORTY-THREE

"IT'S POLITICS AND AGRICULTURE"

Jim: Well, it's funny. I was on The Hill today, and I was meeting with someone in Congress. Some lobbyist took me there to meet this person. I don't even know who it is. I was on The Hill lobbying with some other veterinarians involved with advocating for the Farm Bill.

Dan: Well the Farm Bill's a special project of Jon's.

Jon: Yeah. I'm working on the Farm Bill.

Jim: Really?

Jon: Yes.

Jim: Can you keep the King amendment out of it?

Jon: Keep the King amendment out? Yeah.

Jim: Out of it. Yeah, see if you can do that.

Jon: All right. We'll see.

Dan: Who's that? Peter King from New York?

Jim: No, Steven King from a western Iowa district.

Dan: Oh, that guy, that right-winger guy, the Tea Party guy. . . . He's a knuckle dragger.

Jim: But this King amendment deals with different states having different agricultural practice. He wants to force all states to accept any other state's agricultural practices. You've got a really terrible system. . . . I mean, a lot of bad things could happen regarding food quality and food safety. So basically, the lowest common denominator becomes the rule.

Louis: Yeah, preemption.

Jim: And the argument that we're making—actually, I'd preempt it myself— it's kind of a federalist argument that states should have the right to have their own standards for quality. I've been told it probably won't get in, but you can't let your guard down.

Louis: Yeah. Sure.

Dan: Well Jon, you're like the whistleblower's whistleblower. You protected yourself. You had great support in Congress when you did what you did. You did it by the numbers. You litigated, you stood firm, you looked good. What's your long-standing legacy? What's your contribution, and your legacy for what you've done?

Jon: I hope my long-standing legacy is that I've put the interest of students, families, and taxpayers out front at least at the Department of Education and maybe even among the interest groups where no one else would talk about it. It was either the institutions or the lenders or the collectors that got attention at the Department. That was what it was all about. And by shaking up the system and showing fraud and corruption . . . and then winning court settlements. . . .

Dan: Including a Supreme Court decision—

Jon: And then getting a Supreme Court decision. That, I hope, is a lasting legacy.

Dan: So, it was Oberg I, Oberg II, and Oberg III, right?

Jon: Right.

David: And we're about to see Oberg IV?

Jon: Well, we hope so, but I'm not taking any bets on it.

David: My experience—which has not been my whole career, only the last eight years—with the Department of Education is that they entirely saw the institutions, the schools, and the banks, as their constituency, and not the students. And partly because of Jon, that really started to change. It took us eight years to get the Obama administration to actually start to mean that. In their final year, they kind of did start listening to and protecting students. Now, under Donald Trump and Betsy DeVos, it's swung back again, but at least there's some sense that they should be ashamed that they don't care about students. As a culture there, what they're scared of is that the schools have political power. The banks have political power. They're scared of a member of Congress calling up the secretary and screaming at them. You know, "Bill Smith and your department is messing with our school or messing with our bank."

Jon: That's true.

David: The other specific thing that I think maybe Jon's work helped influence—although I think other things were a factor, too—was that we had this ridiculous student-loan system that was basically paying the banks as if they were lenders when, in fact, they were taking no risk at all. And, basically, they hired every lobbyist in town, Democrats *and* Republicans, to keep that privilege which made no sense. It is a huge giveaway.

Dan: This was the 9.5 [guaranteed subsidy percent]?

David: Well, the 9.5 system created concern about what was called the guaranteed student loan system. Instead of paying the banks a subsidy when they were taking no risks on the student loans, we got rid of that. And I think part of that, part of what Jon did, was to teach people how crooked the lending institutions were. Jon made it easier to push back.

Dan: How did Jon's work influence you when you first entered the fray?

David: When I first got involved in this issue, I was told, "You will never get rid of that system just because the banks are too powerful." So, it was Jon along with the fact that we needed to pay for Obamacare and people started to look and say, "Well here's all this money that we're just giving away."

Jim: So why did the government do that?

Louis: Why did it happen in the first place?

Jim: Yeah. Why did the government agree to let the banks have this freebie?

Jon: Well, it's more historical, actually. How did we get into the student loan business in the first place? Because, you know, you used to have low tuition or you could work yourself through college, and student loans didn't really come into the picture until a few decades ago. And then there were competing systems back then as to whether it would be the federal government or whether the banks would do it, and the banks were chosen. And there was not an alternative for the federal government to get back into it until around 1990. But then you could do either. I testified on The Hill [to kill the bank-based program]. No one else would testify, to tell the committees to just kill the thing, take the savings and put them into grants for students. All the experts were aghast that anybody would actually say that in 2007. And then after my suit details became known. It was the beginning of 2010 that Congress needed a few billion and said, "Oh yeah, here's a place where we can get forty billion by just killing this program and put ten billion toward the Affordable Care Act, to make it budget neutral, and put the rest toward student grants." Now, I had a lot of help along the way from others who made it actually happen.

Dan: So, your legacy is?

Jon: Putting students, families and taxpayers back into consideration.

Dan: Now, did you have problems with the Clinton administration?

Jon: Sure, I did, with all administrations to some extent.

Dan: I'm just wondering, because David said he had problems with the for-profit schools and with the Obama administration. They didn't get it, and you had to explain it to them.

David: Well, they started to get it, but they still didn't have the political will to do it, because every time they listened to us, then they'd listen to Don Graham, then they'd listen to Lanny Davis, then they'd listen to Dick Gephardt, Marc Morial, Trent Lott. . . . They hired lobbyists. They co-opted media outlets. They co-opted nonprofits. Some of America's democratic activists were paid by the industry to shill for them. They could buy anybody they wanted.

And it was our money—paid for by our tax dollars that went to the schools. That was the cycle. Thirty-two billion dollars a year for taxpayers to their industry. They could buy any lobbyist they wanted and that got them more money, and that's why so much of our economy now is just playing the right game in Washington, which gets you this advantage.

Jim: Hey Jon, can we circle back to, before I forget, how were you working on the Farm Bill and in what capacity?

Jon: It's politics and agriculture. My partner in this effort, Doug Hillmer, just retired from the Census Bureau. And we wondered what we could do to challenge Trump, who is a disaster for agriculture. And I said, "Well, let's get a bunch of people together." Doug's a great demography expert, and he could pull all the election data out of every precinct and county and state and say, "Here's where Trump won. These precincts, these counties in Wisconsin, Michigan, and Pennsylvania. They're rural counties." And then he looked historically, and he said, "Obama carried these, but in 2016 they went to Trump." It isn't that these people are of one mind. You only have to move so many of them back. Now, what are the agriculture issues that might bring them back?

Dan: And the 2018 Farm Bill?

Jon: The Farm Bill was up before Congress with huge implications for rural America. Huge implications. Unappreciated. What would be some good policies in the Farm Bill to bring these people back?

Jim: It's like the King amendment. It's the same thing.

Jon: So, we talked to a lot of like-minded agriculture groups and came up with initiatives on the Farm Bill, good for rural America. We talked to a lot of people on The Hill. Let me just tell you frankly, we've been extremely disappointed in the Democratic leadership. We continued to be told, "Don't you dare do anything for those people who voted for Trump, they're the enemies." I replied, "Don't you want to win the next election?"

David: You made progress on the Farm Bill this year and actually legislation passed that was good for farmers. How would that hurt Trump? If it was a good bill, how would that hurt Trump? Because the farmers would say, "Oh, good things are getting better."

Jon: Because we wanted Democrats in the key states like . . .

Dan: Wisconsin, Michigan, Ohio, and Pennsylvania . . .

Jon: . . . to be the leaders and say, "Here's what we stand for. We are for something. We're not just against Trump. We are for these kinds of constructive policies that will help rural America." And let me give you a couple examples: saving topsoil, soil conservation [which Trump cuts in his USDA budgets]. It's not, per se, a political thing. And that rings a bell with rural communities. Jobs, local and regional, are created while building [healthy food] markets. We have economic studies behind us that say, "Hey, it's ready to take off. You just need the right kinds of incentives in your crop insurance. You need to take 'specialty crops' out of bill language and make them mainstream." These are issues that relate to rural people.

Dan: And what was the response from the Democratic leaders you approached?

Jon: We did not get good responses from the Democratic leadership. They said, "No, no, no."

David: So, forget the congressional leadership. It seems to me what you need to do is put together something really persuasive and then start meeting with presidential candidates. Explain your theory. "These are the districts we've looked at. These are the policies that work." If you go in and talk to the farmers, face to face, about this, this could turn some people away from Trump. . . . In Congress, not many laws are passing anyway.

Jon: Well, they're going to pass [a mediocre] Farm Bill. . . . There's a danger in it, that the King amendment might get in, there's a danger that a lot of bad things might get in the bill.

Louis: I agree with that.

Jon: The Senate bill is not as bad as the House bill.

David: Are you sure those Pennsylvanian and Wisconsin farmers are against the King amendment, though? Might they see it as a way, to get their way and to outsell stuff to California that otherwise they wouldn't be able to?

Jim: Let me give you one example of what happened in King's District about eight or nine years ago. I know this guy, a poultry veterinarian. He was part of a facility that is Iowa's number-one producer of eggs. They produce billions of eggs every year. And in King's District there was this one farm, big, gigantic, industrial egg farm that had been kicked out of Maine, so it moved to Iowa. One of my students told me that the place was just filthy, filthy, filthy, but they exported eggs all around the country. That's why they were kicked out of Maine. It turned out that those eggs were contaminated with salmonella. It led to the largest outbreak of salmonella in people from poultry ever—at least from poultry, I know that for sure that it killed some people. A bunch of people had to be hospitalized. It caused the recall of many, many, hundreds of millions of eggs, which caused the price of eggs to go up because of this one place.

Jim: And with the King amendment, California couldn't stop those crappy eggs from going to California. That's an example. And they went around nationwide. . . . So, it's a public-health issue and not just agricultural.

Jon: We wanted Senator [and ranking member on the Agriculture Committee] Debbie Stabenow out there, visibly offering a positive alternative to Trump's USDA. She's the ranking member, Michigan is key. I met with Stabenow's staff director, and the staff attorney.

David: On the [Agriculture] committee staff?

Jon: On the committee staff. We were told that the senators themselves were not going to get out in front of this, that there would be no Democratic initiatives on the Farm Bill whatsoever. Everybody would be on his or her own. Debbie Stabenow's on her own. Heidi Heitkamp's on her own, and so on. And you'll notice that in all Democratic deals [like the "Better Deal"], there is no farm program, no agriculture, no rural economy, no heartland issues.

Jim: It's punishment though, and that's the driver?

Jon: Well, that's—

David: It's crazy, is what it is.

Jon: I've been told by some of the think-tank people, working on the Farm Bill, sympathetic pro-farmer people, who said, "Nobody's working on the Farm Bill." We started to get somebody to work on it, but our funders said no. They will not put any of our resources into doing something for the people who got Trump elected.

Louis: It's Big Ag. It's like that whole eight years of Clinton. It had become a desert. Obviously, they had to respond to the Jack in the Box situation in 1993, involving the *E. coli* bacterium that allegedly killed four children with hundreds more hospitalized. But, ultimately, nothing really changed after that.

CHAPTER FORTY-FOUR

"I'LL NEVER STOP"

Dan: Were you at the Clinton White House then?

David: Yeah, but I worked on the national security staff. I wasn't involved in the Jack in the Box situation.

Jim: How'd you get involved in that?

David: When I first got out of college the big issue was nuclear-arms control. So, after I graduated, I worked at the Arms Control Association, which is a non-profit group here in Washington and for a few other groups like that. Then, after law school and my clerkship with Judge Gerhard Gesell in D.C., I managed to get hired to be counsel at the Senate Intelligence Committee. . . . Eventually a speech-writer job opened up at the White House. Since I had the National Security background and I was a writer, I did that.

Jim: It caught my ear because my sister-in-law is the National Security Council Director for Europe and Russia.

David: Now?

Jim: Now.

Dan: David, what is your legacy? You are a genuine warrior—where literally, on a day-to-day basis you are out there fighting the good fight against these incredibly draconian policies that have resulted from the Trump Administration as carried out by Betsy DeVos at Education.

David: We were building a coalition at the time I got involved. I was at the Center for American Progress, and the project I was working on was a youth project, getting young people engaged in activism and journalism. We were originally sending speakers, funding college or youth journalism—not really doing our own advocacy operation. But it became clear that people wanted our help. So, we started to build-up our advocacy operation. Then all these partners started saying, "We need your help on this issue of for-profit higher education" . . . I remember having a conversation a woman named Pauline Abernathy, who worked at a group called TICAS, The Institute for College Access and Success. Jon knows Pauline.

Dan: Is that when the for-profit-school people started attacking you?

David: Yes. We were getting attacked with all these fake letters that appeared from fake people to all the groups with whom we were building coalitions: civil-rights groups, consumer groups, veterans' groups. The fake letters from the fake people said don't work with me because I was taking money from Wall Street short seller, Steve Eisman. It was just not true. Then they said we were running a multi-million-dollar ad campaign because we spent four-thousand dollars. . . . So, in addition to being attacked and seeing that these people were desperately trying to go after us and make up lies about us—because we were coming after them—I met a woman named Rashidah Smallwood. We had sort of been canvassing around for students or former staff or current staff who would tell us what was going on. She was at ITT Tech in Texas, and she was being told by her bosses to lie, falsify financial-aid forms to bring in more money for the school.

Dan: How did Rashidah help?

David: We brought her to Washington. We did a little event with her, and we tried to go to congressional offices, which were all meeting with the lobbyists for the schools every day. We couldn't find a single office that would meet with her—not a single office would meet with this important whistleblower.

Back then they weren't. Democrats and Republicans were embracing this for-profit-college industry. It was hard to get support. Like I said, it took eight years to get the Obama administration to actually do something serious in terms of both cracking down on schools, saying they shouldn't be getting the money anymore and granting debt relief for students who'd been defrauded.

Dan: What about your friends from your days with the Clinton Administration?

David: We were really at the brink. I will say that right before the 2016 election, I was meeting with the Clinton transition people. They were gonna continue what the Obama administration was finally doing and be really serious about it. And I believed them. I really did. We were actually preparing a secret report called, "Binders Full of Lobbyists," of the forty people that Clinton should not appoint, not just in higher education, but in every issue, because even though they were Democrats, they had represented all these horrible industries all these years.

Dan: What happened?

David: The election happened, and the president of Trump University was elected President of the United States, and the whole thing went to hell. And so now we're back fighting all the policies that Betsy DeVos is now carrying out via people who worked for the same predatory colleges that were doing all the bad stuff before.

Jon: Consequences?

David: As you know, Jon, all the regulations we worked so hard to get established are being canceled. We're nowhere again. But what we do have is a media that understands the issue. We have attorneys general across the country, including some Republicans, who are on guard, fighting against this for-profit college industry. We have more of the students understanding what a scam this is, which is why a lot of people in the industry have now tried this separate scam of turning their schools into non-profits but are actually non-profit in name only.

Dan: In this environment, how do you fight back?

David: It's hard to defeat these crooks. What I was saying about my friend Pauline was that we had a conversation in 2010, and I said, "Pauline, I'm not gonna quit this issue. We have to agree never to quit this issue until we win." Pauline did finally turn to other issues, but we still discuss higher ed. I feel that as long as I'm self-employed, as long as I have the freedom to have a portfolio of issues, I will keep fighting for those getting scammed and injured. I'll never give up on this issue, because it's just such an outrage. It's just blatant stealing of our money.

Dan: What's been the price tag?

David: At the peak, thirty-two billion dollars a year. It's one thing if you took the thirty-two billion dollars and threw it in the river. That's bad for taxpayers to the tune of thirty-two billion dollars. But the money's being used to systematically ruin the lives of people. And I've met so many of these people now, and many owe as much as a hundred-thousand dollars for a worthless degree. That's a hundred-thousand dollars they'll never be able to pay back. As a result, they can't buy a home. They can't get married. So I'll never stop—even though I can't believe how many of the people that I personally worked with in the Clinton Administration or know in other ways, that otherwise have an exemplarily record or a good record of public service, who get paid to lobby and vouch for this industry.

Dan: What was behind the DeVos appointment? What was behind all of that?

David: I think the DeVos appointment was more rooted in a commitment to religious people and anti-public-school people, because her issue is really K-12 not higher ed. But it's not surprising that, given the influence of Mike Pence and all kinds of other people who stand for special interest being in the administration. DeVos, actually herself, was an investor in for-profit higher education as well as K-12. It just kind of went along. She has said things basically about an industry that's proven again and again to be engaged in fraud. She's pointed to the students as the fraudsters. And she's said that we have to get rid of these policies produced to protect students. She actually said, under an Obama regulation, all you would have to do is raise your hand to get so called free money. What she was describing was students getting their federal loans forgiven, in a situation where they'd wasted years. They put in their own money. They'd taken out private loans. They'd wasted their grants and even the GI Bill. It was not free money. It was just potentially getting some measure of recovery after being massively scammed. What she's saying about students, that they're the fraudsters, is such a disgrace. So, I'll never give-up this issue.

Jon: David's work over the years has really put into the vocabulary the idea that the Department of Education is ruining lives. And it really does. It just ruins lives. It ruins families, forever, and that's incredible.

Jim: It almost gives credence—I hate to say this—that they should get rid of it. Republican lawmakers have said that over the years?

Dan: Get rid of the student-loan program? The movement against for-profit colleges?

Jim: Get rid of the whole Department of Education Aren't they moving in that direction right now?

David: The thing that makes sense are grants and loans for people to go to college. That's a good thing. Unfortunately, it's gotten completely corrupted by these crooks. Where there's that much money around, you're always gonna attract crooks.

Dan: What are DeVos's intentions, and how much damage is she doing then?

David: Her intentions are to unregulate the process, and to let these people go back to doing what they were doing, overseeing the unlimited flow of money regardless of performance. In what area of government do we give people money and say, "We don't care about your performance?" And that's what they're doing. No accountability for leaving students in debt, for having the high default rates, for having low graduation rates. So long as you can get an accreditor to say you're a school, you get the money. That's what we were trying to stop. And, to some extent, we have helped to stop some of them. These schools are failing under their own weight. They're struggling now.

Dan: And your remarkable contribution?

David: What I've been able to do—in addition to working with the coalition doing advocacy—is to attract whistleblowers by writing investigative pieces. The more mainstream media's done quite a bit of it, as well. But I'm getting some of the best stuff.

Dan: Yes, you certainly are.

David: So EDMC was sold to former people from Grand Canyon University, who hooked-up with the Dream Center, which is a religious nonprofit in Los Angeles. And they were gonna run it as a nonprofit. But I got calls from inside the company, that the guy that they put in charge of it, who had been running Grand Canyon University, has basically created a network of for-profit businesses that he's using this nonprofit to enrich. They lied to the students about accreditation, they lied to the accreditors, they lied to the Department of Education, and now the whole thing's falling apart. I'm hopeful that I helped expose the problems. I think I helped bring down Corinthian Colleges when I reported that they—enrolled a student that was mentally disabled and couldn't even read and he was enrolled because he wanted to be a police officer.

Dan: So. what do you conclude from this?

David: Whistleblowers beget more whistleblowers. The more you write the more people call you, and the more whistleblowers you get.

Dan: So, when I ask you what the future of for-profit college is, your answer is, "It depends."

David: It depends a lot on who wins the next election. And it depends a lot on whether there's still funding from foundations and generous donors to keep everyone honest, because it's all being done by non-profit groups, continuing the fight, exposing the abuses. We have the civil-rights community, consumer student groups, and increasingly, the veterans' community stronger than ever. But it has to get funded, or we can't do it.

CHAPTER FORTY-FIVE

"SCIENTISTS ARE THE NEW HIGH PRIESTS"

Dan: Jon, how you do view the DeVos situation? What needs to be done? The Trump administration has put a baseball bat in her hand and told her to swing away.

Jon: In my opinion, she's totally a tool of other people. As David said, she's a K-12 person put in there for religious-right reasons, and everything else has just been turned over to industry. Is she culpable? Well, sure she is, but she's not the one with the bat. She's not the main actor here, by any means. She's just a puppet.

Dan: So, when I ask you what's the future of the student-loan program, your answer is also, "It depends, right?"

Jon: There are several possible futures out there.

Dan: Let's say if it were to stay on this course, what would happen? What would happen if, say Trump was reelected in 2020, what happens?

Jon: Well, you'll see increasing inequality in education, in higher education. You will just see expanding inequality and more and more lives ruined through excessive loans and through bad schools.

Dan: You agree with Jon, David?

David: Yes, I do. I think, in some ways, the truth is starting to come out, more and more. DeVos can't control it. But yes, this is about taking a program that was meant to help disadvantaged people, but it actually made them worse off.

Dan: Via a for-profit college?

David: Well, it's not true if they go to a legit school. But, as long as there's no standard, the problem is these schools can make a better promise. They can say, "You can study at home. We'll give you a laptop." Some of the commercials showed that you'd get a woman, two women on your arm, if you joined their school. That kind of coercion is a scam, along with the deceptive marketing, and recruiting, and telling people to go to "that" school when you can get a better education at a community college for a fraction of the cost. And the American taxpayer is paying for it.

Dan: Right. . . .

David: We're paying for their ads. We're paying for their lobbyists. We're paying for their lawyers. We're paying for them to attack me, as was the case with the fake charges leveled by the fake people.

Dan: And Louis, do you have other Department of Education cases? Have you had whistleblower cases?

Louis: Not many, actually. Our biggest case was the sports case, University of North Carolina. Mary Willingham blew the whistle on the University of North Carolina and the NCAA and the Department of Education, It wasn't really involved other than there were some threats, because one of things that she was alleged to have released—I won't say whether she did or not—was an essay that this University of North Carolina basketball player submitted on one of his non-existent courses. It was all those courses that didn't exist. He submitted this essay, like about two paragraphs, on Rosa Parks. It would fail a sixth-grade standard. I mean, it was so sad. ESPN had a show, saying that there was some threat from the Department of Education, which was upset about the player's privacy.

Dan: Generally, are you seeing an institutional failure, particularly with regard to the protection of whistleblowers, by the Inspector Generals' offices?

Louis: Totally mixed bag. Every Inspector General's Office is different, and I would say the majority are probably not helpful. It does depend on who the investigators are too, the people who are actually doing the investigative work. It's not all just the Inspector General, but the luck of the draw.

Dan: But whistleblowing continues to be the counterbalance to all the corruption?

Louis: Yeah.

Dan: How do you see the future of whistleblowing in the midst of the Trump Administration?

Louis: I think it's expanding. It's exactly what David was saying. If you're having impact, when he has impact, he's gonna get other whistleblowers, because the motivation for whistleblowers, just speaking more generally, is to have impact—public-interest impact. As a matter of fact, the early surveys all indicated that the reason that people don't blow the whistle is because they don't think anything's going to change. It's not fear of losing their jobs—although there is that fear—but the larger fear is that nothing will happen, nothing will change. If you can make something happen—whether you're a journalist, public interest advocate, or a government official for that matter—and have impact with the whistleblowers, you just get a lot more of them.

Jim: I can comment on what Louie just said, because I did the official route of informing my supervisors if my concerns at MARC for five or six years, and nothing happened. So then, I had to go to stage two, to contact and work with Michael Moss. The official pathway just doesn't work. At least, it didn't work for me.

Jon: Well, I don't think you're alone.

David: Do you see more under Trump?

Louis: No question about it. You know, we're getting more. We represented the deputy chief of staff of the EPA who just got rid of Scott Pruitt.

Jon: He's one of yours?

Louis: Yeah.

David: He's awesome, he's a waiter in Ocean City, right?

Louis: That's what he's doing, Ocean City, Maryland.

David: What can you tell us that I didn't read in the paper?

Louis: Part of winning that case, well, getting Pruitt thrown out, is really him using his Trump card with all his buddies within that whole Trump World. We're finding that if you can get the right Trump person, it's helpful.

David: At the VA?

Louis: Yeah, Kerner, he's really decent so far. It's not universal that the Trump people are going to be bad. It's a mixed bag. Partly the reason it's a mixed bag is because, in my opinion, Trump has not penetrated very deeply into the various departments and agencies. The number of people that he's appointed is really small and he's behind every other president. In a sense, you have just a few people manipulating things and agencies that don't know what to do.

Dan: What about the role of the IG's office? In Jon's case, Jon educated the IG. In Jim's case, the IG kind of fucked him over.

Louis: In every case you have to educate the IG. Like, at the Department of Defense, the IG is particularly bad. And we just got rid of the guy from CIA.

Jim: There's an IG for the CIA?

David: Yeah. When I worked for the intelligence committee I worked with that person.

Louis: Oh really? The guy who just left?

David: Well, it was back in the nineties that I worked there. My boss on the intelligence committee, the chief counsel, L. Britt Snider, ended up being the IG for the CIA for a while. One of the things that I am interested in—you've got to like Scott Pruitt, he's obviously just a grifter. I think Ryan Zinke is actually one, too, and those are IG matters for sure. The problem is the larger corruption, which is exemplified by Andrew K. Wheeler, the number two EPA is now acting chief. You're not actually committing any offenses that are actually, technically, crimes, but the whole thing is corrupted.

Jim: It's not the whole thing we're talking about here, the industry controls every case.

Louis: The biggest corrupter of government is corporate, the corporate world.

Jim: But government has to be. It's a dance.

Louis: Yeah.

Jim: The corporate, like in the student loans, they would take advantage of what the government offered for these people, right? It's true in the USDA, that hand in glove, the people are kind of left out of it.

Jon: One thing you said that I'm so glad to hear: Your legacy is partly about the improvement of science. I don't think too many people have picked up on that. I think that's an important aspect of what you did. That's why it's so disturbing to me to know that the leadership of a university may be undermining science by always siding with industry. Can you say more about that? . . . I spent years and years in research, scientific method, ethics, and conflicts of interest. I'm just appalled at what MARC set up as an inherent scientific conflict of interest, and nobody really seemed to give a second thought to it.

Jim: I don't think MARC is at this point with the White Coats. I call it stupid science. There is stupidly designed science, MARC certainly did some of that. And there's also stupidly executed science. They're two separate things, but they both result in bad science. Some of those have really bad consequences for people. A lot of policy decisions are based on science. One thing I can tell you—some may agree—in a lot of ways scientists are the new high priests. We say, we want things to be science-based. The reality is you can get anything published, there are something like twenty-eight-thousand journals worldwide, so everything and anything is "peer reviewed sound science."

David: Mostly in China.

Jim: If you want to call it peer reviewed, in the readings they call peer reviewed "science." Actually, it's a meaningless phrase to call it that, because anything can get published. There is a saying, "Peer review determines where you will get published, not if you get published." There are many vanity or "predatory" journals that will be happy to publish your work if you pay them.

David: It's pay to play.

Jim: Most journals now, you pay them, some journals, they insist for you to pay a page charge. There really is no critical review. Just because it's published, it doesn't really add a whole lot of weight.

Jon: What you're facing now is this post-tenure review in which you're put in a no-win situation because—

Jim: I can't *not* perform my duties, because if I don't perform my duties I'll get terminated.

David: Are you going to be talking to the local media about this, or have you?

Jim: Something might happen, I don't know. I want to get it in a high-profile publication. I really want to embarrass my institution, so maybe they won't do it to the next person. Maybe they'll think about it. As my lawyer said, I'm checkmated, and there's nothing you can do.

Dan: What are you going to do then? How do you see your future?

Jim: I don't know what my future is going to be. I want to do something totally different than scientific research. I have a job to do in research, but I don't want to do research anymore. I'd actually rather get into policy. I'd have more impact there.

Jon: What you're doing has much more impact. Should you go back and get your re-certification as a vet?

Jim: I already did.

Jon: Oh, you've already done that. Well, you're set up because your brother-in-law is in the practice.

Jim: I've got a job as a vet if needed.

Dan: Would you be satisfied with that, just going back and being a vet. . . . You've seen Paris, so you want to go back to the farm?

Jim: No, but I want to have a job too, so at least I've got a job. That's important. There is nothing wrong with being a veterinary practitioner. The profession helps many owners and animals. I think if I could practice part time it would be good for me.

Dan: Haven't all kinds of opportunities opened up for you?

Jim: Some have, but I haven't pushed them very far.

Dan: Maybe I'm overestimating the impact of front-page *New York Times* stories. I just sort of think, when you've been involved in a big war, do you want to go back to civilian life, or do you want to stay in the fight? I think, Jim, and I know Jon, and I know you, and Louis. You guys are warriors. Let's face it, you guys are all warriors. You couldn't go back to the life of a private citizen.

Jim: Living in a small town, doing divorce cases.

Dan: You couldn't do that.

Jon: It's not the same thing.

Dan: I just want to understand the fight. There's a fight to be fought.

Jim: Nothing against private vet practice or private legal practice, but that's not my first choice. I'll find something.

Dan: Is there a fight to be fought right now?

David: Animal welfare?

Dan: It's a huge issue.

Jon: And food safety.

Jim: One thing I learned from Amanda Hitt and GAP is. . . . She showed me these figures, which shows this interrelationship in agriculture, Big Ag, animal welfare, and then environmental degradation, like pollution, and then mal-treating people who work in agriculture. The workers are getting their arms chopped off in slaughter plants. Before Amanda, I never saw the intersection between poor treatment of animals, destruction of the environment, demise of rural communities and worker abuse. That's the bad thing. The good part of this interrelationship is, if you lessen the environmental damage of agriculture, a side benefit is that you will make animal welfare better. They're so interconnected. If you improve livestock conditions, you will make things better for farm workers. You can make many things better from any one of those angles. I'd be happy working from any one of those three AG angles:

animal welfare, human welfare, or environmental damage, because they're interrelated, so they're really the same goal. I didn't realize that integration until I talked to Amanda.

Louis: Your counsel says that you have no alternative, right now.

Jim: Well, my counsel told me, "I can't do anything for you until you're fired. I can't take any action." Amanda confirmed that for me. She talked to him about it. He said to me, "You'll lose your job, and then I'm pretty sure you'll win your job back with litigation. But then you're going to pay me a hundred-thousand dollars to get a job back that you don't even really want." So, he recommended that I just get a new job. That's what I'm planning to do.

Dan: After all of this, do you have any regrets? Would you do anything differently?

Jim: I don't regret doing it, but I would have done it differently. I mean, Amanda tried to contact me right after that piece came out in the *New York Times*, but I was on mental lockdown. Basically, I didn't want to talk to anybody.

Dan: With the exception of Michael Moss, the *Times* reporter?

Jim: Yes, except for Michael Moss. I was talking to him, but he's not an admissible advisory person.

Dan: He was an enabler. He was a great enabler.

Jim: But I want to say up front that I'm not a victim. Everything was a known free choice. All the things that have happened are my own responsibility. That being said, I wish I would have had some prior knowledge of how to be an effective whistleblower and incur less damage to myself. My professional, financial and personal lives all took a big hit. But that is how it goes for almost all whistleblowers, so there is really nothing unique about my story.

Jon: I wish I knew you in 2007 or whenever, when you started your diary or whatever it is that you talk about in the movie.

Dan: You still don't have your diary? You lost it?

Jim: I don't know what happened, but I was banned from my former office at MARC office for fifteen months. When I went back to retrieve my personal belongings, they had state troopers accompany me there. I could only go in my office for an hour and take what I wanted. The first thing I went to look for was my little logbook, and it wasn't there anymore. My lawyer predicted that. I can't say that they took it. I have no proof of that, but my lawyer predicted, "It's not going to be there when you go back."

CHAPTER FORTY-SIX

"I DON'T REGRET DOING IT, BUT I WOULD HAVE DONE IT DIFFERENT-LY"

Dan: David, do you have any regrets, or would you do anything differently?

Jon: Why would David have any regrets? He has morals. He's made the right moves.

David: I've never had to pay any personal price. I kind of wish that I had stayed in the rock band that I was in when I was a teenager. Because then I could just give people a good show.

Dan: You lacked enthusiasm for Hillary in her 2016 campaign?

David: I lacked enthusiasm for her in every campaign. I thought she was good for the Senate in 2000. I think she's a good person and a great public servant. But, in 2008, when they asked me if I wanted to help her campaign, I said, "no." I didn't think she could win. I wanted Obama. In 2016, I didn't think she could win, but eventually she was the only game in town. I have concerns that she's a little too associated with the kind of Democrat who stands up for industries and banks. . . But I saw some movement there in 2016, signs she might really stand up for working people. But she was not the best candidate.

Dan: She's a centrist. I saw what you wrote yesterday in your column.

Jim: Do you have a blog or something?

David: I do, *Republic Report*.

Jim: *Republic Report*?

Dan: Also, Jon's blog, too, is wonderful: *Three Capitals: Washington, Lincoln, Berlin*.

David: I mean, I feel like I've been working here for thirty years, and I wish I had gotten some things done. The things I worked on, there were a lot of goals that I wanted to achieve that I haven't achieved in terms of policy issues.

Dan: Like what?

David: Well, the Comprehensive-Nuclear-Test-Ban Treaty was one. I worked on that out of college; I worked on it in the White House. Even with the President's backing, we couldn't get the Senate to ratify a Test Ban Treaty, which so many other countries have ratified—to stop testing nuclear weapons. That was too bad. That's one of many examples. . . . I feel like the best thing is it's been an honor to work with so many great people. It's sad that so many other people I work with, who I think are great people, are on the other side of all these things because they get paid to do it. The overall culture of corruption, there's no real way of stopping it. We badly need comprehensive campaign finance reform, but I think some proposed reforms are not constitutional.

Dan: Surely, not this environment.

David: What I'm for is taking issues where money destroys politics and trying to show people both the wrong headedness of the policy and the corruption behind it.

Jim: Quick question on that, David: Is there any place where that doesn't happen, or happens the least? Just within the federal government?

David: Occasionally we fight for human rights, and there's less money involved there, but that's not always the case.

Jon: I have to stick up here for government. I worked in state government for almost eight years; it was corruption free.

David: On what issues?

Jon: On everything, when Jim Exon was governor. I don't know if you remember him.

David: I do, he was a senator when I was—

Jon: He was a senator. I went to Washington with him after he was governor.

Dan: You were his Administrative Assistant for eight years?

Jon: I was in state government for eight years and that was corruption free, and I was his legislative director for five years in the Senate. Things got done right.

Jim: Are you talking about Jim Exon specifically or government at that time?

Jon: Government at that time. . . . You look at state government and think that's easy, but it's not. Federal government, I remember coming to work in Congress—there was not a lot of corruption in it. I remember when Democrats and Republicans worked across the aisle. There were a few bad apples as they say, a few who were corrupted by money. That was back in the Seventies, and many federal programs actually cleaned up the air and the water in the country. Those kinds of programs were remarkable. Those were remarkable successes. So, corruption is not inherent in government; integrity can be restored. It strikes me the wrong way that we think corruption is all over, and we can't fight it. It's bad, but you've got to fight it. That's why I wish you weren't checkmated, Jim. I wish you had some cards to play.

Dan: Let me ask you, Jon, do you have any regrets? Would you do anything differently?

Jon: No, I have no regrets. By the time I played my cards, my career was in its twilight. I didn't have a whole lot to lose. So, no. No regrets.

Dan: I was at every minute of Jon's trial last fall at the Rocket Docket in the Eastern District of Virginia.

David: I remember; I saw you there, Dan. We sat together.

Jon: That's right.

Dan: Yeah, David came down. The only thing I missed was the verdict, because they ended up delaying this thing for a day. Jon had one hell of a fight, and he was his own best witness. But the defense just twisted and confused everything, whether it was the inspector general's report from the Department of Education or a state auditor's report in Pennsylvania. In my opinion, the judge just simply refused to allow certain key pieces of evidence into the record. Of course, the Rocket Docket by definition moves things forward quickly. I had never seen the Rocket Docket in action before, and it's almost arbitrary when the judge says, "How long is this videotape," which is forty-five minutes—

David: "Cut it down to twenty minutes."

Dan: Right. So, what did you learn from that?

Jon: Well, when you roll the dice, you don't always win.

Dan: But you beat the judge in your case three times and then lost on the fourth.

Jon: We actually discovered corruption, fraud, and perjury. It's corroborated, and it's outrageous. As you know, I was the relator for the federal government in my case against PHEAA. But I can't see DOJ pursuing, say, perjury charges in this civil case. Not having any regrets, I have to say, I didn't throw in the towel until I played the absolute last card that I had.

David: But you settled with all the other loan companies. You beat them without even a trial.

Jon: We beat them in settlement, right. We won seven out of nine. One got dropped out, and we won seven out of nine.

Dan: You're seven, one and one, right?

Jon: We're seven, one and one, right. Seven wins, one tie, one loss.

Dan: And that loss stings.

Jon: Right.

Dan: Because it was unfair.

David: But he won. One holdout doesn't obscure that fact. . . . Could I just say why I think it's different from the Seventies? I mean, there are always crooked people and agencies and mean old bosses and bad members of Congress. But I believe it's because of the effective organizing corporations—through things like ALEC and the Federalist Society—and what they've done to push this anti-regulatory agenda that allows corporations to then act with impunity.

Dan: Yeah.

David: It has weakened workers and consumers in all kinds of ways. But they've just done a masterful job of taking their money and turning it into political power. That corrupts decisions. And now, you have a situation where the Republican Party is entirely owned, and the Democratic Party is about fifty percent owned. It's harder for any positive outcome to ever happen. It's really tough. You need every fact on your side to really prevail on a legislative or administrative fight. That's what I see is the difference.

Louis: Then you have Trump on top of that. There are "the facts." The fact is that if you do have the facts, and you do have the right alignment of judge and jury et cetera. If you have all that happening, you will prevail because we still have a democracy. Then, you have a Trump where, all of a sudden, it's all about deregulation, never about public health and safety. He's already wrapped up forty-two percent of the electorate on this mantra. And then any time there is a dispute about facts, he just says, "fake news," and it doesn't make any difference. To me, that is an assault on truth. Before it was really difficult, but now it's almost impossible in terms of having to deal with that sort of cultural phenomena.

Dan: But, you're very optimistic about the future of whistleblowers, and I'm just curious, how are they going to be protected?

Louis: Well, they have really good protection across the board. As long as you have the agencies themselves that are performing, recognizing that the law that's on the books, then I think we're going to be okay.

David: For government, what's on the books?

Louis: For government? On corporate, too, because you can get into federal district court. Eighty-million people have protections in the private sector.

The people at the slaughterhouse don't. The meat industry has been on this for thirty-to-forty years making sure there isn't whistleblower protection within anything that's regulated by the USDA, especially related to meat.

Dan: One thing, going back to Jon's case, and that is Jon was the relater for the federal government in his case, and the federal government who had lawyers there, were basically of no help at all, were they? In the midst of the trial, or in the preparation for the trial because of the changing of administration.

David: They never took the case. They didn't take it.

Jon: They never took the case.

Dan: They were looking to get one-hundred to two-hundred-million dollars back.

David: Settled. The government got most of the money.

Jon: In the PHEAA case, unbeknownst to me, during the trial, the Justice Department was actually filing a brief on behalf of PHEAA in another case.

Jim: Who is PHEAA?

Jon: That was the defendant in my last case, the loan company for servicing student loans, American Education Services. It's a big nationwide outfit, also known as FedLoan.

David: Do you understand, do you know how the federal whistleblower law works?

Jim: No.

David: Basically, an individual says, inside of a company or an agency, "I know something bad is going on" and files a secret complaint with the court. The government then has to decide if it wants to join your case and prosecute it for you. If they do, you'll probably win the case statistically. If they don't, you will probably lose. But if you win, even though the government stayed out of it, the government gets most of the money.

Jim: Why wouldn't the government get involved if they think it might not—

David: If they don't think it's a good case.

Louis: The problem with the Department of Justice is that it's much more difficult for them to do a case if the Department of Education is against it.

Our litigation director was at that office for thirty years as a litigator, and he described what happened to him when he wanted to take a case against the Department of Energy at Rocky Flats.

Jim: Is that the place in Colorado?

Louis: Yeah. It's just really hard, but he prevailed. They did take that case against the contractor, even though the Department of Energy was against it.

Jon: That was the problem. The Justice Department told me that privately. They thought my lawyers and I would be in a much better position to handle it than the Justice Department acting against the Education Department, with which they were collaborating all the time. They wouldn't have any credibility if they took over the case.

Jim: I can see the logic of that, actually, . . . the strategy of that.

Jon: It wasn't that they didn't think I had a case. They knew I had a case.

Dan: Jim, you and Michael Moss of the *New York Times* were victimized by the IG's office of the USDA. Did somebody get to the IG between the interim and final reports?

Jim: I don't really have any knowledge of that one way or the other. I mean, I saw the final report, and I heard beforehand that the final report would be pablum.. . . . I can't say who influenced that report. I don't have any knowledge of that.

Dan: At the same time Jon, you were left stranded by the IG's office at the Department of Education and DOJ, because they didn't follow up on PHEAA's alleged perjury during the trial, no?

Jon: That's right. The department also didn't let the best IG person testify.

Jim: It's frustrating.

Dan: So again, was it a business interest that corrupted the whistleblower protection in your particular case?

Jon: Well, I think so, yes. In my case, it was pure perjury. No doubt about it.

Dan: No doubt about it. We all witnessed it.

Jon: In Jim's case, I don't know. But it sure looks like business interest corruption.

Dan: Louis, take us home here. What's your upshot? What do you see in the future? And what will be the impact of this administration on everything? I just wonder what the damage is going to be at the end of all this.

Louis: I think democracy is on the line with the 2020 election. And I think the Dems are going to prevail. There's going to be a push back, a pendulum swing on the whole issue of truth.

Dan: Wow. That's a bold statement when the president is such a provable liar.

David: Well do you think that—if the Democrats get a chance to be back in power—they will have learned a lesson that it's time to be truthful and to be less corrupt? Or do you think that they have learned that we're going to have to play hardball, and the only way to win is to engage in the same kind of distortions and to suck up to the companies that were cozying up to Trump?

Louis: What a good question. Well, we certainly have the experience obviously of Clinton and Obama on a lot of issues, but national security, in particular, was very problematic. But at the same time, I'm looking for restoring and defending democracy.

EPILOGUE

A FINAL INTERIM WORD FROM THE AUTHOR

I admire and respect people who use their fame, money, and power to defend and protect those who cannot defend themselves. Some of America's greatest leaders have possessed this noble society-serving trait.

Usually without the fame, money, and power, the same is true of whistleblowers. They are usually average citizens of modest means who, risking retaliation, step out of private or public workplaces to reveal acts of abuses and corruption against fellow workers and/or consumers.

Whistleblowers deserve to be protected.

Walter M. Shaub, Jr., the former director of the U.S. Office of Government Ethics, wrote an op-ed in the *Washington Post*, declaring: "The nation's interests will be harmed if individuals with inside information are afraid to make good-faith reports of suspected wrongdoing. Chilling whistleblower activity jeopardizes the government's critical efforts to detect corruption, large-scale waste of taxpayer money, and threats to public health and safety."[50]

---

50   Walter M. Shaub, Jr., *Washington Post*, "Trump's quest for revenge could mean the end of whistleblowing," February 7, 2020.

Remarkably, the supporters of the self-serving Donald Trump, their roguish Lord and Savior, find an inexplicable nobility in his ability and willingness to wage war against the poorest and the most powerless among us. And, when whistleblowers have stepped into the spotlight to reveal acts of general bad behavior or even specific corruption by Trump and/or the members of his administration, the sheep in Trump's flock have launched effective smear campaigns against them in cynical attempts to destroy their general believability and overall credibility.

With the 2017 inauguration of Donald Trump, an odd assembly of pro-business and anti-government advocates were nominated to the Cabinet and approved by the U.S. Senate, which, along with the U.S. House, was controlled by the Republicans. Many of these appointees actually supported the destruction of the agencies that they were appointed to head, such as Rick Perry, the secretary of the Department of Energy, and Scott Pruitt of the Environmental Protection Agency.

And then there was billionaire Betsy DeVos whom Trump nominated as the secretary of education. A woman with no relevant college degree, no teaching experience, and no experience working in a public-school environment, she had contributed over $200 million to Christian schools and groups. Inasmuch as she disdained public education, she, like her children, had never attended a public school.

Predictably, upon her confirmation by the U.S. Senate, she immediately started to roll back recent education reforms that had been implemented with regard to the student-loan program and for-profit colleges by the Obama Administration. As a top aide, she hired Robert Eitel, whose background was at a for-profit college with a history of deceiving students, as documented by David Halperin. As another aide, she brought on Taylor Hansen, a former lobbyist for the principal for-profit-college association and son of William Hansen, a perennial official in the student-loan industry and most recently director of Strada Education, a loan guaranty company.[51]

Simultaneously, DeVos quickly moved to rescind a department policy so as to allow Strada higher fees on student borrowers.

Like a Mafia family busting out a local savings and loan, the Trump Administration appeared prepared to dismantle and even wreck the Department of Education and other federal agencies while giving nearly everything away to a new and emerging class of American oligarchs—via government contracts, tax breaks, repealed regulations, privatization, and dismantled federal watchdog groups.

Notably, the $25-million settlement in the Trump University case in November 2016 came in the aftermath of a civil RICO litigation, a key weapon used by federal prosecutors in the handling of litigations against Mafia figures.

---

51   Excerpt from a letter from U.S. Senator Elizabeth Warren to Betsy DeVos, March 17, 2017:

Mr. Hansen's recent employment history clearly calls into question his impartiality in dealing with higher education issues at the Department of Education, and raises alarming conflicts of interest concerns.

Mr. Hansen may also have conflicts of interest related to the student loan program. His father, Bill Hansen, is president and chief executive officer of USA Funds (recently renamed the Strada Education Network), a former Department of Education guaranty agency that recently sued the Department to block policy that prohibited guaranty agencies from charging additional fees to defaulted student loan borrowers who promptly enter repayment. On March 16th, the Department announced that it would rescind this policy.

In addition to Mr. Hansen, the Department has reportedly hired Robert Eitel, the Vice President of Regulatory Legal Services at Bridgepoint Education, Inc., to serve as a Senior Advisor in the Office of the Secretary. Bridgepoint Education, a for-profit college company, was-less than six months ago-fined $23.5 million after the Consumer Financial Protection Bureau learned that the school "deceived its students," causing students to "tak[e] out loans without knowing the true cost" and "make payments greater than what they were promised.". . .The company is currently under investigation by the Department of Justice, the Securities and Exchange Commission, the New York Attorney General, the North Carolina Attorney General, the California Attorney General, and the Massachusetts Attorney General.

Meantime, with regard to the three heroic whistleblowers featured in this book, here are my final thoughts.

Jon Oberg

Jon Oberg discovered fraud in the student loan program in 2003 and fought it successfully for many years thereafter, saving taxpayers billions of dollars. He even had a U.S. Supreme Court victory along the way, stripping a student-loan entity of its purported sovereign immunity from lawsuits.

But his achievements were quickly undermined by Betsy DeVos, and her disregard for consumer protection of student-loan borrowers. In 2017, she cut off exchanges of information between the Department of Education and the Consumer Financial Protection Bureau.

The following year, she pre-empted state attorneys general from investigating federal student loan servicers. Then, she instructed servicers not to provide information to anyone about how they were running their programs to the great disadvantage of borrowers. Millions of borrowers are now at the mercy of a servicer that—as Jon Oberg showed through legal discovery and depositions—has repeatedly committed fraud, deception, and perjury. Borrowers are being systematically and corruptly deprived of their rightful and lawful benefits under the Trump Administration.

But, for whistleblower Dr. Oberg, the fight continues.

When the final chapter is written, it will show a crescendo of achievements following the end of his formal litigation against student-loan lenders.

The Pittsburgh *Tribune-Review* on September 1, 2018, revealed the potentially vast consequences of PHEAA's loss of sovereign immunity as it described a student-loan borrower's lawsuit:[52]

---

52   Deb Erdley, *Tribune-Review* (Pittsburgh), "Federal class-action lawsuits target practices of Pennsylvania-based student loan agency, September 1, 2018.

Today, she is a plaintiff in one of 10 class-action lawsuits filed against the Pennsylvania Higher Education Assistance Agency that have been bundled in federal court in Philadelphia. The plaintiffs — borrowers from 10 states — say they represent tens of thousands who have been saddled with additional debt because PHEAA cannot or will not properly process their payments...

The consolidated PHEAA suit is the latest sign of trouble in the student loan arena.

Both PHEAA and Navient, the nation's largest student loan servicer, are awash in lawsuits filed by state attorneys general and angry borrowers who claim the agencies make it difficult for them to remain current in payments...

Between January 2016 and this April, the PHEAA paid $2.5 million for outside lawyers to work on 32 cases alone. The agency also paid more than $1.8 million to settle 29 lawsuits between Jan. 1, 2015, and June 30.

As the tobacco and asbestos industries learned, there is a potential for hundreds of billions of dollars in payouts to those on the losing side in multidistrict class-action suits.

PHEAA did not take this sitting down. It enlisted Secretary DeVos to try to protect it from such lawsuits through so-called federal preemption. It also tried to retaliate against Jon Oberg, as shown in federal district court records.

By reversing a long-standing legal interpretation that student-loan servicers must comply with state as well as federal law, Betsy DeVos attempted to shield PHEAA and others in the student-loan industry from consumer-based lawsuits. Going to bat for the industry over the interests of students was nothing new for her, as she had already effectively undone a student-loan-guaranty agency's litigation loss at the hands of the U.S. Supreme Court in the *Strada* case.

In her March 12, 2018, "Preemption Notice," DeVos also reversed decades of settled policy—embodied in the Department's contracts with loan servicers—by claiming that the Higher Education Act preempts all except the federal government from handling borrower protections.

But on June 27, 2019, a three-judge panel from the Seventh Circuit Court of Appeals rejected the borrower-hostile DeVos action. The panel, made up of judges appointed by Presidents Reagan, Obama, and Trump, gave DeVos short shrift:

> [T]he Preemption Notice is not persuasive because it is not particularly thorough and it "represents a stark, unexplained change" in the Department's position.... [W]e give the document itself little weight.[53]

Although DeVos's preemption attempt now appears in trouble, for over a year it tied up consumer-protection efforts and delayed justice for hundreds of thousands of student-loan borrowers whose best chances of getting their lives back relied on state and class-action litigation. The *Nelson* decision now requires DeVos—if she follows the rule of law—to stand down from blocking borrower entry to the traditional halls of justice.

PHEAA's attempted retaliation against Oberg was not subtle, although it was curious that in their blind anger they conceded Oberg's own points about why he went to trial. Defending its claim that he owed them over $414,000, PHEAA wrote to the federal district court that this sum should be his liability for discovering what PHEAA for years had been trying to conceal:

---

53   *Nelson v. Great Lakes Educational Loan Services, Inc.*, No. 3:17-CV-183. (7th Circuit Court of Appeals, 2019)

Oberg has commented on a public blog he maintains that "indeed one of the main goals of a jury trial" was "[t]o get mountains of [] evidence into the public realm," and that "Wiley Rein [his counsel] did this through painstaking discovery over months and years." In the same post, he referred to litigation against PHEAA as "[p]ursuing truth through discovery for the sake of sunshine." Having succeeded in his apparent effort to obtain "mountains of evidence" during "painstaking discovery" and to provide his desired "sunshine" on PHEAA's practices, Oberg cannot now escape the cost of having imposed that effort....

While PHEAA believes the parties' economic resources should not guide the decision to allow or disallow recovery of costs in this case, it bears noting that Oberg has recovered at least $15 million in settlements with other defendants, making clear that he has the ability to satisfy any taxation of costs against him with monies obtained from this very litigation.[54]

In this filing, PHEAA showed itself perplexed that it cannot ruin Oberg financially. Paradoxically, PHEAA admitted Oberg's motivation was not greed, as it told a jury—but, instead, sunshine.

Oberg would not comment on the filing, beyond saying that he had once tried to settle with PHEAA on costs by offering a charitable contribution of over six figures that could be used for grants (not loans) for financially needy Pennsylvania students. PHEAA did not reply to the offer, he said.[55]

---

54   *U.S. ex rel. Oberg v. PHEAA*: Case 1:07-cv-00960-CMH-JFA (Document 983 Filed 01/02/18)

55   On July 15, 2019, the federal district court for Eastern Virginia reduced PHEAA's bill of costs by $338,873, from $414,308 to $75,435. PHEAA received nearly $50,000 less than Oberg had offered them in settlement as a charitable contribution to financially needy Pennsylvania students.

Clearly, this is still the same PHEAA that the Pennsylvania auditor general condemned as having lost sight of its mission, and whose audit report was not allowed into evidence in a federal jury trial.

To be sure, Oberg said he was impressed by the role many charitable organizations continue to play in "shaping better public policy" through litigation as well as advocacy. He added that, at the federal level, "It's all about public policy and fulfilling what is supposed to be the true mission of the Department of Education, which is to help students and their families, and to do it by faithfully following the rule of law. That is the unending struggle. It's too bad any litigation has ever been necessary, but if that is what it takes, then the recent victories are to be cheered.

"May there soon come a day when no more litigation is necessary to return the Department of Education to its mission."

Rod Lipscomb

Rod Lipscomb blew the whistle on the deceptive practices at a for-profit college where he was a top official. But as soon as Betsy DeVos became Secretary of Education, she named for-profit college executives and lobbyists as her top aides and began undoing regulations that had been put in place to protect students from becoming victims of these corrupt schools. She reinstated a for-profit controlled accreditation agency that had previously lost its status due to poor performance.

The Accrediting Council for Independent Colleges and Schools (ACICS) may yet collapse despite the DeVos attempt to prop it up. In January 2020, the agency acknowledged that it is no longer seeking recognition from the private association that gives legitimacy to accrediting bodies.

To be sure, the whistleblowing of Rod Lipscomb continues to work its salutary effects.

James Keen

Jim Keen was a veterinarian and epidemiologist at a land-grant university, the University of Nebraska–Lincoln, assigned to the U.S. Department of Agriculture's Meat Animal Research Center (MARC). He blew the whistle on poorly designed animal experiments at the center. And he paid dearly for his decision to inform the public, as his university banned him from his MARC office and sent its own police force and the FBI to interrogate him without the presence of counsel.

Keen's choice of messenger to inform the public, investigative journalist Michael Moss of the *New York Times*, proved fateful as it unleashed the forces of industrial agriculture—Big Ag—against them both.

First, rather than supporting his faculty member, the university's chancellor challenged as untrue virtually everything Keen and the *Times* reported. At the time, UNL was actively seeking grants and participation agreements from two of Big Ag's largest companies, ConAgra and Cargill. Cargill, not coincidentally, had been targeted by Michael Moss in more than one of his publications.

Moss is the reporter who won a Pulitzer Prize for his 2009 revelation that *E coli* in a hamburger patty, sourced to food processing giant Cargill, was responsible for the permanent disability of a consumer.[56] Moss then moved from food safety to nutrition in his 2013 book, *Salt Sugar Fat: How the Food Giants Hooked Us*, a national best-seller that targeted Cargill and other food processors.

Cargill was a donor to one of the UNL Chancellor Harvey Perlman's most urgent projects, the new Nebraska Innovation Campus and its Food Technology Center. Another donor was Con-Agra, a huge food processor and, like Cargill, a political heavy-hitter. When Michael Moss's article on MARC appeared, the Innovation Campus was still largely empty and threatened to become a white elephant. The chancellor had to ask the Nebraska legislature for another $25

---

56   Michael Moss, *New York Times*, "The Burger That Shattered Her Life," October 3, 2009.

million to fund it.[57] The Innovation Campus also needed more infusions from Big Ag companies to fulfill the chancellor's promises.

Other participants in the Innovation Campus project were Hershey's, Kellogg's and Nestlé, which had likewise been targeted by Michael Moss in *Salt Sugar Fat*.

A vice-chancellor at the university, Ronnie Green, responsible for its college of agriculture—and who would succeed Harvey Perlman as chancellor—was simultaneously doing his part to promote the interests of Cargill and other big food processors in the state. He called for more cattle on feed in the big feedlots of the kind Cargill needed to supply its many Nebraska slaughterhouses.

Green had trained at MARC. He was also Jim Keen's boss with control over his fate as a member of the university faculty and had a bully pulpit to cast doubt on Keen's conclusions about *E coli* risks in huge feedlots.

Michael Moss's views were anathema to Vice-Chancellor Green, who called Moss's MARC article a "gross misrepresentation."[58]

As for USDA, Secretary Tom Vilsack had many bones to pick with Michael Moss. It was Vilsack who had to deal with the fallout from the earlier "pink slime" controversy and from the national outrage that resulted from Moss's reporting about MARC.

The IG's report was done with full knowledge of the trouble Moss had created for Secretary Vilsack. Interestingly, the final IG report was not published until well after Vilsack had been passed over as the Democratic Party's vice-presidential candidate in 2016. He had been among the front-runners until his ties to Big Ag nixed his chances. That could not have escaped notice by those at USDA who put the final spin on the IG report, clearly an attempt to get in a final word against Moss.

---

57 Martha Stoddard, *Omaha World-Herald*, "UNL officials quizzed over Nebraska Innovation Campus' finances, future, October 10, 2015.

58 Nicholas Bergin, *Lincoln Journal-Star*, "Meat Animal Research Center says it has addressed animal care concerns," June 16, 2015.

Obviously, many powerful interests had it in for Moss. Not so obviously, Jim Keen would be caught up in the crossfire. His university would bring in the FBI to target him as an eco-terrorist in a cynical effort to discredit his whistleblowing.

The USDA inspector-general's investigation of the Keen and Moss allegations warrants special scrutiny. In its first report, it verified most of them. But, in its sequel, it clearly went out of its way to try to discredit Michael Moss, a widely respected journalist. Even defenders of MARC were puzzled at the findings, which can be explained only by a willingness at USDA to do Big Ag's bidding to silence one of its leading critics.

Enter the Trump Administration and the new Secretary of Agriculture, Sonny Perdue. Although Jim Keen's whole professional life as an epidemiologist had been to combat *E coli* in the cause of food safety, the new Secretary moved immediately to eliminate USDA meat inspectors and replace them with company employees. He also moved two USDA offices, the Economic Research Service (ERS) and the National Institute of Food and Agriculture (NIFA), out of Washington, resulting in the departure of the best USDA economists and scientists. The offices, Perdue determined, would be relocated in Kansas City.

Doubtless Secretary Perdue has in mind something along the lines of the MARC model for both the ERS and NIFA: A center with close ties to Big Ag and compliant universities nearby, located in states dominated by Trump-fearing politicians.

Mercifully, Jim Keen survived his ordeal as a whistleblower. He is now a visiting fellow in the Animal Law and Policy Program at Harvard University.

God bless America's whistleblowers, as well as those who honor and protect them.

Dan E. Moldea
Washington, D.C.

AFTERWORD

"CLOSING ARGUMENTS"

Author's Note

At precisely the exact time when the United States is examining alternative forms of education because of a worldwide coronavirus, a handful of whistleblowers and their advocates featured in this book have discovered a historical pattern of massive fraud and corruption within higher education.

For the second edition of this book, I have asked them to give their closing arguments for the November 2020 election.

Jon Oberg

After the election of Donald Trump as president in 2016, a few colleagues asked me, as a political scientist with several years of experience working in the Senate and the Department of Education, if I thought our democratic institutions could hold up against such an unprincipled man in the Oval Office. I said no, our institutions are too weak, and there are too many people who will not stand up for their country.

But I quickly added that we had no option but to try.

My bleak assessment was based on memory of the Abscam scandal in the Senate in the late 1970s, when I first started working there, and being a first-hand witness to student loan corruption in the Department of Education during the George W. Bush administration.

The first two years of the Trump administration only deepened my concerns. I saw that under Secretary Betsy DeVos, nothing would stand in the way of an aggressive agenda, abetted by even more pervasive corruption, to weaken legal and regulatory protections for students, families, and taxpayers that had taken years to achieve over the predatory interests of the student loan and for-profit school industries. When legal objections were raised by victims and good-government advocates, they were customarily met with counter-actions to tie the judicial branch up in knots while the plundering proceeded, making a calculated mockery of the rule of law.

After the 2018 elections, which saw the opposition party gain control of the House, I thought there might be a chance for the rule of law to reassert itself. Indeed, the House held informative hearings on some of the most shameful actions of the DeVos Department.

But the House did not comprehend sufficiently that this was a shameless regime. No politically appointed official was subpoenaed; no one from the Department who testified falsely was charged with perjury; no one who refused to provide documents was punished for contempt of Congress. There were many speeches, but little action to hold the lawless accountable.

The House leadership also made a grave mistake in how it proceeded to exercise and defend Constitutional separation of powers. The House in 2019 should first have censured the President for his abundant violations of law, then opened impeachment hearings but held the articles of impeachment at the House until the votes in the Senate could be counted on for conviction and removal.

When it became apparent that Donald Trump, through his inept handling of the coronavirus pandemic, was about to cause the loss of huge numbers of

American lives and do irreparable damage to entire sectors of the American economy (including higher education), sufficient votes would likely have been forthcoming in the Senate to remove him. But the House had squandered its opportunity, and the country will suffer the consequences forever.

This is America. Our institutions' tools are still available, but for how long? We simply must do better.

David Halperin

By the summer of 2020, Betsy DeVos and her top education aide, Diane Auer Jones, the former for-profit college executive, had worked to reverse most of the college accountability reforms implemented under President Obama. They had trashed the gainful employment, accreditation, and borrower defense rules, and rejected most borrower defense claims already filed by ripped-off students. They restored the ability of for-profit colleges to use mandatory arbitration clauses to block students from bringing lawsuits against them.

DeVos also reversed Obama decisions to dump lax college accreditor ACICS and to reject the non-profit status of the predatory CEHE college operation. And she had gutted the Department of Education's enforcement effort, putting in charge a lawyer from the Cooley firm, which has represented many of the worst schools.

Diane Jones is so shameless that she installed her own former assistant at the Department as the sole student representative on DeVos's outside advisory panel, the National Advisory Committee on Institutional Quality and Integrity (NACIQI), and also acted to gut the power of that body. And the VA suspended from GI Bill eligibility three predatory chains caught by the FTC fleecing students, when the law required it to do so, but soon reversed that decision.

More of the worst school chains have abruptly closed, leaving students locked out, but many bad actors remain.

We keep fighting for students, and our coalition keeps getting stronger. The coalition, led by veterans groups, managed to press Congress to pass, with bipartisan support, a resolution to restore the Obama borrower rule, but Donald Trump vetoed it. Our allied legal teams, along with state attorneys general on our side, have beaten DeVos over and over in court, and now they're suing to strike down the new DeVos anti-reforms.

The opportunity to elect a new president in 2020 would allow us to turn things around dramatically. It's still tough to get reforms under a Democratic administration, but it would be a lot better than Betsy DeVos and the former head of Trump University.

The investigation into Dream Center Education Holdings, which my articles, based on whistleblower accounts, launched, has been advanced by committees of the House of Representatives, media outlets, and lawyers representing students, and it has shown beyond doubt that DeVos aide Diane Jones mismanaged the process while engaging in a cover-up, repeatedly lying to Congress along the way. Jones is trying to take formal action against a Dream Center accreditor, Higher Learning Commission, to deflect blame from herself and the Department, but students won a huge victory in July 2020 when NACIQI, which is dominated by Republicans, voted 9-2 to reject punishing HLC after advocates in our coalition, including me, addressed the panel.

With the assistance of more whistleblowers, I have helped expose more abuses at other for-profit college operations—Florida Career College, Keiser University, American Intercontinental, Colorado Tech. Working with the Harvard Project on Predatory Student Lending, I'm also exposing efforts by predatory schools to exploit fears and unemployment in the COVID-19 pandemic and enroll a new generation of struggling Americans into high-priced low-quality education programs. And I'm looking at the lobbyists who are trying to grab even more taxpayer dollars for bad-acting schools as part of the COVID relief acts.

People always ask me, how do you find all these whistleblowers? My response is, how can I stop finding so many of them? Reporting on higher education is my job barely a day a week, and I can't keep up with all the former staff and even top executives who reach out to tell their stories of unbelievable abuses against students and taxpayers. All I can say is that thorough reporting, attention to detail and accuracy, protection of anonymous sources, and the clearest writing I can muster while writing as fast as I can, seem like the components of a big magnet that attracts people who want to share their truths.

Louis Clark

As higher education reformer David Halperin has chronicled here, the U.S. Department of Education is continuing to devolve into an operation that favors both private education and for-profit educational enterprises. Working with whistleblowers over the last decade, he has won one hard-fought battle after another on behalf of student victims, whistleblowers, and taxpayers. Most of these reforms, regretfully, have now reached the Department's cutting room floor at the hands of Secretary Betsy DeVos who has dedicated much of her philanthropic life to promoting private Christian education and charter schools as well as extolling the value of private versus public educational services. These troubling results, as well as the selection of DeVos herself to the top education position in the land, are not surprising developments given Trump's own history as a founder of the fraudulent Trump University—a bogus educational operation that according to the New York Attorney General actually fleeced over $40 million from 5,000 gullible students and left them with nothing more than real estate platitudes and an empty promise of a photo-op with Trump in return. Not satisfied with gutting one Obama-era educational reform after another, Trump even issued one of his rare vetoes to kill a bipartisan congressional reform bill that would have helped protect student borrowers from predatory for-profit college abuses.

In Halperin's additional comments for the renewed publication of this book, he notes that he is barely able to keep up with the number of new whistleblowers who are seeking him out to share their truths about the rampant corruption that plagues the for-profit college industry. He surmises that his accurate and reliable reporting, willingness to keep confidences, quick responsiveness and clear prose all have acted as a magnet to draw a continuing and growing number of whistleblowers to him. With my nearly 43 years of experience at Government Accountability Project, where we have helped over 8,000 whistleblowers, I would add one major element to Halperin's self-analysis of why whistleblowers seek him out; that is, he is clearly having an impact with the information that whistleblowers are providing him.

Large surveys of federal employees and our own legal practice are in sync. We have found that the major reason the clear majority of employees remain silent when confronted with corruption is not so much fear of retaliation, but rather the fear of futility. Many, if not most, potential whistleblowers do have apprehension that their bosses will retaliate. But the even greater fear that is by far the most likely to keep employees from speaking up is that they will take the risk of disclosing corruption and nothing will happen as a result. It is that cynicism that is the most deadly to all reform efforts and democracy itself.

It is notable that whistleblowers might not prevail in the short run. They do not even have to have a better than even chance of success. As long as these whistleblowers are able to sound the alarm to a significant portion of the public, to groups that deeply care about the concerns, and to key policy-makers, whistleblowers will continue to come forward with critical information about a corrupt enterprise and those who are aiding and abating the wrongdoing. This is why it is so important that all of us who share the concerns whether as a participant, reformer, victim, or taxpayer take action in support of true reform and truth-tellers.

Last year, for example, we all learned how one whistleblower could directly help launch the impeachment and resulting Senate trial of only the third President in history. Even though the Ukraine whistleblower never testified in Congress and remained confidential throughout, this individual became a catalyst for so many others to step forward and testify despite the powerful tactics employed by the President, Attorney General, and Secretary of State to silence them.

Relatedly, at this very moment at the Department of Justice, prosecutors and investigators are reaching out to us from the anti-trust, criminal, civil fraud, and civil rights divisions. They are outraged at the conduct of Attorney General Barr in closing criminal cases that should be prosecuted, using bogus anti-trust investigations against disfavored industries and specific companies, and—infamously—clearing the street of legal protestors through use of pepper spray so that Trump could hold the Bible aloft (upside down) in an election photo op. Attorney General Barr, in response to some of these whistleblowers, has shown every indication that he intends to use the power of his position to go after whistleblowers with criminal prosecutions—a foreshadowing of his willingness to do whatever is needed to shield this President from a full reckoning for his behavior as well as having to provide an orderly transfer of power. I expect these truth-tellers will help write the history that will assign the Trump era to a special place of national infamy.

Whistleblowers continue to show what we at Government Accountability Project and Dan Moldea have known for over four decades: even though an array of very powerful and ruthless leaders can cause a great deal of harm to an entire nation, one or two whistleblowers working with journalists, public interest advocates, experienced counselors, and elected and unelected policy-makers can by contrast move mountains. Along with Halperin, the other whistleblowers whom Dan Moldea has so effectively and eloquently portrayed in this book—Jon Oberg, James Keen and Rodney Lipscomb—has each in his own way shaken up the corrupt status quo and exposed elements of higher education that must not continue. As renowned social anthropologist Margaret Mead wisely stated, *"Never doubt that a small group of thoughtful, committed citizens can change the world; indeed, it's the only thing that ever has."*

Made in the USA
Monee, IL
28 February 2021